Ngā Waka o Neherā

Ngā Waka o Neherā
The first voyaging canoes

Jeff Evans

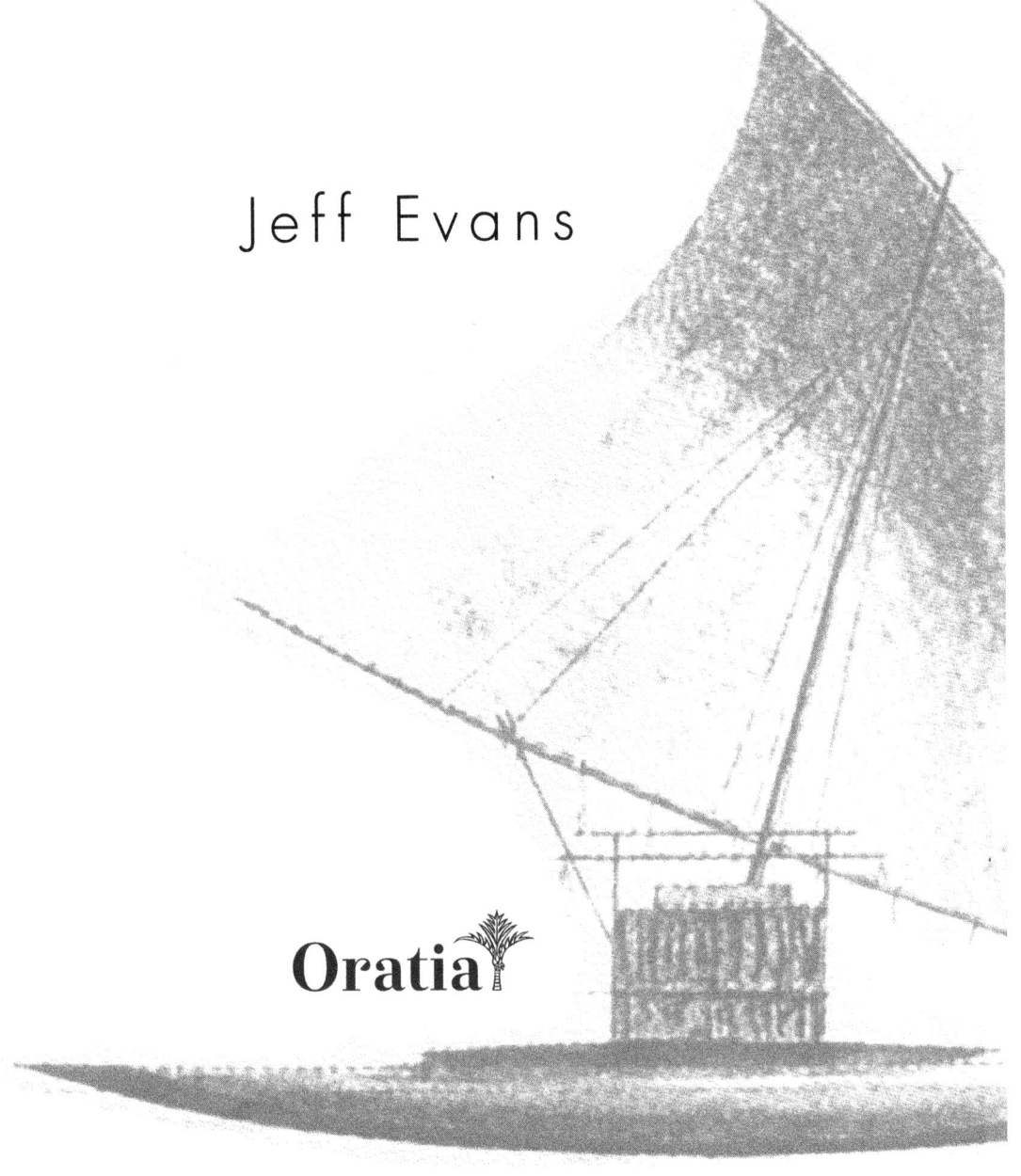

Oratia

Published by Oratia Books, Oratia Media Ltd, 783 West Coast Road, Oratia, Auckland 0604, New Zealand (www.oratia.co.nz).

Copyright © 2016 Jeff Evans
Copyright © 2016 Oratia Books (published work)

The copyright holder asserts his moral rights in the work.

This book is copyright. Except for the purposes of fair reviewing, no part of this publication may be reproduced or transmitted in any form or by any means, whether electronic, digital or mechanical, including photocopying, recording, any digital or computerised format, or any information storage and retrieval system, including by any means via the Internet, without permission in writing from the publisher. Infringers of copyright render themselves liable to prosecution.

ISBN 978-0-947506-05-6

First published 2000 by Reed Books
Second edition 2009 by Libro International
This edition 2016 by Oratia Books

The cover shows a detail from Kennett Watkin's 1912 painting *The Legend of the Voyage to New Zealand*, Auckland Art Gallery Toi o Tamaki.

Printed in Australia

CONTENTS

Acknowledgements	6
Foreword	7
Introduction	9
The waka	13
Nga waka o Maui	194
Nga waka o Rata	198
The maps	200
Bibliography	207
Index	215

ACKNOWLEDGEMENTS

This book is the culmination of years of research and writing over which time I have been fortunate to receive advice and assistance from a number of people.

Initially, encouragement from Te Warena Taua (formerly of the Auckland Museum), Roger Neich (Auckland Museum) and Ian Watt (formerly of Reed Publishing) gave me the confidence and impetus to write this book. Without their input the project would not have got off the ground.

Thanks go to the following people and libraries for their assistance during my various stages of research: Janice Chong and her team at the Auckland Museum Library; Manuela Angelo and her team at the Hector Library; the Alexander Turnbull Library; and the National Library. Suggestions and advice from the numerous staff I beleaguered with my requests for ideas on further research material were invaluable.

A special thanks also goes to Hoturoa Kerr of Te Tari Maori, Te Whare Wananga o Waikato, for writing the foreword.

Once the 'easy' part of researching and writing the book was completed, Peter Janssen and Alison Southby at Reed Publishing displayed the patience of saints when assisting me to tidy up and present a workable manuscript. A heartfelt thanks to them both.

Finally I need to thank my long-suffering wife Fuli, who did everything from rescuing my work when the computer crashed to putting up with my absence when I locked myself away night after night trying to keep up with the writing timetable, and for reading and re-reading my work in the process, finding what seemed to be hundreds of spelling and grammatical errors. Thank you.

FOREWORD

E ngā mana e ngā reo, tēnā koutou katoa. Ki ngā mātua ki ngā tūpuna kua wehe atu ki te wāhi ngāro, whakawhitia ngā moana tau atu rā ki Hawaikinui, ki Hawaikiroa, ki Hawaiki-pāmamao.

For hundreds of years Māori have recited stories of the seafaring adventures of their ancestors. Despite the theories of many anthropologists and scholars the feats of these ancestors have remained as something to be admired and believed in. However, as time has continued on in it's ever advancing way many people have grown up in the belief that only a handful of intrepid voyagers made it to Aotearoa in a band of seven waka that travelled together in a fleet type of voyage. This romantic image of the arrival of Māori to these shores is often the only description that reaches New Zealanders as they pass through the educational processes of this country.

If one took the time however to look closely at the stories and songs that describe the voyages and the eventual settlement of Aotearoa by the Māori one will find a wealth of information and a startling number of accounts of waka that travelled here. The idea of seven waka voyaging together pales into insignificance when one is confronted with the numbers of voyaging waka that can be traced through traditional sources.

In his efforts to trace the seafaring heritage of his own family and to record this information for them, the author has written a book that illustrates just how many waka played a part in the settlement history of this country. Those waka we are all familiar with are encountered, but we also find waka whose history has faded to the point where only the names remain. This in itself should be seen as a challenge to all those interested in the waka history of Aotearoa. It challenges us to find out more about the voyaging heritage of our ancestors. It challenges us to seek answers whether it be through asking acknowledged experts in those fields or researching old history books and song recordings. No doubt some people will know stories that differ in some aspects to those that this book presents. Be that as it may, the list of ancient waka names that this work provides reinforces the voyaging heritage of a people who were once the bearers of significant technological and scientific know-how.

We were once a voyaging people. As Captain Cook found out, our ancestors discovered minute specks of land in a vast ocean centuries before his own people would venture beyond the sight of land. Eventually we will all make that final voyage across the vast ocean to Hawaiki-nui. In the meantime we can still voyage with our ancestors through their stories and we can continue on personal voyages of discovery as we trace the lost traditions and stories of those waka who remain with us in name only.

Books such as this, coupled with the renaissance in traditional voyaging and navigational techniques by Hawaiians and Māori with the construction and successful journeys of waka such as Hokule'a in the 1970s and Te Aurere in the 1990s will certainly maintain the seafaring histories of not only Māori but Polynesian culture for many generations to come.

'E kore au e ngaro, he kākano i ruia mai i Rangiātea'

Hoturoa Kerr
Te Tari Māori
Te Whare Wānanga o Waikato

INTRODUCTION

This book came about from a desire to bring together as many of the written traditions as possible for each of the waka that voyaged to Aotearoa during the earliest period of Polynesian exploration and migration to Aotearoa. In each case, as much information has been presented for the reader as possible, allowing an 'across the board' view of details recorded for each particular waka tradition. After each entry a list of the sources used is listed for those wishing to look further into any particular tradition, or for those who may wish to question any information offered. I have avoided a personal commentary in all but one or two entries, leaving it to the reader to choose between the varying versions.

Naturally there will be many points that will be strenuously debated, and any discussion is to be encouraged. It should be noted, however, that this is a collection of traditions gathered since Europeans first arrived in Aotearoa, and as with any oral tradition, there will be contradictions with contemporary traditions. Suffice to say there are problems surrounding collecting written traditions and oral traditions alike. Misinformation can be provided, and important details can be lost or inadvertently corrupted as tradition passes from one mouth to another. Taking this into account, it would seem pointless to argue whether a statement recorded over 100 years ago is valid, when the challenge comes from a source quoting oral history.

On the other hand, some sources used have been questioned in the last decade or two, with claims against their authenticity strongly voiced. Such works as *The Ancient History of the Maori* and *The Lore of the Whare Wananga* have been largely discredited, with claims suggesting large portions of both works were either falsified or have had so much European input as to make them invalid for historical purposes. Despite such claims, all information gathered has been included, with references used for each entry listed. This will allow those who wish to delve deeper the opportunity to study the original reference.

My main disappointment during the research for this book is that I did not have the resources to investigate the wealth of information available in the Maori Land Court Minute Books. There is without doubt a huge amount of waka tradition entombed within the leaves of the Minute Books, and I would encourage anyone with enough time and willpower to seek it out.

On a personal note, before the idea of compiling the numerous traditions recorded in earlier works into one volume came into being, my objective was to pass on any information I could gather to my daughters about their Maori ancestry. Once I started to search for information on their particular waka, the deluge of recorded traditions and part traditions on waka I had never heard of (remember the seven-waka migration fleet theory?) was virtually never ending. It seemed every book ever written about the Maori contained at least a passing reference to one or more ancestral waka.

Gathering information from such a wide pool of sources was both a blessing and a curse. The names of many waka have been preserved in such valuable volumes as *Nga Moteatea* and the numerous works of J. Herries Beattie, with little or no other information remembered or available. At the other end of the scale, the better-known waka, such as Te Arawa, Tainui and Aotea, have a huge amount of information written about them, either supporting other information, or offering alternative versions.

In recent years, a number of contemporary academics, among them Margaret Orbell and David Simmons, have made claims that many of the waka traditions passed down over the centuries were memories of voyages that were made by ancestors along the shores of Aotearoa, and not voyages made directly from the Pacific Islands. There has been a large amount of support for their claims, and it is perhaps worth taking the time to read their offerings. (Simmons, *The*

Great New Zealand Myth; and Orbell, *Hawaiki — a new approach to Maori tradition*).

Because the majority of the texts sourced have been printed without the use of either macrons or double vowels, I have resisted the temptation to adopt the modern trend of editing with macrons, and have left the text as originally printed.

Jeff Evans

THE
WAKA

AEA-KA-HURU-MANU

It is briefly mentioned in White's *Ancient History of the Maori* that Tu-taka-hinahina, Rukutia, Marama, Ahia and Matoa-tipua travelled in their waka Aea-ka-huru-manu to see Maui after he had fished up Ha-hau-whenua (possibly an ancient name for the North Island of New Zealand) from the sea.

The name similarity between this waka and the Huruhurumanu suggests that they may be one and the same vessel. The Huruhurumanu is noted in South Island traditions as being one of the earliest exploring/migration waka.

The Ancient History of the Maori, Vol. 3, p. 117.

AKEAKE

Little is recorded of this waka, other than that it landed at Whakatane.

Sketches of the Ancient Maori Life and History, p. 38.

AKIKI-A-TE-TAU

Name variation: Ariki-a-te-tau

The Akiki-a-te-tau is briefly mentioned in W.E. Gudgeon's *The Whence of the Maori*, with the only details being the chief's name, Tamatea-kai-ariki.

JPS, Vol. 12, p. 129.
Treasury of Maori Exploration, p. 265.

AOAO-NUNUI

Name variation: Rangi-aoao-nunui

The Aoao-nunui was a waka that belonged to Tiki-te-pourangi, and is mentioned in two laments recorded from the Taranaki area. The following is an abstract from the second verse of a lament for Tonga-awhikau, a member of the Ngati Ruanui tribe, as composed by Te Rangi-Mauri. The translation given is by Hare Hongi.

> E iri E Papa! i runga Rangi-totohu, i runga Rangi-kekero,
> Koe waka uru mate, no Uru, no Ngangana, e-i.
> Kauraka e utaina ki runga te Aoao-nunui,
> Ko te waka tena o Tiki-te-pourangi,
> Me uta o iwi ki runga Rangi-takou.

> You are born high, O father, on Rangi-totohu,
>   and on Rangi-kerero,
> The waka of death, of Uru, of Ngangana, alas,
> Do not place him upon Te Aoao-nunui,
> That is the waka of Tiki-te-pourangi.
> Let your bones be placed on Rangi-takou.

JPS, Vol. 5, pp. 112–13.
Nga Moteatea, Vol. 3, pp. 259, 435.

AOTEA

I will begin with the version of the Aotea waka tradition as told by Hetaraka Tautahi to S. Percy Smith in November 1900. Other accounts follow.

The introduction accompanying the legend given by Tautahi notes that he was a kaumatua of the Nga Rauru tribe, and claimed direct descent from Turi, captain of the Aotea. At the time of the interview, Tautahi was 70 years old and blind, and had sought out a representative of the Polynesian Society to ensure 'a true account [of the tradition] should be furnished' to them. (Smith admits that a few smaller details were missed in his text, because his shorthand was unable to keep up with the flow of information from Tautahi!)

No mention is made in Tautahi's account of the construction of the Aotea, which will be touched on in the additional information section. It is, however, remembered that an ongoing war between Turi and Uenuku was the cause of Turi's migration to Aotearoa. During a battle over the ownership of land at Awarua, Turi and his people defeated Uenuku and his tribe, Tini-o-Uenuku, and in the process Uenuku's younger brother, Kemo, was killed by Kewa, Turi's younger sibling. Despite being badly beaten, Uenuku seemed intent on escalating the hostilities and murdered Turi's son Potiki-roroa to revenge the death of Kemo.

The next move was Turi's, and he killed Uenuku's son Awe-potiki at a stream named Waimatuhirangi. After killing the boy, he gouged out his eyes and cooked them accompanied with pohata (a native cabbage). When the food was ready, he invited Uenuku himself to the feast, conceivably feigning a conciliatory gesture, and offered him first choice of the food. While Uenuku was eating, he asked Turi if he knew the whereabouts of his son Awe-potiki. Turi's reply, suggesting that he was perhaps 'within the belly of Toi' (Toi-te-huatahi, an ancestor of Turi's) was sufficient for Uenuku to realise the awful truth. He immediately returned to his village, no doubt very distressed. Later that night Turi's wife, Rongorongo, overheard Uenuku reciting a karakia-makutu (a curse) that asked the gods to destroy Turi and Ngati Rongotea, over whom he was chief. Rongorongo hurried back to Turi and told him all she had heard.

Despite defeating Uenuku and his tribe in the previous battle, Turi was certain that his tribe would eventually be destroyed by the superior numbers of the Tini-o-Uenuku, and decided on a plan to abandon the island. He asked Rongorongo to visit her father, Toto, and appeal for the use of his waka, Aotea. In return Rongorongo was to present him with the dog-skin cloak named Puke-ko-whatawhata-a-rangi. (It has been remembered that the cloak had been made from the skins of eight dogs: Potaka-tawhiti, Pukeko-whata-rangi, Whakapapa-tuakura, Matawari-te-huia, Kakariki-tawhiti, Miti-mai-te-rangi, Nuku-te-apiapi and Miti-mai-te-paru.) After questioning his daughter as to the sudden need for the Aotea, and being told of the dire consequence should they not leave immediately, Toto readily agreed to his daughter's request and made ready the waka.

Those remembered from the crew were:

Turi	*chief*
Kauika	*navigator*
Rongorongo	*Turi's wife*
Kewa	*Turi's younger brother*

Tuau	*priest*
Turanga-i-mua	*Turi's son*
Tane-roa	*Turi's son*
Tu-taua	*Turi's son born during the voyage*

Hoi-matua	Urunga-tai
Kahu-papae	Te Kahui-kotare
Hou-areare	Puhi-potiki
Kahu-nui	Te Kahui-po
Tu-te-rangi-pouri	Potoru
Rangi-te-pu	Tapu-kai
Hau-nui	Te Kahui-kau

The tribes at Hawaiki that these men represented were: Ngati Rongotea, Ngati Kahu, Ngati Rangi, Ngati Tai and Ngati Kauika.

Several major gods accompanied the Aotea on its voyage to Aotearoa: Maru, Te Ihinga-o-te-rangi, Kahu-kura, and Rongo-mai, while the minor gods Haere-iti and Rehua were also represented. The mana transported in the Aotea was said to have resided in three hand-carved and hollowed stones called whatu. The vessels were named Huna-kiko, Kohatu-mua, and Kohatu-te-ihi. They were considered precious links by the voyagers between Hawaiki and Aotearoa.

Among Turi's personal possessions were:

Te Roku-o-whiti	his paddle
Te Anewa-o-te-rangi	his spear
Te Ririno-o-te-rangi	his bailer
Te Awhio-rangi	and his adze
	(also claimed by other waka)

According to this legend, the anchor of the waka was Akiaki-whenua, and the anchor-rope was Wharona-o-te-rangi. It is also remembered that during the journey four taniwha are said to have escorted the Aotea. Their names were Toi-te-huatahi, Ikaroa, Tangaroa and Rua-mano. (Toi-te-huatahi was one of Turi's ancestors.)

Before the waka commenced its southern voyage, an awa was recited to help calm the seas that the waka would encounter. The following translation is of the awa reputedly used for the Aotea as given by Tautahi (translation by S. Percy Smith).

Aotea is the waka,
Turi is the man on board,
Te Roku-o-whiti is the paddle.

Close to the side, the paddle,
Encircle the side, the paddle,
Forward, standing, the paddle,
Forward, flying, the paddle,
Forward, springing, the paddle,
Forward, flapping, the paddle.

The paddle! up is the paddle, O Rangi!
The paddle of whom?
'Tis the paddle of Te Kau-nunui.
The paddle of whom?
'Tis the paddle of Te Kau-roroa —
The paddle of the great heavens above.
Now the (course of the) waka rests
On Tipua-o-te-rangi —
On Tawhito-o-te-rangi —
On the place of Rehua's eyes
Horizontal will I place the handle
Of my paddle, Te Roku-o-whiti,
To cross over, rattling along,
To fly along, rattling along,
To be light, rattling along,
The up-rising, the up-lifting,
The thrusting in, the dragging hither,
The whirling, the turning round,
Of the spray of the water,
Of this paddle of mine.
Like the far-off sky,
Like the uplifted sky,
Like the great expanse of Tu,
Now does the way part.
The way of this first-born chief,
The way of this section of the tribe,
The way of the great heaven of above.
Name the handle of my paddle, then,
(After) Kautu-ki-te-rangi.
'Tis the heaven elevated.

'Tis the heavens uplifted.
'Tis the heavens that stretch hither.
'Tis the heavens where stands dread.
'Tis the heavens where stands the trust.
'Tis the heavens where stands the tapu.
Be sacred!
Now does the way part,
The way of Tane-matohe-nuku,
The way of Tane-matohe-rangi,
The way of Kau-nunui,
The way of Kau-roroa,
The way of this chief,
The way of the great heavens above,
Hold on (the course) to Rehua —
To the son in the world of light,
O Rongo-ma-tane!
Lift her up, Hae!

It is claimed that at some stage during the journey, Potoru tried to influence Turi's judgement by arguing strenuously that they should abandon the sailing instructions passed down from Kupe, and sail towards the sunset. After much debate, Turi agreed to change course, and despite personal misgivings, sailed the Aotea further west. After the change of direction, the waka soon found itself in a part of the ocean known as Tautope-ki-te-uru. Before Turi could reset the course, the waka was caught in a phenomenon known to Maori as Te Korokoro-o-te-Parata. Turi, in a desperate effort to save the waka, began reciting the following ancient karakia.

Tenei hoki taku taketake,
E Rongo-ma-Ruawhatu,
Whanaua iho i runga i te pu whakamaroro hau,
Amo ake au i taku toki,
Ko te Awhio-rangi, Waihorua,
I hoki ki runga,
I hoki ki raro,
I hoki ki te whai-ao,
Ki te Ao-marama,
Maru a! ka hura,
Tangaroa! unuhia.
Unuhia i mua waka,

I roto waka,
I a Tane-mahuta,
Ki te whai-ao,
Ki te Ao-marama,
E Rongo whakairihia . . .

The karakia had the desired effect and the waka was saved. Turi then commenced another karakia that was used to empty the Aotea of the sea water that had threatened to sink her.

Once the waka was safe, Turi turned to Potoru and accused him of attempting to kill him, then threw him overboard. The god Maru saw this and went to Potoru's aid. Not only did this interference save Potoru's life, but it also helped persuade Turi to let him back aboard the Aotea.

Tautahi also mentions that during the voyage a 'tapuae, or incantation, was used after weathering Tawhiti-nui, the great waves, and after killing the taniwhas, Tutangata-kino, Tuhuatahi and Mokohikuwaru, with the axe, Te Awhio-rangi'. Several other karakia were recited to protect the Aotea during the voyage. There are twelve karakia recorded in an article by John Houston featured in volume 44 of *The Journal of the Polynesian Society*, pages 36–47. The karakia were used at various times, such as during the building of the Aotea, the hauling of the waka to the ocean and when the bailer was being fashioned. These karakia were also provided by Hetaraka Tautahi.

During the voyage from Hawaiki to Aotearoa, the Aotea stopped off at Rangi-tahua. It is not clear whether this happened before or after the saga with Te Korokoro-o-te-Parata, but it is remembered that Turi erected an altar on the island and sacrificed two dogs to appease the gods. While Turi and his companions were at Rangi-tahua, the waka Kurahaupo was wrecked at the island. Several of the crew are said to have joined the Aotea at this time, including Ruatea and Hatonga. (There is much debate over the claim that the Kurahaupo was wrecked at Rangi-tahua. *See also* Kurahaupo.)

From Rangi-tahua, the Aotea sailed directly to the west coast of the North Island. The waka first made land somewhere between Kawhia and Aotea, and was hauled up on the beach, bow facing the sea. This was to allow the rite known as Whaka-awhiawhi to be performed; it was apparently used to destroy any evil in the new country. (Kawhia is supposedly named after this rite — Ka-awhia). From here, Turi and his fellow travellers journey overland, naming several places including Mokau, Ure-nui, Wai-tara, Mangati, Oakura, Wai-ngongoro and Patea as they made their way south. Turi and his people finally settled in the vicinity of Patea.

Two main houses were built by Turi's people. Matangi-rei, on the south side of Patea, and Rangi-tawhi, in the approximate locality of the Patea railway station (as it was in 1900). The garden that the kumara were cultivated in was near Rangi-tawhi, and was called Hekeheke-i-papa.

Among the tribes that claim ancestors from the Aotea are: Ngati Ruanui, Nga Rauru, Whanganui, Ngati Apa and Mua-upoko.

ADDITIONAL INFORMATION

In Hawaiki

It is sometimes claimed that the Aotea had a sister waka built from the same tree. In a passage from *Treasury of Maori Exploration*, the second waka is named as Matahourua, and her captain was Reti. Through marriage to Toto's daughter Kura-maro-tini, Kupe was given possession of the Matahourua, and later voyaged to Aotearoa. A second reference, found in *Maori Place Names*, states that 'the Aotea and the Ririno were hewn from the same tree, which grew on the bank of a river called Wai-harakeke'.

Two other names have been supplied for dogs that were sacrificed for the cloak Puke-ko-whatawhata-a-rangi: Tuhina-po and Tuhina-te-ao. It has also been suggested the correct spelling for Matawari-te-huia is Mata-whare-te-uia. According to sources quoted in *Maori Art*, the names of two of the bailers have been recorded as Tipuahoronuku and Rangi-ka-wheriko. Also given is a list of the cargo transported to Aotearoa in the Aotea, including: kakau (a type of kumara), karaka seeds, para-tawhiti fern, perei (an edible orchid), edible rats, pukeko, and kakariki. From *The Story of Aotea*, we can add to the cargo list taro, hue, aute and dogs.

We learn in *The Coming of the Maori* that another paddle from the Aotea was named Kautu-ki-te-rangi. It is also said that Turi's wife, Rongorongo, was responsible for transporting nine seed kumara in her double belt. Ancestors of the Aotea crew have since refered to kumara by the name Tatau-o-Rongorongo (belt of Rongorongo). Another paddle named from the Aotea was Rangi-horona.

The crew

In Tautahi's version of the legend, he names Potoru in the crew. It is interesting to note that there was a man by the name of Potoru who captained the waka Ririno. Another obvious link between the Aotea and Ririno is the name of the Aotea's bailer — Te Ririno-o-te-rangi.

Other crew collected by Augustus Hamilton and listed in his book *Maori Art* are:

Tura	Tutawa	Tapo
Hou-taepo	Rangi-potaka	Takou
Tama-te-ra	Tuanui-o-te-ra	Uira-ngai-mua
Tanene-roro	Hine-wai-tai	Kura-mahunga
Haupipi		

An explanation before one of the waiata featured in volume three of *Nga Moteatea* claims that Haupipi joined the Aotea from the wrecked Kurahaupo. It also states that the full name of Hau-nui was Hau-nui-a-Paparangi. In some versions it is stated that Turi's child Tane-roroa (or Tane-roa in Tautahi's text) was a female. Pungarehu is named as the leader of a party sent ahead of the main expedition by Turi to plant the karaka seeds, as the migrants journeyed south from their landing place.

According to a list given in *The Story of Aotea*, other hapu that have ancestors among the Aotea crew include:

Ngati Haupipi	Ngati Ruanui
Ngati Kahunui	Ngati Haupihipihi
Ngati Taroa	Ngati Riuwaka
Nga Rauru	Ngati Rangipu
Ngati Maru	

From the same source we can add to the crew: Potanui, Tama-ki-te-ra, and Tu-tawa-whanau-moana (almost certainly the full name of Turi's son, spelt Tu-taua by S. Percy Smith).

Those listed as the crew of the Aotea in John Houston's *Maori Life in Old Taranaki* include Pou-poto and Rakeiora, a tohunga. The family groups Te Kahui Kotare, Te Kahui Po, and Te Kahui Kau are also named. The tradition Houston gives states that the priest Tuau was married to Turi's sister. Tuau had not planned to voyage on the

Aotea, but had been tricked by Turi. Apparently Turi had asked his brother-in-law to accompany the waka to the harbour heads, promising to drop him off before the waka reached the open ocean. Unfortunately for Tuau, before he realised he had been deceived, the Aotea was well offshore, and Turi could not be persuaded to return to land.

The voyage

A spelling variation for the area of ocean that nearly claimed the Aotea is Te Tai-tope-ki-te-uru. According to Takitimu sources, the Aotea stopped over at Rangi-tahua to refit the waka's wash-boards, which had worked loose during the voyage. Rangi-tahua is believed to be one of the islands in the Kermadec group. Sometimes it is said to be Sunday Island; other suggestions for the island's name are Kotiwhatiwha and Motiwhatiwha.

A solitary tradition supposedly collected from Whanganui and Ngati Ruanui sources claims the Aotea stopped at two islands during its voyage to Aotearoa. The first was Rongo-rupe, and it is suggested that this was the island later known as Tuanaki. Tuanaki is believed to have sunk beneath the sea about the turn of the nineteenth century. The second island was Rangi-tahuahua — an obvious reference to Rangi-tahua.

The legend of the waka Ririno states that its captain, Potoru, argued with Turi over the correct sailing directions to Aotearoa and sailed off, either to be wrecked, or in a few versions to land at or about Nelson. (*See* Ririno).

Another taniwha stated to have escorted the Aotea during its southern voyage was Tu-tangata-kino.

Landfall in Aotearoa

According to some, the land about Patea was already occupied when Turi and his party arrived. Among those named as living in the vicinity were the people from the waka Ariki-mai-tai. Other sources suggest that Taikehu (Taiehu) and his tribe were the first inhabitants to give the original name for the Patea River as Te Awa-nui-a-Taikehu.

The claim that the Aotea first made landfall in the vicinity of Aotea and Kawhia is disputed in *Takitimu*, in which it is claimed that the Aotea was the only waka to make landfall directly on the West Coast. The landing place named was Patea.

In a statement attributed to Karipa-te-whetu of Te Ati-awa, it is claimed that the Aotea stopped off at Kaipara on its journey down the west coast of the North Island, and some of the crew remained there with people of the Mahuhu waka.

Other accounts claim that the Aotea first made landfall on the east coast, before voyaging through the Waitamata and Manukau harbours and down to Aotea harbour.

As in some other well-known legends, the crew of the Aotea are said to have been fooled by the blooming pohutukawa into throwing their faded red head-dresses into the ocean, only to discover that they had been deceived by flowers inappropriate for garlands.

The man who was thrown overboard by Turi, and later saved by Maru, is sometimes named as Tapo. In other accounts it is said that at some distance from Aotearoa, Turi threw Tua-nui-o-te-ra overboard because of gross insolence. When the Aotea finally made landfall, Tua-nui-o-te-ra's footprints were reputedly seen in the sand, much to Turi's dismay. The footprints were easily recognisable, because of Tua-nui-o-te-ra's club foot.

According to *The Coming of the Maori* the icon named Hunakiko was taken from its protective cover and displayed at both Oakura and Maraekura during the overland trek to Patea. It is also stated that the full name of Patea is Patea-nui-a-Turi. (A detailed list of places named by Turi during his overland journey is given on page 28 of *Maori Life in Old Taranaki*.)

The Coming of the Maori, pp. 41, 47, 55, 61.
JPS, Vol. 9, pp. 211–28.
JPS, Vol. 12, p.58.
JPS, Vol. 44, pp. 36–47.
Maori Art, p. 29.
Maori Life in Old Taranaki, pp. 19, 23, 28.
Maori Place Names, pp. 153, 165.
Maori Religion and Mythology, Vol. 2, p. 506.
Nga Moteatea, Vol. 3, p. 377.
The Peopling of the North, p. 32.
The Story of Aotea, pp. 99, 109, 118, 120, 124, 147.
Takitimu, pp. 69–70.
Treasury of Maori Exploration, pp. 78, 79, 81, 83.

AOTEAROA

In her book *Two Worlds*, Anne Salmond relates that 'The descendants of Huarere [son of Tama-te-kapua] and Hei intermarried with local people on the peninsula [Whanganui-o-Hei, Mercury Bay] who claimed descent from Mokoterea of the Aotearoa waka'. In one particular reference, Mokotorea is mentioned as the first man to sight the North Island of New Zealand. From him come the ancestors of Ngati Mahuta.

In another tradition, this time from the Chatham Islands, it is stated that a waka by the name of Aotearoa voyaged in the company of Mapouriki, Rangi-ahua and Te Ririno to the Chatham Islands directly from Rarotonga. The Aotearoa is variously mentioned as having been captained by Maui and by Kupe, which is probably merely a testament to the waka's early arrival.

The Great New Zealand Myth, p. 174.
JPS, Vol. 23, p. 76.
Tuhoe: Children of the Mist, p. 679.
Two Worlds, pp. 28–9, 192.

ARAHURA

The waka Arahura is attributed with having brought the greenstone image of an ancient god, also called Arahura, to Aotearoa. The chiefs on board the waka are said to have been Pe-ki-te-tahua, Rongo-ka-he, Rangi-tatau, Hine-raho, Te Rangi-temau, Tae-whenua, Te Mikimiki (Mingimingi), Atua-a-whaka-nihoniho, Te Atua whaka-taratara and Whaka-rewa.

The Ancient History of the Maori, Vol. 2, p. 179.
Maori Art, p. 30.
Maori Lore, p. 296.

ARAI-TE-URU

Name variations: Arai-uru, Taki-te-uru, Arai-te-tonga

Tradition tells of a voyager from Hawaiki named Rongo-i-tua, who introduced kao (dried kumara) to the Kahui-tipua people during a feast. So captivated were his hosts by its sweet taste that they immediately started planning an expedition to procure a supply of kumara to cultivate for themselves.

Soon afterwards one of the local men, Tua-kakariki, found a large totara log washed up on a beach. Delighted with his find, Tua-kakariki hurried back to his pa. While he was away, Rongo-i-tua came across the very same tree and seeing no mark of possession, climbed up and excreted on it as a sign of ownership. Later he confronted Tua-kakariki, claiming that the tree had followed him from Hawaiki and that he had proof that it was his. The two men went to the tree and there Tua-kakariki was shown Rongo-i-tua's mark.

Once Rongo-i-tua's ownership of the log had been established, the Kahui-tipua agreed to assist him in the construction of a waka to be used on a voyage to secure kumara. The size of the log was such, however, that it was soon apparent that two ocean-going waka could easily be constructed from it and the Arai-te-uru and the Manuka were built side by side.

The Manuka, manned entirely by Kahui-tipua people, is said to have set out before the Arai-te-uru and successfully returned with a cargo of kumara. Unfortunately for the Kahui-tipua, the tubers failed to germinate due to the extreme cold of the South Island climate. Rongo-i-tua, aware of the frailties of the kumara, learnt a sacred karakia from the people of Hawaiki to protect the kumara and returned to Aotearoa some time after the Manuka, possibly in the company of the waka Takitimu. The Arai-te-uru made its first landfall at Whitianga-te-ra where part of its cargo was unloaded. Soon after unloading some of the kumara at Whitianga-te-ra the waka was caught in a fierce storm and was forced southwards.

According to a version given to J. Herries Beattie, during the stormy southern passage one of the crew, Moko-tere-a-tarehu, was washed overboard at the mouth of the Waitaki River, and further on Pohu was also lost. As the Arai-te-uru continued to be blown south along the east coast of Te Waipounamu, some of the cargo was lost overboard at Kai-hinaki, a beach near Hampden. The evidence is still to be seen in the form of huge boulders shaped like kumara kits along the seashore. These boulders are commonly known as the Moeraki Boulders. Finally, the exhausted crew were no longer able to handle the waka in the massive seas and Arai-te-uru was wrecked at Matakaea (Shag Point). In some accounts all the crew except Hipo were saved, and most of the precious cargo was turned into stone at the site of the wreckage. Hipo is still in the petrified waka, now a reef just off Matakaea. The kumara, along with hinaki and other possessions of the crew are to be seen as boulders of all sizes strewn around the reef and along the nearby coastline. The sail of the Arai-te-uru is also still visible, petrified under the ocean, close to the waka.

It is also remembered in *Treasury of Maori Exploration* that a waka named Arai-te-uru was 'carrying the Ahi-tapu-a-Uenuku, a sacred fire kindled by a famous tohunga at Hawaiki. This fire was taken up the Waikato river and buried. It took the form of a seam of lignite coal. Subsequently it was dug up by Tamatea-pokai-whenua and used by him to good effect.' Elsewhere, J. Herries Beattie, when discussing names for wind directions in the South Island, was told by an informant that 'he believed that the waka Arai-te-uru famous in southern Maori history was in the Cook Islands known by the name Arai-te-tonga' (the inference being that both uru and tonga were variations for the same word).

Crew Lists

Aheihura	Aroaro-kaehe	Aroaaro-kaihe
Ao-nui	Ao-raki	Hape-ki-tu-a-raki
He Kura	Hepo	Hipo
Hika-aroaro	Hiku-roroa	Kai-tangata
Kake-roa	Kaki-roa	Kiri-kiri-ka-tata
Manga atua	Matakaea	Maukaatua
Moko-tere-a-tarehu	Nga mau-tau-rua	Paha-tea
Pakahiwitahi	Pakihiwitahi	Pikihiwitahi
Poko-hiwi-tahi	Pateatea	Piri-a-mokotaha
Pohu	Puke-tapu	Ri-tua
Tapuaenuku	Tata-i-tu	Tawera
Te Heni	Te Hiwi	Te Horo-koa-tu
Te Maro-tiri-a-te-rehu	Te Wai-o-te-ao	Tikoumu
Wairuapo	Whakai-a-pakura	

The Ancient History of the Maori, Vol. 2, p. 179.
Folklore and Fairytales of the Canterbury Maoris, pp. 25–6.
The Great New Zealand Myth, p. 206.
Hawaiki: A New Approach to Maori Traditions, p. 62.
JPS, Vol. 12, p. 129.
JPS, Vol. 24, p. 108.
The Morioris of the South Island, pp. 35–9.
Tikao Talks, p. 63.
Traditional Lifeways of the Southern Maori, p. 197.
Treasury of Maori Exploration, pp. 55, 57–8.

ARATAUWHAITI, TE

Te Aratauwhaiti was possibly one of the first migration waka to reach the shores of Aotearoa, making land at Whakatane (previously known as Kakaho-roa). The captain is said to have been Tiwakawaka, and those remembered in the crew were Tiwakawaka's wife Haumia-nui, his brothers Toikairakau and Hirawe, and crew members Maku, Areiawa, Turuturu, Tokomauku and Himoki, each of whom had rocks named after them at the entrance of Whakatane River. It is stated that the land was uninhabited when the waka reached Aotearoa, and that the migrants built a pa named Kapu-te-rangi. (In the entry for Paepae-ki-Rarotonga it is claimed Toi-te-tuatahi also built a pa at Whakatane, called Kapu-te-rangi, during his search for Whatonga.)

There is considerable debate in Transactions of the New Zealand Institute, volume 37, page 122, as to the correctness of the claim that Toikairakau and Maku were members of the Aratauwhaiti crew, with the genealogical evidence quoted suggesting it to be false.

Transactions of the New Zealand Institute, Vol. 37, p. 122.
Whakatane and District Historical Society Inc. Memoir #1, p. 71.

ARATAWHAO

This waka was built by Hoaki and Taukata to enable their return to Hawaiki to acquire kumara. (The story of their voyage to Aotearoa in search of their sister Kanioro and her husband Pou-ranga-hua has been recorded in the tradition of the Hinaki-pakau-o-te-rupe.) After introducing kumara to the inhabitants of the Kapu-te-rangi (or Tapu-te-rangi) pa, near Whakatane, the brothers were induced to build a voyaging waka in which to return to their homeland and procure a selection of the vegetable tubers for cultivation. It was agreed that a new waka would be built and sailed to Hawaiki where kumara grew in great abundance.

A large totara log was selected, and Hoaki and Taukata commenced construction. The log had been found washed up on a beach near the mouth of the Whakatane River, and from this tawhaowhao (driftwood) the waka was named. The adzes used to form the mighty waka were named Te Manokohuka, Te Waiheke and Te Warawaratai-o-Tane. As soon as the weather permitted, the waka was made ready for the voyage to Hawaiki and a crew selected. Those remembered of the crew are:

Hoaki	*navigator*
Tama-ki-hikurangi	*chief*

Tama-rakei-ora	Te Whatu-pouri
Te Whatu-potango	Tata-puku
Kauae-puku	Nuku-taria
Pouranga-hua	Whatu-kiore
Ira-te-wewenga	Tikitiki-o-te-rangi
Awa-hei-roa	Ue-apa
Awa-hei-nui	Awa-morehurehu
Awa-nui-a-rangi	Te Puka
Tama-ki-te-ra	Tahu-o-rehu
Mawake	Puhi-ariki

It was decided that Taukata would remain at Kapu-te-rangi while Hoaki navigated the waka to Hawaiki. It is often suggested that this was insisted on by Tama-ki-hikurangi to ensure that Hoaki would assist him and the crew return to Aotearoa after the outward voyage. Some other accounts say Taukata preferred to stay with his sister Kaniora.

On the eve of the voyage, Pou-ranga-hua decided to visit his grandchild Kahu-kura at Kirikino. As he left, he asked that the waka await his return, as he was eager to voyage to Hawaiki. The reason the departure of the waka was not delayed for Pou-ranga-hua has not been recorded, but he was very distraught when he returned to find the Aratawhao gone. So determined was he to voyage to Hawaiki, that he summonsed Te Manu-nui-a-rua-kapanga to transport him to his desired destination (*see* Ruakapanga).

There are few references to the journey itself, although it is remembered that Tama-ki-hikurangi was able to strengthen his position in the eyes of his fellow tribesmen by a sleight of hand. Having overheard Puhi-ariki, one of the lesser chiefs of the tribe, trying to persuade some of the crew to leave him behind by secretly casting off in the middle of the night, Tama-ki-hikurangi formed a plan to make himself look indispensable. During the night prior to the departure he crept down to the waka and bored a hole in the bottom of it near the position he would assume as chief of the tribe. He then plugged the hole and hid the bailer. The next morning he assured everyone that he had the bailer and not to worry. In due course the Aratawhao departed, and Tama-ki-hikurangi put his plan into action. He dislodged the plug and let the waka start to fill with water. As those around him began to panic, he re-plugged the hole and emptied the water, thus saving the day. He repeated this on more than one occasion, thus convincing the crew that he, Tama-ki-hikurangi, had saved them all from a watery grave.

The following karakia are taken from Elsdon Best's *Notes on Ancient Polynesian Migrants*, and are said to have been used by the crew of the Aratawhao. The first is a tata, recited while bailing water from the waka.

> Pa atu hoki taku tata
> Ki te riu tapu nui o te waka
> E haere nei
> Rei kura, rei ora
> Rei ora te mahaki
> Ka turuturua, ka poupoua
> Ki tawhito o te rangi-e.

This second karakia, called an awa, was used to calm the seas and make the way smooth for the waka.

> Tu mai awa, tu mai awa
> Ko koe kei takahia noatia e au
> Ta peau nuku, ta peau rangi
> Whati ki runga, Whati ki raro
> Ma uru marara
> Pera hoki ra taku manu nui na Tane
> Ka tatau atu ki roto nuku ngaere
> Mai whiwhia, mai a rawea
> Mai a whakatakaia
> Ka taka te huki rawea
> Koro i runga, koro i raro
> Koro i Tawhirimatea
> Ki kona hoki koe tu mai ai
> Ka hura te tamatea nunui
> Ka hura te tamatea roroa
> Te kauwaka nuku, te kauwaka rangi
> Te ai a nuku, te ai a Rangi
> Te kura mai hukihuki
> Te kaweau tetere
> Kawea a nuku, kawea a tai
> Oi! Tumatakokiritia
> Hoatu waka ki uta
> Hoatu waka ki waho

Ngaru hinga atu, ngaru hinga mai
I runga te tama-wahine
I raro te tama-tane
Huki nawenawe
Tenei te awa ka whakairi
Ko irirangi te waka
Ko irirangi te tangata.

The karakia below is known as a rukutia, and was recited to ensure that the waka remained seaworthy during the long and arduous voyage.

Rukutia
Rukutia te waka e haere nei
Rukutia te kei matapupuni
Rukutia i te ihu mata pupuni o Tane
Rukutia i te kowhao tapu nui o Tane
Rukutia i te mata tapu nui o Tane
Rukutia i te rauawa tapu nui o Tane
O te waka e haere nei
Tumatakokiritia
Rei kura, rei ora
Rei ora te mahaki-e
Ka turaturua ka poupoua
Ki tawhito o te rangi
E manawa mai ao-e
Hoatu waka ki uta.

The final karakia recorded is a rotu, and was chanted to pacify the winds.

Hika atu ra taku ahi
Ki te hau e riri mai nei
E rotu mate, rotu mate aio he
Tawaha ana ra
Te hau e riri mai nei
E rotu mate, rotu mate, aio he
He marangai te hau
E riri mai nei
Haere i tua, haere ia moana nui
Haere i a moana roa

Haere i a moana te takiritia
Ki te whai ao, ki te ao marama.

A number of the Aratawhao's karakia which are very similar to the four recorded here appear in the book *In Ancient Maori Land* (pages 10 and 11).

When the Aratawhao reached Hawaiki, Hoaki was greeted by his father, Rongotau, who was the rangatira of the island. After the ceremonies of greeting were completed, and the inevitable celebrations were over, it was agreed by Rangitau to supply Tama-ki-hikurangi with prize kumara. They were supplied by Maru-tai-rangaranga, a chief with well-renowned cultivations at Pari-nui-te-ra and Ngaruru-kai-whatiwhati. It is generally agreed that neither Hoaki nor the Aratawhao returned to Aotearoa, but that the waka Mata-atua was used by Tama-ki-hikurangi and his crew to transport the kumara instead.

In one tradition, credited to certain sections of Ngati Awa, the Aratawhao is said to have escorted a fleet of waka to Aotearoa which included Mata-atua, Takitumu, Nukutere, Te Arawa, Rangi-matoru, Turereao, Tokomaru, Kurahaupo, Tainui and Tauira. It is doubtful whether this fleet actually existed as a whole, but it is possible that the legend was designed to imply that Hoaki of the Aratawhao passed on the sailing instructions to the navigators of the waka listed. When the navigators followed the directions, Aratawhao was considered to be escorting them.

The tribes descending from the Aratawhao and Mata-atua are Ngati Awa, Te Ure-wera, Ngai-te-Rangi and Te Whanau-a-Apanui.

The Coming of the Maori, p. 33.
In Ancient Maori Land, pp. 10–11.
JPS, Vol. 3, p. 69.
JPS, Vol. 12, p. 170.
JPS, Vol. 75, p. 204.
Transactions of the New Zealand Institute, Vol. 37, pp. 130–6.

ARAUTAUTA, TE

Name variation: Ara Umauma

Legend says that the Whakatohea ancestor Tarawa sailed to Aotearoa in his waka, Arautauta, and accompanied by his two taniwha made land at Waiotahi Beach, between Opotiki and Ohiwa

Harbour. On arrival, Tarawa is said to have placed his taniwha in the spring O-potiki-mai-tawhiti and then travelled inland to Motu. There he met and cohabited with Manawakiatu, daughter of Tauwharangi, of Ngati Maruiwi tribe, and they had two children, who were the progenitors of the present Ngai Tama tribe.

Whakatane and Districts Historical Society Inc. Memoir, #8, p. 18.

ARAWA, TE
Name variation: Mahanga-a-Tuamatua

The tradition of Te Arawa is one of the most comprehensive to have been recorded. The version given in the main passage is based on Stafford's *Te Arawa* text.

The reason for the voyage of Te Arawa was the departure of Houmaitawhiti and his people from Hawaiki, following a long-running conflict with Uenuku. The trouble between the two parties started soon after the slaying of Houmaitawhiti's dog, Potakatawhiti, by Uenuku. Toitehuatahi, one of Uenuku's fellow tribesmen, had seen the dog unearthing some discharge from Uenuku's ulcer that had been secretly buried. In accordance with custom, Uenuku killed the dog, and he and Toitehuatahi then ate the remains.

Soon after, two of Houmaitawhiti's sons, Tamatekapua and Whakaturia, went searching for the dog. It wasn't until they reached the neighbouring village where Uenuku lived that they heard the familiar cry of their dog. Despite searching all over the village, they were unable to locate the animal. They were on the verge of giving up when they heard the dog yelping from Toitehuatahi's stomach, and discovered the awful truth. Unable to challenge Uenuku and Toitehuatahi in combat, the two boys returned to their village and decided that the best revenge would be to steal fruit from a poporo tree in Uenuku's garden (the tree is often refered to as te poporo whakamarumaru o Uenuku — the sheltering poporo of Uenuku). To avoid detection, Tamatekapua and Whakaturia climbed up on their stilts and walked to Uenuku's garden, without leaving footprints to incriminate them.

The ruse worked successfully for several nights, until so much fruit had been taken that Uenuku knew that someone must be stealing it. Furious, he went about setting a trap to catch the thieves. The next night his suspicions were confirmed when he caught Tamatekapua and Whakaturia in the act. Rushing from their hiding places, Uenuku and his colleagues cornered Whakaturia in the garden, but were unable to capture Tamatekapua. The unfortunate Whakaturia was taken by his captors and hung from the rafters above the fire of the tribe's meeting house. Uenuku had decided that Whakaturia would die a slow death in the smoke of the fire, as he and his people celebrated in song and dance below.

It wasn't long before Tamatekapua learnt of his brother's predicament, and quickly devised a plan of escape. Climbing the outside of the whare, Tamatekapua spoke to Whakaturia through the thatch. He told his brother to jeer at the performance of those below and boast to them that he was a far superior dancer. As Tamatekapua had suspected, Uenuku and his people immediately lowered Whakaturia and ordered him to dance for them. He danced for some time, and soon his captors had let down their guard enough for him to dash to the door, where Tamatekapua waited outside. Once Whakaturia had leapt through the door, his brother bolted it, and the brothers escaped. Uenuku, in a rage at being outsmarted by the boys, assembled a large force and attacked Houmaitawhiti's village. After a violent struggle in which many were killed, Uenuku was finally defeated, and forced to retreat to his village.

Not long after this, Houmaitawhiti decided that his people would migrate to Aotearoa. A large tree was felled, and the craftsmen Rata, Wahieroa, Ngahue and Parata were selected to fashion a mighty voyaging waka. The adzes used were called Tutauru and Hauhauterangi. Tradition remembers that the following karakia was recited before the final blow to sever the tree used to build Te Arawa from its stump.

> Kakariki powhaitere
> Kotia te pu waiho i konei.
> Kotia te kauru waiho i konei.
> E ai hoki au i te umu a Te Tuhi,
> Kihai i tae ki nga pu, ki nga take,
> Ki nga wananga, ki nga tauira.
> Patua kuru, patua whao,
> Patua te toki a Taiharuru.
> Piki ake hoki au nei ki runga,
> I te whare-hukahuka-nui a Tangaroa,
> I whatiia ai e Nukutaimaroro.
> E Nukutaimaroro pera hoki ra

Ko au ko Hinetuahoanga, e kimi ana,
E hahau ana i te whanau a Rata.
Ko Rata i mate mai i te awa i Pikopiko i whiti.
Mate! Maranga mai, ka whiti!
Nuku e! Ta taua rangi
Whano! Whano!
Haramai te toki!
Haumi e!
Hui e!
Taiki e! i!

It is said in some accounts that the Tainui was built at the same time as Te Arawa. The following waka-hauling chant is recorded in Te Arawa and features the names of both waka to back up this claim.

Time caller
Toia Tainui, Te Arawa
Kia tapotu ki te moana
Koia i hirihiri te mata whatitiri
Takatakatu mai i taku rangi tapu

Time caller	*Response from haulers:*
Ka tangi te kiwi	kiwi.
Ka tangi te moho	moho.
Ka tangi te tieke	tieke.
He poho anake	te tikoko, tikoko.
Haere i te ara	Tikoko.
Ko te taurua te rangi	Kauaia.
Ko te hao tane	Kauaia.
Homai me kawe	Kauaia.
Me kawe ki whea	Kauaia.
A ki te take	Take no Tu.
E Hautoia	Toia.
Hau riri	Toia.
Toia ake te take	Take no Tu.
Koia rimu haere	Kauaia.
Totara haere	Kauaia.
Pukatea haere	Kauaia.
Homai te tu	Kauaia.

Homai te maro	Kauaia.
Kia whitikia	Kauaia
Taku takapu	Kauaia.
Hihi e	Haha e.
Tipi e	Tata e.
Apitia	Ha.
Ko te here	Ha.
Ko te here	Ha.
Ko te timata	E ko te tikoko pohue.
E ko te aitanga a mata	E ko te aitanga o te hoe manuka.
Ko au, ko au	Hitau e.
Mate ko te hanga	Hitau e.
Turuki, turuki	Paneke, paneke.
Oioi te toki	Kauaia.
Takitakina	I a.
He tikaokao	He Taraho.
He parera	Ke-ke-ke-ke.
He parera	Ke-ke-ke-ke.

After the two voyaging waka, Te Arawa and Tainui, had been completed and the appropriate ceremonies attended to, they were dragged to the shore of the bay called Whenuakura for finishing and provisioning.

Just prior to departure, Tamatekapua is credited with two acts that have been well recorded, and that marked him as a man of deceit until his death. In the first, Tamatekapua stole the wife of his fellow tribesman, Ruaeo. Having secretly desired Ruaeo's wife for some time, Tamatekapua formed a plan to ensure Ruaeo would be left behind when Te Arawa sailed. Tamatekapua asked Ruaeo to return to the village to collect the adze Tutauru, which Tama claimed was under the sill of his whare. Unbeknown to Ruaeo, the adze was already safely onboard the waka, and by the time he returned to the shore, Te Arawa had sailed.

In the second act of deceit, Tamatekapua asked the high priest Ngatoroirangi and his wife Kearoa (Keataketake), who were due to voyage on Tainui, to visit Te Arawa to perform the rites that would ensure the waka safely reached its destination. As soon as Ngatoroirangi and his wife were aboard, Tamatekapua ordered the anchors to be lifted, and the waka shot off on its voyage to Aotearoa.

Because of Ngatoroirangi's knowledge of the seas and stars, he was regarded as the navigator for the trip, and as such spent the majority of his time sitting on the whare that is said to have been built across the two hulls of Te Arawa. Ngatoroirangi was well aware of Tamatekapua's roving eye, and had tied a length of cord to Kearoa's hair each night that he spent on the whare roof, so that he could tell if she was entertaining anyone. Tamatekapua, always willing to take up the challenge, soon managed to untie the cord. He then retied the cord to a beam, so that Ngatoroirangi still held a taut cord. Unfortunately for Tamatekapua and Kearoa, however, Ngatoroirangi soon discovered their act of deception when he returned to his bed earlier than expected, leaving no time for Tamatekapua to retie the cord in Kearoa's hair. When asked who had visited her, Kearoa simply replied, 'Who other than Tama?' Hearing this, Ngatoroirangi flew into a fury and called upon the gods to destroy Te Arawa and every soul on her. The waka was drawn into a whirlpool called Te Korokoro-o-te-Parata (Te Waha-o-te-Parata). As the waka sank further and further into the heart of the whirlpool, all the provisions loaded on Te Arawa, save a small basket of kumara which Whakaotirangi saved, were lost overboard. It was not until the waka was almost completely lost that Ngatoroirangi took pity on the women and children and calmed the waters. The following karakia is said to have been that used by Ngatoroirangi to save the waka, and is recorded in *Te Arawa*.

> Takina te kawa,
> He kawa tua-tahi,
> Takina te kawa,
> He kawa tua-rua,
> He kawa tua-toro,
> He kawa tua-wha,
> He kawa tua-rima,
> He kawa tua-ono,
> He kawa tua-whitu,
> He kawa tua-waru,
> He kawa tua-iwa,
> He kawa tua-ngahuru.
>
> Takina te kawa,
> He kawa ma Tangaroa,
> Ka pipi,

Ka wawai,
Ka hoaia,
Ka whanake i raro i ona taranga,
Tutuki te rangi,
Eke,
Eke,
Eke Tangaroa
Eke panuku,
Hui, e!
Taiki, e!
Unuhia te pou,
Ko te pou mua,
Ko te pou roto,
Ko te pou te wharaua,
He aturangi-mamao,
Hekeheke iho i runga i o ara,
Takikiwhara,
Te ara o Ngatoro,
He ara whano ki te po,
Te po-nui,
Te po-roa,
Te po-matire rau,
Te po-whaiariki,
A ko taku waka ko Te Arawa,
Ngahue i te Parata,
Eke,
Eke,
Eke Tangaroa,
Eke panuku,
Hui, e!
Taiki, e!

Tena to tu tau e Rongo ka whawai,
Te kawa Tuai-Nuku,
Tua-i-Rangi,
Tua-i-Papa,
Tua-i-Tane,
Rua Nuku,
A tuai,
A tuai.

Fortunately for those on board Te Arawa, the remainder of the voyage to Aotearoa was without incident, and the waka soon reached the coast near Whangaparaoa, Cape Runaway.

On first sighting the pohutukawa in flower several of the crew threw away their faded red-feather head-dresses. It wasn't until they approached the tree that they discovered that the flower wasn't suitable for making head-dresses. Try as they might, those deceived couldn't persuade Mahina, who had gathered up the discarded headwear from the beach, to give them back.

While exploring the beach and surrounding lands, one of the crew came across the carcass of a recently stranded whale. Upon closer inspection, Tamatekapua discovered that the crew of another waka (the Tainui) had beaten them to it, and had tied a flax rope to the whale to claim ownership. Unperturbed, Tamatekapua ordered his men to plait a rope of their own, dry it over a fire, and tie it to the jaw of the whale. Next he had an area of the scrubland cleared, and using old and dry pieces of timber from about the place, built an altar that looked remarkably old. Tamatekapua then confronted Hoturoa and the crew of Tainui, claiming the whale as Te Arawa's, pointing to the 'older' rope and altar as his proof. Despite knowing the truth in their hearts, Hoturoa and the crew of Tainui left the whale to Tamatekapua, and sailed north.

Soon afterwards, Te Arawa also voyaged north, stopping at a small island in the vicinity of Moehau (Cape Colville), called Te Poito-o-te-kupenga-a-Taramainuku. At the island, Ngatoroirangi deposited a sacred mauri stone he had carried from Hawaiki as a guardian for Te Arawa and her crew against evil. As the waka was about to leave the island, Tamatekapua announced that he would return to Moehau to live out his days once the waka had finished its voyage. Other chiefs also picked out land for themselves as the waka travelled along the coastline.

The next stop for Te Arawa was Reponga (Cuvier Island). Here two birds named Takereto and Mumuhou were freed. Each of the birds had a distinctive cry, and it was believed that navigators could tell from them whether the forecast was for fine or foul weather, depending on which bird sang. After the brief stop over at Reponga, the waka sailed back south along the coast. When Te Arawa neared the outlet of the stream called Wairakei, Tamatekapua again claimed land for himself. Motioning towards Maketu, he is said to have likened the headland to his nose. This action of describing the land as a part of his head made the claim sacred, and ensured none from his crew would argue the point. Other chiefs among the crew, including Tia and Hei, soon took Tamatekapua's lead, and all the coastal land from Maketu to Katikati was claimed by Te Arawa.

The next stopover was at Maketu where the waka entered the river mouth of the Kaituna. The bow of the vessel was anchored on the rock subsequently named Tokaparore, while the stern was tied to the rock Tuterangiharuru. Soon after Te Arawa anchored at Maketu, the waka Pukeateawainui made landfall nearby. The captain of the Pukeateawainui was Ruaeo, who had voyaged to avenge the insult Tamatekapua had thrown in his face. While the crew of Te Arawa slept, Ruaeo and his men silently surrounded them. Ruaeo then approached the waka, and with a thump of his weapon on its side, woke the startled crew. He immediately challenged Tamatekapua to a fight, which Tamatekapua eagerly accepted. After a long and fierce battle, Ruaeo managed to pin his adversary down, and taking a handful of vermin, avenged Tamatekapua's insult by rubbing it in his hair. Ruaeo then left his wife, Whakaotirangi, to Tamatekapua as compensation for the final insult.

Among those remembered from Te Arawa's crew are:

Hatupatu *	Haukapuanui	Hei *
Hopo	Hurikoko	Ihenga *
Ika *	Kahumatamomoe *	Kawatea
Kawatutu *	Kawauri	Kearoa *
Kurapoto *	Kuraroa	Kuri-niho-popo, Te
Maaka *	Mapara *	Marupunganui *
Mawate *	Naki	Ngatoroirangi *
Oro *	Paeko	Penu
Pou	Rongokako	Rongomai *
Rongomaiwhaia	Rongopuruao *	Ruarangi
Ruarangimuria	Tahu	Taikehu *
Taininihi *	Tamatekapua *	Tamateranui
Tamaterawhakarapa	Tangihararu	Tangihia *
Tarawhata	Tapuika *	Taunga *
Tia *	Tuarotorua *	Tuhoromatakaka *
Tutauaroa *	Uea	
Uenukuwhakarorongarangi *		Uruika *
Waitaha *	Whakaotirangi *	Whaoa

* Considered by Stafford to have sufficient traditional evidence to confirm their having migrated on Te Arawa.

The following version of the burning of Te Arawa was collected by Elsdon Best from 'the Maori school of learning', as opposed to others from 'ordinary' sources, which claim the destruction of Te Arawa was an act of aggression. (It is sometimes said that Raumati threw a flaming dart on to the roof of the waka house).

After the historic voyage of Te Arawa from Hawaiki, the waka was hauled up on land in the vicinity of the mouth of the Kaituna, and placed in a waka house built especially for her. Presently a party of travellers, lead by Raumati, chose to visit the site of the famous waka, while passing through the area. For one reason or another the waka was unattended as the group approached the waka house. After inspecting the reknowned waka, the party moved off some distance to cook food and rest. Unfortunately for them, the winds turned, and their fire quickly raced out of control. Before they could move the waka, the fire caught hold of its shelter, and the waka was destroyed. Despite it being an accident, Raumati and his group were hunted down and annihilated by Tamatekapua and his men.

ADDITIONAL INFORMATION

The waka

According to Tuwharetoa tradition, the Te Arawa was built from two huge trees picked out by Tia and Hei from a forest owned by Kurapoto. The waka was built especially to convey a selected group from the tribe to Aotearoa.

It is stated in *Maori Lore* that Te Arawa was originally owned by Puhaorangi. It is claimed that the adzes Tutauru and Hauhauterangi had been made from a block of pounamu, which Ngahue had found during his exploration of Aotearoa, when he had voyaged there in his waka, Tawirirangi.

The following description of Te Arawa was given in *Historic Maketu*:

The Arawa was really a double-hulled waka, capable of carrying 200 or more people with a certain amount of lading. It was magnificently carved as to prow and stern. Above, across the two hulls which were lashed together and estimated at not less than 120 feet long, was built a deck called 'pora.' This deck was in the forward part of the waka and on it was built the cabins or pakokori, while right forward was a shrine or sacred place for the performing of incantations by the priest or tohunga. Below were carried some effects and the food for the voyage. On board, as part of the equip-

ment besides paddles, were elaborately-carved bailers, called 'tata.' There was also a special steering paddle used by the navigator, but the Arawa and other waka of the fleet did not depend on the paddlers but upon sails rigged from a mast and sprit and shaped like a inverted triangle. They were made of plaited material. The Arawa probably had three sets of sails and masts, foresail, mainsail, and mizzen, for she was reputed to have a terrific turn of speed.

In the entry for Mahanga-a-Tuamatua, it is explained that Ngata suggested that Te Arawa and Tainui may have been two hulls of the same double waka *(see* Mahanga-a-Tuamatua). It is also noted in *Tuwharetoa* that Te Mahangaatuamatua was an ancient name for Te Arawa, and that principal chiefs on both Tainui and Te Arawa were descendants of Tua-matua.

The waiata that follows is for waka hauling and was collected by White from Te Arawa sources. It is stated that it was used when Te Arawa was dragged to the seashore prior to launching.

Toia Te Arawa tapotu ki te moana!
Ma wai e to? Ma te whakaranga ake!
He tara wainuku; he tara wairangi.
Tinia, momoa. Naumai, naumai e Tane!
Ka kau taua, kia matakitakina koe
E te tini o te tangata.
Naku koe i tiki atu i te wao nui o Tane —
He tane miroi, he tane koakoa,
He tane rangahau. E patua mai ana
E te komuri hau na runga o Waihi.
Panekeneke ihu o te waka,
Turuki, turuki! Paneke, paneke!

The next waiata is quoted in *Tuwharetoa,* and is claimed by Te Kapooterangi to have been chanted by Ngatoroirangi moments before Te Arawa and Tainui were launched.

Tainui ano Tainui,
Te Arawa ano Te Arawa.
He rangi kia paku,
He rangi kia pake,
He pake rohutu.
Rohutu ra i mau ai te tieke.

Hei te tieke!
Hei te tieke!
Haramai te toki!
Haumi e! Hui e!
Taiki e — i!

It is claimed that this waiata was sung by Houmaitawhiti to his sons when they visited him prior to their voyage.

Tuatua mai,
Te Whiwhia mai,
Te rawea,
Turou parea Tangaroa,
I te orooro,
I te oromea,
I tukitukia ai koe,
Itataia ai koe,
O i!
Kiri o Tangaroa!
O i!
Tere te waka nei,
Tere angaia,
O i,
Tutaki ki tenei manuka,
Tutaki ki tenei ngahoa
Tupu ki toto.
Kia hono koe, E Tama!
Ko to hono tawhito.
Purua o taringa kia turi,
A kia hoi,
Kei whakarongo koe
Ki te korero iti,
Ko te korero iti,
Ko tahuri na
Ko te hau aitu
Kihai te kanohi i titiro
Ko te taringa i whakarongo.

According to Tuwharetoa tradition, the reason Tamatekapua originally asked Ngatoroirangi and his wife Kearoa aboard his waka was to release Te Arawa from a state of tapu, so women could safely travel on her. In some versions of the Te Arawa tradition, Tamatekapua sends Ruaeo back to his whare to collect his comb, rather than the adze Tutaura.

The voyage

According to sources quoted by Buck in *The Coming of the Maori*, Ruaeo used 'magical powers' to confuse the appearence of the evening stars, and thus slow Te Arawa's progress, while he prepared his waka for the chase. In the Tuwharetoa version of the voyage, Te Arawa stopped off at Rarotonga en route to Aotearoa to reprovision and make minor repairs. When the waka left Rarotonga, it is said to have left from the mouth of the Waitekura stream. From the same source comes the following karakia. It is claimed that Ika tried to save Te Arawa from the depths of Te Korokoro-o-te-Parata by reciting it.

> Tenei tokanuku, te kiri o Tane;
> Ko taipito, ko taingahoa.
> Hoa ita, hoa ita.
> Te kupu tenei hoki te ruruku
> Ka mau, ko te ruruku nui na Ika.
> Rukutia mai hae kia u.
> Tapu te raka kia u
> Rukutia nga atua kia u.
> Tapu te rakakia u.
> Rukutia Tainui, Te Arawa,
> Kia u!
> Tapu te raka kia u.
> Rukutia nga tangata kia u.
> Tapu te raka kia u!
> E — i!
> E rangi e!
> Ko Rangi taua iho,
> Ko Rangi taua ake,
> Ko Rangi tau apiti te tuahiwi,
> Te Tuahiwi o te Rangi
> Ka moumoua te kaokao o Tane,
> Tena toka whenua.
> Whakamau atu te ruruku

Ki te ihu o te waka;
Whakamau atu te ruruku
Kei te ihu o nga tangata.
Turou parea.
Pera hoki ra Tangaroa.
I te horomea
I tukitukia ai, i taitaia ai.
O — oi!
Kani Tangaroa!
Whano, whano!
Haramai te toki!
Haumi e!
Ui — e!
Taiki — e!

In some accounts of the voyage, it is said that Te Korokoro-o-te-Parata was a shoal that Te Arawa washed up on, while others claim it was the name of a fierce storm encountered mid-ocean. One account of Ngatoroirangi's karakia states he called upon the gods, Maui-mua, Maui-roto, Maui-taha, Maui-pae, and Maui-taki-taki-o-te-ra when he wanted to destroy Te Arawa. The same source claims that he showed no mercy until he heard the voice of his nephew, Uenuku-whaka-roro-nga-rangi, call out for him to save the waka.

The landfall

Evidence collected by Judge J.A. Wilson from early Maori Land Court cases suggested that Te Arawa first made landfall at Whangara, before sailing north in the company of Tainui to the Bay of Plenty. It is claimed in many versions that it was Tauninihi who threw his red feather head-dress away when Te Arawa first neared the coast of Aotearoa. Another version (in *Treasury of Maori Exploration*) suggests that it was Rua-rangi-murua and Ika who threw away their kura, or head-dresses. Maihi te Kapua te Hinaki of Ngati Paoa and Ngati Whatua claimed that Whakaotirangi was Hoturoa's wife, and that Tamatekapua was challenged to a fight at Orawharo, a pa on the island Motutapu, by Hoturoa. It is remembered that Hoturoa beat Tamatekapua so badly that the crews of the two waka had to intervene before Tamatekapua was killed. The island Rangitoto, in the Hauraki Gulf, was named after this encounter, the full name being Te Rangitoto o Tamatekapua. It is also stated that the islands of the Hauraki Gulf were collectively referred to as Nga Poitu-o-te-kupenga-a-Taramainuku. The names of two of the kura thrown away by those on board Te Arawa were Tu-he-po and Tu-he-ao.

It is said that Te Arawa carried five separate mauri from Hawaiki. The first was the stone left at Moehau; the second was a manuka tree planted at Whakatane; the third was a rengarenga (lily) placed on an altar at Whangara; the fourth was the flint stone used by Ngatoroirangi to make Tongariro erupt on one of his later journeys; and the final one was the altar known as Ahurei at Kawhia, Maketu.

According to sources quoted in Grace's *Tuwharetoa*, soon after the Tainui left Whangaparaoa, the crew of Te Arawa tried unsuccessfully to launch their waka. Due to an incantation cast by Ngatoroirangi, the waka was immovable, and no one in the crew had the mana to undo the witchcraft. Fortunately, the waka Mataatua had landed nearby, and Toroa, the captain, was able to recite the following karakia to free the waka.

> Whakamoe, whakamoe au maroro whenua,
> Hina pera hoki ra
> Ko Ruiho,
> Ko Ruake,
> Ko Manu,
> Ko Weka,
> Ko Toroa,
> Ko Ruaihona,
> Ko Tahingaotera.
> Tenei te maro ka huru,
> Huruhuru nui no te wahine,
> Tutapori atu, tutapori mai,
> Wero noa, wero noa
> Wero noa Tamatekapua
> I tona rakau.
> I te rakau na te wai?
> I te rakau na te tipua
> I tiki ki Hawaiki.
> I homai nei hei rakau mo taku waka
> Mo Waimimiha.
> I mate i Tukaniwha.

I mate i Tutaua.
Whano, whano,
Haramai te toki,
Haumi e,
Hui e,
Taiki e!

In a tradition given by Takaanui Tarakawa of Tainui and Te Arawa, it is claimed that some time after Te Arawa reached Maketu, Oro, Maka, Uruika, Kurapoto and others, with the assistance of Ngatoroirangi, sailed the waka south and discovered Te Awa-a-te-atau. The waka was manoeuvred through the river mouth, and landed at a spot named Niao. From there, the crew explored in all directions. The waka was finally returned to Maketu by Ngatoroirangi and 'his companions'.

The crew of Te Arawa were of the Nga Ohomairangi tribe of Hawaiki. Among the tribes descending from the crew of Te Arawa are Ngati Porou, Rangitihi, Ngati Pikiao, Ngati Rangi-wewehi, Tuhourangi, Ngati Wahiau, Ngati Tuwharetoa, Ngati Kearoa, Tapuika, Ngati Ha, Waitaha, Ngati Rangitiki, Ngati Uenuku-kopako, Ngati Tama, Poutawa, Ngati Huarere, Ngati Apa, Ngai Tahu, and Ngati Whakaue.

The name of the place Whakaotirangi planted her kumara is remembered as Te Rokiroki a Whakaotirangi.

The waka Whatu-ranga-nuku has very close ties with Te Arawa, and it is claimed that those of the Nga Ohomairangi who did not sail in Te Arawa herself, voyaged in this waka.

The Ancient History of the Maori, Vol. 5, p. 9.
The Coming of the Maori, pp. 39, 44, 50, 273.
Fragments of Ancient Maori History, p. 5.
Historic Maketu, pp. 4–5.
JPS, Vol. 1, p. 221.
JPS, Vol. 2, pp. 233–6.
JPS, Vol. 3, p. 47.
JPS, Vol. 34, p. 294.
JPS, Vol. 60, pp. 82–3.
Maori Art, pp. 30–1.
Maori Lore, p. 224.
The Maori–Polynesian Comparative Dictionary, p. 20.
Te Arawa, pp. 2–9, 11, 13–20, 471, 475–6.
Te Ika a Maui, p. 290.
Treasury of Maori Exploration, pp. 100, 103, 107, 108, 258.
Tuwharetoa, pp. 29, 30, 39, 41–3, 50–1, 53, 56.
Whakatane and District Historical Society Inc Memoir, #1, p. 82.

ARIKI-MAI-TAI

This waka is considered to be an early arrival, with the descendants of its crew well established in the Waitara district and the area surrounding Hawera and Patea when Manaia of the Tokomaru waka and Turi of the Aotea waka arrived independently in the district. Manaia is said to have killed aborigines at Waitara, and Turi, on his arrival, enslaved the men and took the women who inhabited the lands near the Waimate plain, north and west of Hawera.

History and Traditions of the Taranaki Coast, p. 74.
The Maori–Polynesian Comparative Dictionary, p. 20.

ARORANGI

Although this waka is reputed to have stayed in Rarotonga, it is mentioned alongside many of the better-known migration waka in Percy Smith's *Hawaiki: the Original Home of the Maoris*.

> *The migration of Naea came from Avaiki to Iva (supposed to be Nukuhiva in the Marquesas) and from Iva to Tahiti, and thence to Rarotonga. This was before the time of Tangiia and Karika. The following are names of the waka of Naea and his tere [flotilla]: Tainui, Turoa was captain; Tokomaru; Te Arawa; Kuru-aupo; Mata-tua; Takitumu; Okotura; Muri-enua; Arorangi; Rangiatea; Ngaio; Tumu-enua and Mata-o-te-toa; Tamarua being captain of Tumu-enua and Aia captain of Mata-o-te-toa. The last two named were called fighting waka, and the first eight went to New Zealand, the remainder staying in Rarotonga.*

(It is doubtful whether the above-named fleet actually sailed together, as it is generally accepted that the majority of those waka named that went on to Aotearoa voyaged independently.)

Hawaiki: the Original Home of the Maoris, p. 265.

AWARUA

The Awarua is mentioned in *The Story of Te Waharoa* as having landed at Matata. Nothing else is recorded.

The Story of Te Waharoa, p. 252.

AWE-KUMU

This ancient waka is mentioned in passing as having been left behind at Hawaiki when the Aratawhao (or more probably the crew who returned in the Mataatua) voyaged back to Aotearoa with her precious cargo of kumara. It is not remembered why the Awe-kumu was left behind, or whether she made the voyage to Aotearoa at a later date (which may explain why the waka is remembered in Maori tradition).

JPS, Vol. 12, p. 170.

HAERE

Although tradition states that the Haere returned to Hawaiki without any of its crew remaining in Aotearoa, it is remembered that this was the waka of the chiefs Tu-ngutu-tangata and Tungutungu-o-te-Rangi.

JPS, Vol. 1, p. 217.
JPS, Vol. 12, p. 129.

HAHAU-TUNOA

'Ko Hahau-tunoa te waka o te Kahui-rua'. This line is from a waiata that is said to have been sung on 11 December 1887 when the adze Te Awhio-rangi was displayed to over 300 members of Nga Rauru, Whanganui and Ngati Api tribes. The adze had been unseen for seven generations as it lay in a tapu resting place near Okoutuku, until a stranger unfamiliar with the sacred places of the district stumbled upon it while searching for hakekakeka (a fungus). The translation is, 'Hahau-tunoa is the waka of Kahui-rua', a people associated with the distant past.

JPS, Vol. 9, p. 231.

HAKIRERE

The Hakirere waka occurs at least three times in Maori traditions: firstly, in the story of how the taro arrived in Aotearoa; secondly, as a war waka to seek revenge for the death of Tuwhakararo; and lastly, as part of a fleet of waka that sailed to Hawaiki Rangi-atea.

The Nga Rauru and Ngati Ruanui ancestor Maru came across the taro plant growing on a distant island while exploring the Moana-nui-a-Kiwa. Upon returning home, he showed his people this new plant and induced them to return to the island Wairuangangana (or Wairuangaungau) to procure roots of the plant for cultivation. In due course two waka — the Hakirere, captained by Maihi, and the Pahitonoa, captained by Rauru — set out to retrace Maru's course. On the outward journey disaster overtook the Pahitonoa and it was wrecked in a mishap, with the survivors rescued by the crew of the Hakirere.

The expedition continued in the remaining waka and successfully landed at Wairuangangana, where the local population agreed to give some taro and the instructions for its cultivation to Maihi and Rauru. With the careful storage of the crop and the appropriate karakia, Maihi was able to return safely to his people and successfully introduce taro to the land. To support the above tradition, a waiata published in *Nga Moteatea* claims that both the kumara (refered to as Tu-tahi) and the taro (whaka-tau-weru) were brought on the Hakirere and that both were cultivated in the garden called Kura-tau (or Tepapa-Kuratau).

In the second occurrence of the name Hakirere, a fleet of waka was built by Whakatau-potiki and his brothers to avenge the death of their brother Tuwhakararo, who was murdered at the hands of the Ati-Hapai tribe. During the attack Whakatau-potiki and his men inflicted widespread death among their enemies and burnt the wharekura known as Te Uru-o-Manono, to the ground. Some of their waka were Whiritoa, Tapatapa-hukarere, Toroa-i-Taipakihi, Hakirere and Mahunu-awatea. The Hikutoto was said to be the waka in which Whakatau voyaged.

In the third recording, given by Hetaraka Tautahi, the waka is named along with Rangi-taki, Takere-o-toitaha and Pahi-tonoa as having reached 'as far as Hawaiki Rangi-atea', while other waka in the fleet voyaged on (presumably to Aotearoa).

The Ancient History of the Maori, Vol. 2, p. 151.
JPS, Vol. 3, p. 105.
Maori Art, p. 37.
Nga Moteatea, Vol. 3, p. 307.
Polynesian Mythology, p. 62.
The Story of Aotea, p. 113.

HAPE
Chatham Islands

One of seven waka built by the Rauru people, but left in Hawaiki at the time of their voyage to colonise the Chatham Islands. The other six waka were: Tama-Kororo, Tupu Ngaherehere, Mata-rangi, Tohoro-i-ongongo, Karangatai and Tihauwea (a waka of witchcraft).

JPS, Vol. 5, p. 18.

HAWAI, TE

Te Hawai, renamed Kurahaupo, is the waka in which Whatonga searched for his grandfather Toi-te-tuatahi after Toi himself had sailed to Aotearoa from his Pacific homeland to search for his storm-lost grandson. Whatonga obtained the waka from a man named Turangi and fitted it out for a long deep-sea voyage.

The following description of Te Hawai is from Buck's *The Coming of the Maori*:

The waka had three blunt joins (hami tuporo), twenty six thwarts (taumanu), two bailing places (puna wai) and two anchors. Wash boards were added to the bow and it was painted with red ochre (kowhai whenua) mixed with shark oil. A crew of sixty six experienced men were given appointed places in the waka.

(*See also* entries for Te Wao and Kurahaupo.)

Nga Waka Maori, p. 10.
The Maori, p. 50.
The Coming of the Maori, p. 26.

HIKUTOTO

The Hikutoto is named as Whakatau-potiki's waka during his voyage to avenge the death of his kinsman, Tuwhakararo (usually named as Whakatau's brother, but occasionally as his father). (*See* Hakirere.)

The Ancient History of the Maori, Vol. 2, p. 151.

HINAKI-PAKAU-O-TE-RUPE

Name variations: Nga-tai-a-Kupe, Tutara-kauika

The waka Hinaki-pakau-o-te-rupe was sailed to Aotearoa by the brothers Taukata and Hoaki and their sister Tuturi-whatu in search of their sister Kanioro and her husband Pou-rangahua. Although it is not clear how Kanioro had reached Aotearoa, it is unlikely that Pou-rangahua had visited Hawaiki to get her because, as subsequent events will show, his people were unaware of the existance of the kumara prior to Hinaki-pakau-o-te-rupe's arrival at Turanga.

On arriving at Turanga, the voyagers made their presence known to the tangata whenua, who immediately prepared a huge feast of delicacies from the forests. During the feast, Taukata, who was unused to the local food, took some dried kumara from his belt and after mixing the kumara with water, handed the paste-like substance to Tama-ki-hikurangi, chief of the tribe. Tama-ki-hikurangi was delighted with this new food and immediately requested that a voyage to Hawaiki be planned to fetch some kumara for cultivation, which Hoaki agreed to lead. A new waka, Te Aratawhao, was adzed and prepared for the voyage to Hawaiki. (For an account of the voyage, *see* Aratawhao.)

A footnote in Reed's *Treasury of Maori Exploration* reads:

As might be expected, there are variations in names and events. In J.H. Mitchell's Takitimu, Hoaki's brother is Rongo-taua, while their sister Kani-oro he says was brought to Aotearoa by Pou-ranga-hou who lived at Kirikino near Turanganui. Their waka was said to be Tutara-kauika.

It will be noted that this story is very similar to that of the Arai-te-uru.

How the Maori Came to Aotearoa, p. 36.
Treasury of Maori Exploration, p. 224.
Tuhoe: Children of the Mist, p. 695.

HIRAUTA

It is remembered that the migration waka Hirauta left Hawaiki for Aotearoa under the command of Kiwa, possibly accompanied by the waka Mangarara. Having landed at Turanga, the crew of the Hirauta and their descendants remained in the Poverty Bay area, later intermarrying with those of the waka Horouta to form the major tribes of that region.

JPS, Vol. 12, p. 130.
Maori Art, p. 31.

HOROUTA
Name variation: Orouta

The exact history and movements of the Horouta, like those of so many waka, have been lost over time. The Horouta is primarily remembered for its voyage to Hawaiki to procure kumara for Toi, although, as evidenced by the large list of crew members collected by Gudgeon, it is likely that it was also used as a migration waka. (In White's *The Ancient History of the Maori*, volume 2, he quotes his sources as saying that Uenga-pua-ariki was the chief who voyaged to Aotearoa in the Orouta, and the ancestors of Ngati Ruanui came with him.) Admittedly few details of the migration voyage remain, and those that do are often well and truly entangled in the 'kumara expedition' tradition.

In a Ngati Porou tradition dictated by Pita Kapiti, it is said that two men named Kahukura and Rongoiamo travelled to Aotearoa by way of a rainbow. The rainbow was constructed by several people standing in Hawaiki, and bending over so that their hands reached the North Island of Aotearoa, in the vicinity of Whakatane.

The two men evidently made contact with Toi, and during a feast were introduced to the local food. Unimpressed with the ti, mamaku and aruhe placed before him, Kahukura asked for some bowls containing a small quantity of water. Rongoiamo then took some dried kumara, and after mixing it with the water introduced the food to Toi. Toi was so excited by the food that he immediately arranged for the Horouta to be readied for a voyage to Hawaiki to collect kumara for his own cultivation. (It is suggested in Kapiti's version that the Horouta had actually been built in Aotearoa by Toi.) Kahukura agreed to return to Hawaiki to gather suitable kumara for transportation back to Aotearoa, and Rangituroua was given the honour of being the tohunga for the journey.

Before the waka sailed, Rangituroua is said to have recited the following kawa-moana, or prayer to ensure a safe voyage:

Hau toto, hau toto,
Ko Tu, hekea ana,
Ko Rongo, hekea ana,
Ko te ngahau o Tu,
Utaina taku kawa nei,
He kawa tua-maunga,
Ka wiwini, ka wawana,
Tara pata tu ki te rangi,
Au e ki,
Whano, whana,
Hara mai te toki,
Hauma, Hui e, Taiki e.

The final rite preformed prior to the Horouta's departure was the reciting of the karakia used to define the ara-moana, or ocean path that would be taken. The following is the Horouta's ara-moana:

Tura mai te tura,
Kakapa te manu i uta, he paki hau,
Tauranga ko tawhiti nuku,
Te whakamakautia he ariki tapu,
Kia inu ia i te wai o Whakatau,
Mate toka i mua, mate toka i roto,
Tu whanawhana, tu maihi, tu makaro,
Tu te Whairamu,
E ai hoki te hirihiri,
Kei te kohukohu i runga,
Koi rangi tukua, koi rangi horoa,
Tane tukua, Tane takoto,
E ai hoki tenei mata tohu.
Uru whakapupu ake te uru o te whenua,
Te tau arohakina ki waho,
Ki te uraura o te ra,
Ki te werawera o te ra,
Whakarere ki tai marehua ki waho,
Taku hoe nei, ko Rapanga-te-ati-nuku,
Ko Rapanga-te-ati-rangi;
Na Tai-pupuni, na Tai-wawana, na Tai-aro-puke,
Hua taku hoe nei, he hoe tahurihuri,
He hoe karaparapa,
Ki taha tu o te rangi,

Aue ki; Whano, Whana.
Hara mai te toki, Hauma,
Hui e, Taiki e.

The next karakia to be recited by Rangituroua was offered when Hawaiki had been sighted by the crew of Horouta.

Mano ki te Hawaiki,
Ka tu hakehakea,
Mai te kowiwini, mai te kowawa,
He toki minamina, he toki mai anarea,
Ka hirahira,
Ko aitu mai o tangata,
Ki te pu o te rakau,
Ka ui iho ka ui ake,
Ka ui tua te kaha o Tangaroa,
Ko au matakaka, ki tua o Hawaiki,
Katea te rawaka mai,
Ko Tane ka haruru rutu,
Whano, Whana, Hara mai te toki,
Hauma, Hui e, Taiki e.

On arrival at Hawaiki, it was found that the cultivated kumara had already been harvested and deposited in storage pits in a village named Huiakama. Unwilling or unable to fight the local inhabitants, Kahukura sailed the Horouta around to a nearby cliff. Here he took his ko (digging stick), which was named Penu, and struck the side of the cliff as he recited incantations. Kumara fell from the cliff and filled the hold of the waka. The pakura (swamp hen) and the Polynesian rat also fell with the kumara into the waka, inadvertently joining the kumara for the voyage to Aotearoa.

Before the return voyage was made, Kahukura announced that he would not return with the waka, but would instead remain at Hawaiki. He instructed the crew to ensure that the precious kumara not be allowed to come into contact with aruhe (fern root). Pawa (Paoa) then took command of Horouta and safely guided the waka back to Aotearoa. The voyage was apparently uneventful, with little or no information remembered about the southern journey.

The first landfall for the Horouta is unclear. Most versions suggest Ahuahu (Great Mercury Island), although some accounts state the waka first touched land at North Cape before continuing south to

Ahuahu. When the Horouta landed at Ahuahu, a woman named Kanawa went ashore and gathered some fern root. Unnoticed by any of her fellow passengers, she smuggled the root aboard. Later, during the journey south along the coastline, the Horouta was caught in an unexpected storm. Suspecting someone had disobeyed Kahukura's command, the tohunga soon discovered the culprit, and threw the woman overboard. As Kanawa struggled in vain to save herself, she capsized the waka by hanging on to its bow. (In some accounts, it is stated that the waka went aground on the reef Tukirae-o-kirikiri, or Tukerae-o-Kanawa, and that was the cause of the wreck.)

Despite this near disaster, the kumara remained safe, and was taken ashore. The waka was also manoeuvred through the surf to the shore, where Rangituroua recited the following prayer as the crew turned the waka right-side up:

E iki, e iki, te tura uro whiti,
E iki, e iki, te tura uro whiti,
Hiki nuku e, hiki rangi e,
Hiki nuku e, hiki rangi e,
Ha ha, ka hikitia tona ure,
Ia ia iaia, Ha i i i.

Once the waka had been beached and inspected for damage, it was found that the top-stakes had been irreparably damaged and would have to be replaced. Pawa himself travelled inland to seek the timber required to repair the waka, which was found on a mountain subsequently named Maungahaumi. In order to transport the timber to the ocean, Pawa is said to have relieved himself into the streams Waioeka, Motu and Waipaoa. By the time he had finished, the streams had become rivers, and the timber was easily floated to the seashore.

The kumara carried by the Horouta was dropped off at, or at least subsequently transported to, several places, including Ahuahu, Whangaparaoa, Turanga, Nuku-tau-rua, Heretaunga, Te Whaka-whitinga, Kaikoura, Whangara and Waiapu. The garden at Waiapu was named Whaka-rara-nui, and its position is marked by a hutukawa tree, named Otekomaitawhiti. The sacred mapau rod named Atiatihinga also took root in the vicinity of the garden.

The Horouta's final destination is said to have been Muriwai, just south of Turanganui. One account names the exact spot of the waka's landfall as Pakirikiri. Another informant claims that the Horouta lies at the bottom of the Muriwai lagoon.

ADDITIONAL INFORMATION

The waka

It is suggested in many texts that the Takitimu and the Horouta were in fact the same waka — Takitimu being re-named Horouta for its second voyage. Ngata, in an argument denouncing this particular theory, suggests that Horouta and Takitimu were possibly the joint hulls of a double waka. He came to this conclusion because the traditions of both waka were so intertwined, and shared so many crew. He also noted that there was a Cook Island tradition that the two formed a double waka. It has also been suggested in another article by Ngata that there may have been quite a fleet accompanying Horouta during its voyage to Aotearoa.

In an account of the *History of the Horouta Waka* given by Pita Kapiti, it is suggested that the Horouta belonged to Toi-te-huatahi, was built in Aotearoa, and after voyaging to Hawaiki to collect kumara, returned to Aotearoa in the company of other waka. Additional comments made, state that Toi-te-huatahi lived at Whitianga (Mercury Bay), and that his 'house' was named Hui-te-rangiora.

Best, in *Tuhoe: Children of the Mist*, states that some traditions claim that the Horouta was in fact the Aratawhao, renamed for the return voyage to Aotearoa.

A statement by Tikao claims that the Horouta and Manuka were built from the one tree, and the two waka sailed off to Hawaiki to procure kumara. (It is usually said that the sister waka of Manuka was Arai-te-uru.)

The naming of the waka

There are several accounts explaining the naming of the Horouta, each closely tied with the Takitimu waka. The most popular account suggests that Horouta and Takitimu were built about the same time by the craftsmen Rua-wharo and Tu-pai. One waka was named Puwhenua (later to be re-named Takitimu), while the other was at first unnamed. Soon after their launching ceremonies had been completed, the two waka are said to have joined Te Arawa, Tainui and Mataatua for trial races on the lagoon Pikopiko-i-whiti. During the race the Puwhenua was so fast that it easily outraced the other waka. So impressive was its win that one of the spectators sitting on the hill, Puke-hapopo, which over looked the lagoon, was heard to say the waka was 'speeding past' or 'eating' the land. Word got down to the crews as they returned to the beach of the comment, and the crew of the unnamed waka adopted the phrase horo uta (horo — speed or eat, uta — land) for the name of their waka.

In a version recorded in *Maori Lore*, the warrior Tamatea had aquired three waka after defeating the Tu Rahui people, and a further waka after conquering the Pu-whaka-awe people. It was decided by Tamatea that he and his tribe should migrate to Aotearoa, and the four waka were subsequently raced on the stretch of river called Poko-poko, to assess their sailing ability. Tamatea, Pawa, Tai-kehu, and a number of other chiefs were overlooking the river from a nearby hillside. Tai-kehu is said to have been overheard commenting that one of the waka was 'eating or swallowing' the land. Upon hearing Tai-kehu's comment, Tamatea is said to have gifted the waka to him, and presumably suggested that the waka be named Horouta.

After the events of the day, however, Tamatea's tohunga were said to have persuaded him to keep the waka for himself, and to make it tapu. Only chiefs, gods, and priests were permitted on board the Horouta, and absolutely no cooked food was allowed on her.

On the day chosen to embark upon the migration, the priests chanted a sacred karakia over Tamatea's waka, and for some reason not alluded to, re-named the waka Takitimu. They then transfered the name Horouta to the waka of Tai-kehu and Pawa.

The crew

During its long voyage to Aotearoa, Pawa (Paoa) was in command of the Horouta, and according to some, Kiwa was the tohunga. (Kiwa is also claimed in some accounts as the captain of the Takitimu.) Others among the crew remembered in a list compiled by Judge W.E. Gudgeon were as follows.

Males
Awapaka	Hounuku	Hourangi
Hiwara	Houatea	Hauararo
Houtakitaki	Hikitapua	Hine-raukura
Hakutore	Ira	Koneke

Karotaha	Kura	Mahu
Manurewa	Mahaututea	Mawhakeururangi
Matangi-rauarangi	Makawa	Nenewha
Ngarangikahia	Parutu	Pouheni
Taiaroa	Tapoto	Te Paki
Tutepakihirangi	Te Hirea	Tamatahaia
Tahukarangi	Tarana	Tokipuanga
Te Amaru	Tunurangi	Te Ikirangi
Takiwhenua	Tangitoronga	Tararoti
Takirangi	Taikehu	Tapuke
Taneherepi	Te Hatoitoi	Tahore
Te Manawaroa	Rongotopea	Rerepari
Rangitarona	Rourouatea	Wahapaka
Whioroa	Whakapuku	

Females

Hine-mataotao	Hine-kapuarangi	Hine-huhunurangi
Hau-ki-te-rangi	Hine-kau-i-rangi	Hine-hakirirangi
Koia	Ki-te-rangi	Mapuhiarangi
Tangihia Waitutu	Tangaroa Kaitahi	Te Roka
Waitaramea	Whakite	Whitiauaunau

From other sources come the following ancestors, also named as having sailed on the Horouta.

Te Poutama	Iri-a-rangi	Te Kahutakiri
Tama-whiro	Tama-ki-te-rangi	Te Hekenga
Oipiria	Te Rakau-pango	Te Kotore-o-hua
Tangi-torona	Hiki-tapua	Makawa
Tari-toronga	Tao-roa	Taipupuni
Tai-wawana	Rangi-tu-roua	Hine-akua
Pairangi	Hine Haakirirangi	

Those among the major tribes claiming descent from the Horouta include Ngati Kahungunu, Ngati Porou, Tuhoe and Ngati Hau.

In the book *In Ancient Maori Land*, Best states that one of his informants claimed:

Whata-kiore and Ira-te-wehenga, and Whatu-pouri, and Ue, and Whatu-potango, and Tama-ki-hikurangi, returned from Hawaiki.

They assembled and came on board the sacred waka which is called Horouta. The pilot of that waka was Kahukura-i-te-rangi, who stood with one foot upon the ocean and the other upon the land, and when his face appears like an arch in the heavens, that is Kahukura bending down and behind him is his wife, Te Atua-wharoro-mai-te-rangi.

Those named in the above passage are said to have voyaged to Hawaiki in the Aratawhao.

The voyage

In one account, it is stated that the kowhai was carried in the Horouta. Another claims tools including a mapau, named Ateateahenga or Atiatihinga, used in planting ceremonies, and two hutukawa plants named Te Rohutumaitawhiti and Otekomaitawhiti were also on board.

Before the voyage, it was decided that the paddles, Akau, Piripiri, and tapaki, would be used by Tai-pupuni, Tai-wawana, and Tai-aropaki respectively.

The rainbow constructed by Kahukura was made up of: Kahukura's mother, Hine-te-wai, on the bottom; on top of her lay Kahukura's father, Rongomai; next came Te Paoka-o-te-rangi; above him Totoerangi arched; then Kahukura himself; Tahawai; Kaurukiruki: and finally Here-umu.

The landfall

In a version of the Horouta's landfall, given in *Treasury of Maori Exploration*, it is said that Pawa's overland trip had two objectives. The first was to gather timber for the repair of the waka, while the second, and possibly more important reason, was to track down one of the crew who had absconded from the party soon after the Horouta had been dragged onto the beach. Hine-kau-i-rangi was eventually found by Pawa and his men, and later had a very important role in the kumara planting ceremony at the garden named Manawaru.

From *Te Arawa*, we learn that the crew settled at Omeheu, on the left bank of the Rangitaiki River, between Matata and Te Teko.

The Ancient History of the Maori, Vol. 2, pp. 180–1.
The Ancient History of the Maori, Vol. 3, pp. 67, 97.
The Coming of the Maori, pp. 34, 57–8, 64.
Echoes of the Pa, p. 121.
In Ancient Maori Land, p. 10.
JPS, Vol. 1, pp. 231–2.
JPS, Vol. 7, p. 111.
JPS, Vol. 12, p. 122.
JPS, Vol. 21, pp. 153, 155, 156, 159.
Kahungunu, October 1992, p. 23.
Maori Art, p. 31.
Maori Lore, pp. 289, 290, 300–1.
Sir Apirana Ngata Memorial Tribute, p. 76.
Takao Talks, p. 62.
Takitimu, pp. 22, 23, 25.
Te Arawa, p. 481
Treasury of Maori Exploration, pp. 212, 241, 243–4.
Transactions of the New Zealand Institute Vol. 37, p. 127.
Tuhoe: Children of the Mist, p. 690.
Tuwharetoa, p. 55.
Two Worlds, p. 121.
Whakatane and District Historical Society Inc Memoir #4, pp. 8, 11.

HOTU-TAIHI-RANGI

Name variations: Hotu-te-ihi-rangi, Hotu-te-ihi, Hotu-te-ihu-rangi

The waka Hotu-taihi-rangi is mentioned in two waiata listed in *Nga Moteatea*. In both cases the waka is said to have belonged to the well-known Maori ancestor Whiro. Below is the second verse and translation from the Ngati Porou apakura (lament) given in volume two of *Nga Moteatea*.

Kia mate ia nei koe, e hika,
Ko Atamira te waka, Ko Hotutaihirangi,
Ko Tai-o-puapua, Ko Raro-tua-maheni,
Ko Araiteuru, Ko Nukutaimemeha;
Ko te waka i hiia ai te whenua nui nei.

You are gone indeed, dear one
(for your) waka there are Atamira, Hotutaihirangi,
Tai-o-puapua, Raro-tua-maheni,
Araiteuru, and Nukutaimemeha:
The waka which fished up this widespread land.

The notes following this waiata state that Atamira is a figure of speech for a stage or platform upon which the dead are laid; Hotutaihirangi is the waka of Whiro; Araiteuru is a waka which made landfall in the South Island; and Nukutaimemeha was the waka of Maui. Both names Tai-o-puapua and Te Raro-tua-maheni are forgotten, but in the context of the verse are very probably early waka as well.

> **ADDITIONAL INFORMATION**

Among the many traditions collected by J.F. Stimson during his time in Tahiti are several relating to Hiro. In one it is claimed that Hiro owned a waka named Hotu-taihi-nui. He had built the waka himself, from the great tree Ihi-matoa, which grew in his own forest.

Nga Moteatea, Vol. 2, p. 7.
Nga Moteatea, Vol. 3, p. 123.
Songs and Tales of the Sea Kings, p. 157.

HOUAMA, TE

The Houama is one of three waka in which Nuku-tama-roro and his men chased Manaia and the remnants of his tribe to Aotearoa. Manaia was a powerful chief over the Ngati Purauwha and Ngati Wairehu tribes in Hawaiki who had been at war for some time with the tribe of Nuku-tama-roro, whose brother, Tomowhare, he had killed during the fighting. Dreading the total annihilation of his people, Manaia had the voyaging waka Tokomaru fitted out and secretly fled seeking the sanctuary of Titiri-o-te-moana (Aotearoa).

Nuku-tama-roro, upon learning of the flight of his sworn enemy, ordered three waka to be prepared to chase Manaia. The Houama was the fastest, being a single waka with an outrigger attached for stability. The other two, Tangi-apa-kura and Waimate, were both double-hulled vessels. As well as three well-armed crews, Nuku-tama-roro took along three tohunga, Aweawe-nuku, Kowao-roa and Hau-paroa, to ensure the success of the chase. Despite the speed of the Houama, the Tokomaru was able to keep ahead of the chasing waka, and after stopping off in Rarotonga along the way, reached Aotearoa first.

The pursuers first landed at Arapawa Island in Cook Strait. From there the tohunga Hau-paroa directed the expedition around to D'Urville Island, where they found the remnants of a recently lit fire. From this they concluded that the Tokomaru had only just departed, and under the direction of their tohunga they chased the Tokomaru northward. Although the Tokomaru sailed as fast as she could in an effort to escape, the Houama caught up with her in the vicinity of Mana Island and way-laid her until the Tangi-apa-kura and Waimate arrived. A fierce sea battle commenced just off Pukerua and continued until dusk when the two forces broke off hostilities, Manaia landing at Paekakariki, while Nuku-tama-roro and his force stayed afloat. During the night, while Manaia's warriors rested, his tohunga Te Aowhaingaroa raised a storm by karakia forcing Nuku-tama-roro's fleet to be washed ashore with much chaos and loss of life. In the morning the two leaders sued for peace, with Nuku-tama-roro deciding to return home. The two double-hulled waka were dismantled and prepared as outrigger waka, and the five waka returned to Hawaiki.

The Coming of the Maori, p. 31.
The Lore of the Whare Wanaga, Vol. 2, pp. 132–3.

HURUHURU-MANU

Name variations: Wakahuruhurumanu, Wakahuruhuru, Wakahurumanu, Whakahuruhurumanu

The Huruhurumanu is considered an ancient waka, perhaps one of the first to voyage to Aotearoa, and is prominent in South Island traditions. Probably because of its antiquity, there have been many conflicting claims.

In one account, Te Operuarangi, who lived in a land distant to Aotearoa, travelled to a nearby island to get the Huruhurumanu from its owner, Te Moretu. Taiehu was named as the captain, his adze was Paki-tua, and the guardian spirit of the waka was Tu-kai-tauru. Those who travelled on the waka were known as Te-tini-o-te-para-rakau. Elsewhere it is claimed that it was the Maeroero people of the South Island, or the ancestors of the Waitaha tribe, who voyaged in Huruhurumanu.

Tare Te Maiharoa claimed the following as members of an ancient waka, thought to have been the Huruhurumanu: Kopuwai, Pukutuaro, Komakohua, Te Karara-haurau and Pouakai. All subsequently named as giants or monsters in traditions with individual deeds attributed to them. Perhaps their real place in history has been distorted by the passage of time.

Other sources give Tukete as the captain of the waka, and say that he went on to achieve the reputation of a great navigator in the Huruhurumanu, and that during the voyage to Aotearoa the crew met fifty gigantic seas that threatened to swamp their waka. As the journey continued the crew were able to smooth the sea, presumably with karakia, so that in the years to come the Uruao and other waka were able to voyage safely in the wake of the Huruhurumanu.

In a rare association with the North Island, it is said that the voyage commenced at an unidentified place named Patu-nui-o-aio and ended safely at North Cape, where the crew settled. There they built a pa called Ritoa (Ritua) and remained until they were over-run by another tribe.

As a final note to further add to the confusion here, there is also a legend that names the captain of the Waka-orurea as Te Huruhurumanu.

(*See also* Aea-ka-huru-manu.)

JPS, Vol. 24, p. 107.
JPS, Vol. 27, pp. 139–40, 144, 152.
Our Southernmost Maoris, p. 157.
Maori Place Names, p. 120.
Tikao Talks, p. 58.
Treasury of Maori Exploration, p. 8.

IKA-ROA-A-RAURU

The waka Ika-roa-a-Rauru is mentioned in Ngata's *Nga Moteatea* as belonging to Maia, a brother-in-law of Uenuku. Maia is supposed to have fled Hawaiki in fear of Uenuku and landed with his freight of hue at Turanga.

Nga Moteatea, Vol. 3, p. 325.

I-TERE

Originally called Karaea-kura, this waka was renamed I-tere after Tai-te-atai and his grandfather Tai-taraka had commissioned Ngatoroirangi and Tamatekapua to refit the old waka at Iva-nui. Soon after embarking on his maiden voyage as captain, Tai-te-atai encountered a waka captained by Maio (from Taiti-iva-iti), also on a voyage of discovery. Travelling together, the two waka eventually came across a third, named Takoto, captained by the explorer Te Ra-tu-mai-tonga. It was agreed that the three waka would proceed to the house of Tai-te-atai's parents on the bank of the Vairoa river in Taiti, and there resupply and rest before recommencing their exploration.

Soon after the waka had left Vairoa, they were overtaken by a violent storm, and the fleet was scattered, Maio landing in Manuae, while Te Ra-tu-mai-tonga was carried as far as Tonga. I-tere managed to make it to Aitutaki, which was then known as Araura. After many more voyages, Tai-te-atai renamed his waka Tainui, and made Oturoa (Hoturoa) captain.

JPS, Vol. 64, pp. 193–4.

KAHA-TU-WHENUA

The Kaha-tu-whenua is said to be one of the earliest waka to bring migrants to Aotearoa, particularly to the Taranaki region. Tai-kehu is said to have been captain.

Treasury of Maori Exploration, pp. 49, 87.

KAHUI-MAUNGA

Name variation: Kahui-mounga

The only information recorded about the Kahui-maunga is that it was captained by Tai-kehu. (Tai-kehu (Tai-ehu) features as the captain in several different waka traditions.)

JPS, Vol. 16, p. 191.
Treasury of Maori Exploration, p. 109.

KAHUITARA

The Kahuitara is noted in Lesley Kelly's *Tainui* as being the waka in which Monoa came to Aotearoa.

It is unclear if it is the same as the Kahutara, with some sources claiming it to be an earlier arrival.

Tainui, Whakapapa Sheet 1.

KAHUTARA

According to one tradition, the first inhabitants of Aotearoa landed at Ngamotu on the Taranaki Coast in three waka: the Kahutara, the

Taikoria, and the Okoki, commanded by Maruiwi, Ruatamore and Taitawaro respectively. Three other chiefs on these waka are also remembered: Poho-kura, a younger brother of Tai-tawaro; Pana-nehu; and Tamaki. The descendants of the three crews were later known as Tini-o-Maruiwi, Tini-o-Ruatamore, Tini-o-Taitawao, Tini-o-Pananehu, Koaupari and Te Wiwini.

According to Best in *The Maori as He Was* these three vessels had been swept away from their homeland by a westerly storm, and after a long drift voyage reached the Taranaki coast. They called their homeland Horanui-a-tau and Haupapa-nui-a-tau.

In describing their physical appearance and material culture, Best continues:

They are said to have been a people of spare build, thin shanked, with flat noses, distended nostrils and generally unpleasant appearance. Their eyes were peculiarly restless, their hair upstanding. They lived in rude huts, wore little clothing and were an indolent people — fond of hugging the fireside.

Transactions of the New Zealand Institute, Vol. 48, p. 455.
The Maori as He Was, p. 24.
Treasury of Maori Exploration, p. 48.

KAI-KANOHI

Name variations: Poutini, Tuhua

Kai-kanohi was the waka in which Hine-rau-haraki, Hine-rau-kawa and Te Kohi-wai fled from their husband Tama (alternatively named as Tamatea, Tama-taku-ariki, Tama-ki-te-rangi or Tama-ahua) soon after their arrival in Aotearoa on the waka Tairea. The Kai-kanohi was later found by Tama overturned in the Arahura River during the search for his wives. One of his wives had been transformed into pounamu in the river, and when he found her, his tears penetrated the stone to produce the tangi-wai, or teardrop effect in the pounamu. The other two wives hid behind a waterfall and escaped their husband.

Treasury of Maori Exploration, p. 204.
Treasury of Maori Folklore, p. 358.

KAPAKAPA-NUI

In 1860 Te Neke identified the migration waka Kapakapa-nui and Te Rangaranga as belonging to the Atiawa tribe of Taranaki.

JPS, Vol. 16, p. 189.

KAPAKITUA

The Kapakitua is said to have been captained by Tai-ehu, and the tribe descending from its crew were the Hawea. The sacred adze of the captain was named Awhio-rangi.

Treasury of Maori Exploration, p. 265.

KAPUA-HORAHORA

Name variation: Kopua-horahora

The Kapua-horahora is only remembered by name, with no other information recorded.

Treasury of Maori Exploration, p. 265.

KAPUA-RANGI

Kapua-rangi waka was built at Rangi-whaka-oma by Ngake during a contest with Kupe to decide who could build a waka the fastest. Kupe easily beat off the challenge of Ngake, and named his own waka Rangiwhakaoma in honour of the venue for the competition.

Ancient History of the Maori, Vol. 3, p. 93.

KARAEA-KURA

According to Cook Island legend, Karaea-kura was the original name of the Tainui before it was first renamed I-tere and subsequently Tainui.

JPS, Vol. 64, p. 192.

KARAERAE

Name variations: Takareira, Takaria

There are at least three legends in which a waka by the name of Karaerae features in Maori tradition.

In the first account, the ancestors of the Ngati Kopeka hapu of the Waitaha tribe came from Hawaiki in a waka named Te Karaerae, said to have left Hawaiki at the same time as Takitimu and Horouta. The chiefs of the waka were Te Ao, Rongo-mai-whenua, Pu Waitaha and Kahu-koka, and it was the latter who carried with him a basket of kumara seed, wrapped in the leaf of the koka plant. (It is said he was given the name Kahu-koka because of this deed.)

The Karaerae made landfall just north of Waipiro, on the East Cape, at a place named Tai-harakeke at Mataahu. After some time there was a dispute over fishing grounds between the newcomers and the Te Wahine-iti people, who were tangata whenua, which forced Te Ao and his fellow tribesmen to move on. From their East Cape homes these people migrated to the Chatham Islands, where they settled, but no mention of the waka utilised for that journey is recorded (presumably it was Ta Karaerae).

In the second version, the Karaerae is captained by Te Ahu-ruru (Te Ahuru), and during its journeys is said to have called at Rarotonga. Upon leaving that island the waka was never heard of again; presumably it became lost at sea.

In the final legend, Karaerae was built while Tamatea-ariki-nui, captain of the Takitimu waka, and some of his crew were living in the cave named Te Ana-whakairo (reputed to have paintings lining the walls and thought to be in South Canterbury). Having stayed in the south for some time, and after the death of his wife Turihuka, Tamatea wanted to return to the North Island to see out his days. During the voyage north Te Karaerae stopped at Kapiti Island, where the waka was re-provisioned and checked over for seaworthiness. Further up the coast at the mouth of the Whanganui River they saw smoke rising inland (it is said to have been steam from the mighty mountain Tongariro), and they landed at a place called Putiki (opposite the township of Wanganui). After staying with the tangata whenua for an appropriate length of time, the crew of Karaerae paddled and poled her further upstream to a place subsequently named Papa-a-waka-o-Tamatea-ariki (place of the waka of Tamatea). No further mention is made of Karaerae in the tradition after this.

As Tamatea and his men went further inland to Taupo, they did, however, have use of another waka at Taupo, thought to have been named Ua-piko or Uepiko, which was subsequently wrecked at Huka Falls. There are contrasting accounts of the outcome of this disaster, with one stating that all but Ririwai were drowned. A more popular version proclaims that Tamatea and most of the crew survived the falls and before they continued on their trip, they left behind Kahukiwa (a god perhaps?) to care for the wrecked waka. In most legends concerning Tamatea he sees out his days at Hokianga.

How the Maori Came to Aotearoa, p. 88.
JPS, Vol. 23, pp. 79–80.
JPS, Vol. 24, pp. 16–19.
Maori Art, p. 37.
Treasury of Maori Exploration, pp. 192, 209.

KARAMU-RAU-NUI

The Karamu-rau-nui is named as one of several ancestral waka by Hetaraka Tautahi of the Nga Rauru tribe in a recorded interview in November 1900, while he was dictating his people's version of the migration of the Aotea waka (*see* Takere-o-Toitahi for the full list of names). Mention is also made of the Karamu-rau-nui in Salmond's *Two Worlds*, where it is told that the well-known headland Mahia-mai-Tawhiti (Mahia Peninsula) is also known as Tuara-hiwi-otienga, 'after the back of the captain of the ancestral waka Karamu-rau-nui'.

JPS, Vol. 9, p. 213.
Two Worlds, p. 145.

KARAMURAURIKI

The Karamurauriki is sometimes interchanged in Maori oratory with the Tatataeore, both being waka of misfortune and death that took the wairua of the departed to Hawaiki. In poroporoaki (farewell speeches) for the dead, descriptions of the preparation of the waka are often made, including the lashing on of the tau-ihu (bow piece) and the decoration of the tau-rapa (stern piece) with streamers of white albatross feathers. The poroporoaki would end with the orator calling upon the Karamurauriki to return and collect the souls of the dead for their last voyage.

The Coming of the Maori, p. 61.

KARANGATAI

Chatham Islands

Karangatai was one of seven waka recalled in Moriori legends that were left behind when the Rauru people fled their homeland and migrated to the Chatham Islands in the two vessels Rangihoua and Rangimata. The seven waka (Karangatai, Tama-kororo, Tupu-ngahere-here, Mata-rangi, Tohoro-i-ongongo, Hape and Tihauwea) were remembered over the generations by the respective karakia of each waka that had been carried with the Rauru people to their island refuge.

JPS, Vol. 5, p. 18.

KATOKO

Chatham Islands

It has been suggested that the Katoko was used as the secondary hull for the double waka Pouariki. The little information available reads, 'He whakapiri no Pouariki. An adjunct — lie close together — of Pouariki.' Pouariki was a migration waka used to convey immigrants to Chatham Island about the same time that the Rangihoua and Rangimata were voyaging to the same destination.

JPS, Vol. 5, p. 17.

KAUAE-TAKA

A mythological waka crewed by Pupuke, the Kauae-taka belonged to the reptile god Mongoraiata or Mangaroa, and stayed on the other side of the heavens.

Maori Art, p. 31.

KAUAU

Another waka with very few clues to its history, the Kauau is remembered as 'Kauau a Turi' — Kauau belonging to Turi.

Maori Art, p. 31.

KAURIA

All that is recorded relating to this waka is that the chief Wharewharenga-te-rangi and his contemporaries voyaged on the Kauria and established the Ngati Hako tribe at the headwaters of the Waihou River.

JPS, Vol. 12, p. 166.

KIMI

Chatham Islands

The Kimi is said to have voyaged to the Chatham Islands under the captain Rangihou in latter times, along with a second waka named Rangimata. Several other waka are said to have been lost at sea during the migration.

Transactions of the New Zealand Institute, Vol. 22, p. 76.

KOKAKO

It is remembered that Ihenga-ariki was captain of the Kokako, which has generally been associated with the Taranaki region. As an interesting aside, when Kupe was exploring Aotearoa, he is said to have seen two birds, a kokako and a tiwaiwaka (fantail) near present-day Patea. The two 'birds' seen by Kupe could have been two waka flying through the ocean.

JPS, Vol. 16, p. 190.

KURAHAOA

An informant of J. Herries Beattie confided to him that in 1869 he had been on a large mound between O-Tamatea and Waimeha catching weka with 'old Aperahama Hutoitoi', who told him 'that the name of the hill was Ka-tata-o-Kurahaoa (the bailers of Kurahaoa). My informant could give no further information, nor any particulars about this waka'.

JPS, Vol. 24, p. 110.

KURAHAUPO

Name variations: Kuraaupo, Kura-pau-popo, Kura-te-po, Kura-wau-po, Kurawhapo, Kuruatepo, Kuruhaupo

Two waka with the name Kurahaupo feature in Maori traditions. In the first of the traditions, Whatonga obtained the waka Te Hawai from Turangi and, after renaming it Kurahaupo, voyaged to Aotearoa in search of his grandfather, Toi. According to a version of the voyage recorded by Best, the Kurahaupo was sailed first from Hawaiki to Rarotonga, where Whatonga heard that Toi had sailed on to Aotearoa. Following the ara-moana (sea path or route) of Toi's waka, Te Paepae-ki-Rarotonga, Whatonga eventually reached the shores of Aotearoa, making his first landfall at Muriwhenua. The waka was then sailed down the west coast and landed at Tonga-porutu, in northern Taranaki. Whatonga was able to learn from the local inhabitants that Toi was living in the Bay of Plenty. Despite a number of his crew opting to stay and live among their hosts (Maungaroa, Te Hatauira, Korehewa, Moko, Pou, Te Auaha and others), Whatonga managed to voyage to the East Coast via North Cape.

During this section of the voyage, Whatonga and the remaining crew stopped off at a spot in Northland to collect food and water. Here one of the group, Otuako, died (and the locality was subsequently named after him). Further south, the Kurahaupo put in at Moharuru (Maketu), where the chief Matakana entertained Whatonga and his men. It was while the crew of the Kurahaupo were enjoying Matakana's hospitality that Whatonga finally learnt the whereabouts of his grandfather. The waka was sailed to Whakatane, where Whatonga was re-united with Toi at the pa Kaputerangi. After staying at Toi's pa for some time, Whatonga decided to find lands for himself, and relaunched the Kurahaupo. He sailed to Turanganui where Popoto, Mahutonga and (in some versions Tu-ranga) settled. After staying for a while, Whatonga travelled on to Mahia.

The following is a list, collected from several sources, of those said to have been on the Kurahaupo:

Whatonga	Mahutonga	Tama-ahua
Taramanga	Popoto	Te Hatauira
Tokaroa	Korehewa	Moko
Pou	Te Auaha	Te Awe

Orutu	Rau-matangi	Te Hape
Tauarau	Tu-kapua	Te Akaaka-whenua
Maungaroa *	Ruatea *	
Hine-ahu	(wife of Tama-ahua, from Ahu)	
Hine-tangi-akau	(wife of Tama-ahua, from Rarotonga)	

(* Maungaroa and Ruatea are usually associated with the second Kurahaupo)

(*See also* Paepae-ki-Rarotonga and Te Wao.)

ADDITIONAL INFORMATION

It is claimed in *The Lore of the Whare Wananga* that when Whatonga came to Aotearoa he brought with him a papa-tatau (inscribed stone) from the sacred house Whakamoe-ariki. According to tradition, a house was erected for the papa-tatau at O-akura. It is remembered that the pa-paepae of the house was made from kiri-kara (possibly some kind of basalt), and was red in colour. It is also stated that Mahutonga had charge of the gods Ruamano, Tunuiateika and Maru, who were evidently represented in the form of physical images. In a part of the Kurahaupo tradition recorded in *Treasury of Maori Exploration*, Ruatea is said to have stayed at Rarotonga when the Kurahaupo stopped off at that island, and he was replaced by the Rarotongan Te Awe.

In the second tradition, the Kurahaupo was a migration vessel. Some sources say it was originally named Tarai-po, having been renamed prior to voyaging (*see also* Tarai-po). Details of the voyage of Kurahaupo vary considerably from source to source, but generally the northern tribes believe that the Kurahaupo was wrecked at Rangitahua during the voyage to Aotearoa. The waka was subsequently repaired, and sailed on to northern shores, with alternatively Pi, Po, or Ruatea as captain. The Taranaki version agrees that the waka was wrecked, and their geographical proximity to tribes descending from the Aotea crew could point to their ancestors having continued on to Aotearoa after the wreck in the Aotea. Taranaki state that Te Moungaroa was the captain of the Kurahaupo. A third group, whose members live between Whangaehu in the north and Horowhenua in the south, claim that Ruatea was the chief of Kurahaupo.

Rangitane tradition, as stated in McEwen's book *Rangitane*, is as follows.

The ancestors of the Rangitane now resident in the Manawatu came in the Kurahaupo waka which was hewn with celebrated greenstone axes out of a tree which grew in the Tawhitinui Forest. She was made at the same time and place as the Arawa, and was commanded on her voyage by three chiefs. Ruatea was the principal chief, and acted as steersman. Whatonga had charge of the fore part of the waka, and Popoto, a minor chief, was stationed in the centre, his duties being to urge the crew to greater exertions, and to see that there was no 'skulking' . . . The Kurahaupo landed at a little bay inside Mahia Peninsula called Nukutaurua, where according to the legend she was turned into stone by Hau.

(This passage is followed up by a claim from McEwen stating that every Rangitane elder he had known in the 40 to 50 years prior to the publication of the book had 'supported this version of the Kurahaupo story'.)

McEwen later explains that according to sources quoted by Buick in Old Manawatu, Hau had offended his relatives prior to the departure of the Kurahaupo, and had been left behind when the waka set sail. By way of his 'exceptional powers', Hau was able to reach Nukutaurua before the Kurahaupo, and managed to sink her by means of a karakia some small distance from shore. None of the crew are said to have perished, but the waka sank, and subsequently turned into a reef.

Information collected for the *Muriwhenua Fishing Report* on northern ancestral waka stated that the Kurahaupo was almost wrecked at Rangitahua when the timbers were loosened or damaged. Most of the crew transferred to the Aotea, but a few men stayed behind to repair the vessel. In one version, it is said that after successfully repairing Kurahaupo, Pi navigated the waka to Aotearoa, being guided part of the way by phosphorescence, which was seen in the ocean (the informant suggested the name of the waka was from the 'strange light in the darkness' of the phosphorescence).

The following ancestors have been remembered, although some of their places can be argued for either crew.

Te Moungaroa	Ruatea	Rongoueroa
Nga kura-matapo	Hatonga	Hau-pipi
Akuramatapu	Tukapua	Te Hatauira

Turu (Turu-rangi, Turu-rangi-marie)		Taumauri
Pou-poto *	Popoto *	Pi
Po *	Po-hurihanga *	Popo *
Pou *	Pou-poto *	

* Possibly alternative names for the same man.

Te Moungaroa, Akuramatapu, Tukapua and Turu are usually said to have joined Mataatua after their waka was wrecked at Rangitahua. It is recorded that Hatonga and Haupipi transferred to the Aotea.

Among the many tribes that claim descent from the Kurahaupo crew are: Ngati Hau, Ngati Apa, Taranaki, Ngati Ruanui, Ngati Kahungunu, Ngati Awa, Rangitane, Ngati Kuia, Ngati Tumata-kokiri, Te Aupouri, Te Rarawa, Mua-upoko, Ngai Tara, Ngati Ira, Ngati Momoe.

The voyage

Te Kahui Kararehe of Taranaki stated that the captain of Kurahaupo was Te Moungaroa. According to Te Kahui, the waka broke up before it left Hawaiki, and Te Moungaroa, Turu, Akuramutapu and Tukapua transferred to Mataatua for the voyage to Aotearoa. This version was repeated by Takaanui Tarakawa, who added that the Kurahaupo was subsequently repaired in Hawaiki, and voyaged to Aotearoa with Te Rangihokaia as captain. Tarakawa also claims that the name of the waka was changed to Te Rangimatoru prior to the voyage, so that the previous owners couldn't claim her.

In one account, the waka accompanied Horouta during the voyage, and landed at Ohiwa. The god Tu-kai-te-uru is stated to have been the guiding deity. (Te Hoka-a-te-rangi and Te Tangi-whakaea are also named as having been captain of the waka.)

Other versions given for the *Muriwhenua Fishing Report* claim that Po-hurihangi was the captain, and the waka was successfully beached and tied to a rock known as Te-wa-o-te-Kura (since shortened to Wakura). After a night of resting, the crew, who belonged to Ngati Kaha, returned to the waka in the morning to find it waterlogged. With the aid of the local Te Ngaki people, the waka was dragged ashore to a village at the mouth of the Waitangi stream, and left. (It is explained that the tribal name, Ngati Kaha, was taken from 'the header rope (kaharoa) of the great net belonging to Po-hurihanga and brought with him on the Kurahaupo waka. Their waka was sinking, and the damage was repaired at the Kermadec Islands, using Po's kaharoa to bind the loosened timbers together'.)

Elsewhere it is said that Kurahaupo was wrecked at Rangitahua under the command of Ruatea. Fortunately for the crew members, they were able to join the crews of Aotea and Mataatua. Another version of the legend has the wrecking of the waka happening on a second migration voyage, when the vessel was sailed back to Hawaiki to pick up those of the tribe that had not been able to fit on the waka for the first trip.

According to Takitimu tribal knowledge, Popoto was the commander of Kurahaupo, and Ruatea was the priest. A Tainui tradition alluded to in *Whakatane and District Historical Society Inc Memoir #4*, states that Taumauri was the commander of Kurahaupo. It is often said that Te Moungaroa carried a kura to Aotearoa, kura being 'power of oratory, authority over land, power of invocations in time of war, power for good, power over environment, power over some of the atua, power over all things on earth'. (From *Treasury of Maori Exploration*.) Another source states that the kura was a physical object, and that it was rescued by a diver after the Kurahaupo began to break up at Rangitahua.

The landfall

Information collected by the *Muriwhenua Fishing Report* researchers included physical evidence in the shape of a rock at Takapaukura, which is said to be the remains of the Kurahaupo. The marks of the waka's timber are apparently still visible. They also collected a tradition that the Kurahaupo came from Waerota Island. The site of the Kurahaupo's wreck during its voyage to Aotearoa is stated variously as Te Au-o-kura or Whenuakura; while an alternative name for the island where the Kurahaupo was wrecked is Motiwhatiwha.

It is also recorded that after Te Moungaroa had landed in Aotearoa aboard the Mataatua, he claimed that Kurahaupo had been bewitched, and that was the reason for its mishap at Rangitahua. He declared that the other chiefs who had voyaged to Aotearoa were jealous of his kura. A source quoted in *Maori Place Names* stated that the Kurahaupo was finally wrecked on the west coast of the South Island. It is also claimed in *How the Maoris Came to Aotearoa* that 'the Kurahaupo ended her adventures in the sounds of Marlborough'.

It is suggested in *The Coming of the Maori* that some details, such as Maungaroa and Te Hatauira being in the 'first' Kurahaupo's crew, have been added to the Whatonga story by certain parties to add substance to their version. Other details have had to be amended or added as well: the claim that the Kurahaupo sailed down the west coast, before returning north, may be in this category.

The Ancient History of the Maori, Vol. 2, p. 182.
The Ancient History of the Maori, Vol. 4, p. 35.
The Coming of the Maori, pp. 26–9, 31, 54, 337.
How the Maoris Came to Aotearoa, p. 106.
JPS, Vol. 3, p. 70.
JPS, Vol. 9, p. 218.
JPS, Vol. 12, pp. 124–5.
JPS, Vol. 23, p. 15.
JPS, Vol. 24, p. 53.
Maori Art, p. 32.
Maori Life in Old Taranaki, pp. 21, 29.
Maori Lore, p. 295.
Maori Place Names, pp. 127, 159.
The Maori–Polynesian Comparative Dictionary, p. 20.
Maori Religion, 2, p. 213.
The Maori Waka, pp. 392–3.
Muriwhenua Fishing Report, pp. 255, 256, 263.
Rangitane, pp. 10–14.
The Story of Aotea, p. 214.
Takitimu, p. 45.
Te Arawa, p. 11.
Treasury of Maori Exploration, pp. 63, 66–7, 94, 230, 245–6.
Treasury of Maori Folklore, p. 191.
Whakatane and District Historical Society Inc Memoir #4, p. 20.
Whakatane and District Historical Society Inc Memoir #7, pp. 21–2, 26.

KURA-TAWA

The Kura-tawa is remembered only by name. No other information is recorded.

A Leaf From the Natural History of New Zealand, p. 49.

MAHANGA-A-TUAMATUA

The Mahanga-a-Tuamatua is considered in some circles as an ancient name for the waka Tainui and Te Arawa. Ngata suggested to John Te H. Grace in the following recorded conversation that the two waka were in fact a double waka — an 'ihu waka tau'.

> *One hull was under the control of Hoturoa and the other under Tamatekapua. Ngatoroirangi being high priest of the tribe was automatically tohunga and navigator. It was not until the vessel reached some point before arriving in New Zealand that the hulls were unlashed. This double waka was Te Mahanga-a-Tuamatua.*

Ngata said he was of this opinion because of the abundance of traditional history that was common to, and claimed by, both waka. For instance, there was the story of Whakaotirangi and her basket of kumara. Both claim her as a passenger and, therefore, the honour of bringing the kumara to this country. Te Arawa people refer to her kumara basket as te kete rokiroki a Whakaotirangi (the secure basket of Whakaotirangi), and Tainui make reference to it as te kete rukuruku a Whakaotirangi (the small basket of Whakaotirangi). Both have the same kumara lore. The accounts of the whale at Whangaparaoa and the discarding of the kura are identical. Each waka claims the honour of putting the birds Mumuhou and Takereto ashore at Cuvier Island, and both vessels have the same dragging chant; the Te Arawa version is, 'Toia Te Arawa tapotu ki te moana' (Haul Te Arawa the covered waka to the sea), while Tainui merely substitute Tainui for Te Arawa.

Tuwharetoa, pp. 54–5.

MAHUHU-KI-TE-RANGI
Name variation: Mahuhu

Usually referred to by its shorter name Mahuhu, the Mahuhu-ki-te-rangi was captained by either Whakatau or his son Rongomai. The majority of the crew settled in the vicinity of the Kaipara Heads. Claims put before the Waitangi Tribunal in the 1980s and 1990s suggest that Whakatau was the main chief on the Mahuhu-ki-te-rangi: 'Ko Mahuhu-ki-te-rangi te waka; Ko Whakatau te tangata' (Mahuhu-ki-te-rangi is the waka; Whakatau is the man), although this saying does not rule out the possibility that Whakatau was the chief of the tribe, Rongomai the captain of the waka.

The following tradition, pieced together from several interviews collected between 1887 and 1889 from members of Te Uri-o-Hau tribe, claims that Rongomai was the captain of the Mahuhu-ki-te-rangi. As will be seen in the story, it is possible that Whakatau is named as 'te tangata' in some Treaty claims because of Rongomai's untimely death.

The Mahuhu, captained by Rongomai, came from the hautiu (northwest), from a place named Waerota. The reason Rongomai left his homeland has been put down to a feud with his younger brother Rongoatu over family matters. The main points of dispute seem to have revolved around the garden known as Te Pare-o-tonga and ceremonies for the cultivation of crops, and of family occupation areas and boundaries. In an unusual turn of events, it was the elder brother Rongomai who decided to leave the family land and seek a new beginning elsewhere. He had a new waka built and named it Mahuhu-ki-te-rangi, apparently after the cultivation ceremonies (whaka-mahuhu) which were the root of the brother's discord. The waka's cargo included several types of plants, among them seed of the hue, tubers of the uwhi (yam), taro, kumara, ti, aute plants (paper mulberry) and also the coconut.

As the Mahuhu-ki-te-rangi departed it is claimed that Rongomai called to his younger brother, 'E Noho! Ko to taua mara he tuakana mou!' (Remain, let our cultivation be an elder brother for you!) To which Rongoatu retorted, 'Haere! E taku tuakana kumara — ou Kumara he teiha mou!' (Depart, my elder kumara-brother — may the kumara be a younger brother to you!) Rongoatu's reply was full of meaning, and is today shortened to 'tuakana kumara', a whakatauki (proverbial saying) applied to selfish people, particularly an elder brother placing himself before a younger relative.

From Waerota, Rongomai sailed the Mahuhu to Waeroti, and then on to Mata-te-ra where he heard stories about a fabulous new land — Aotearoa. It was decided to voyage to this new land where a new life could be started.

After the voyage south from the tropics, the Mahuhu-ki-te-rangi first made landfall at Takou, near the North Cape, but found the land inhabited by a people whose name was Kui. Rongomai then sailed his waka to Whangaroa, and on to Whangaruru, Ohiwa and perhaps as far south as Waiapu on the East Cape, with one or two crew members staying at each port of call. Unable to find any suitable land for his people to settle, Rongomai decided to return to the north. They sailed the waka back to Takou, and then on to Parengarenga, where still more of the crew disembarked. From

Parengarenga the Mahuhu-ki-te-rangi rounded the North Cape and sailed down the west coast as far as Taporapora, an island that once stood inside the Kaipara Heads, where the remainder of the crew settled.

Some time after his arrival at Taporapora, Rongomai drowned in a fishing accident after he had neglected some uru-uru-whenua ceremonies. His remains were gnawed at by araara (trevally) and tamure (snapper) before being pounded by the waves onto the rocks near Waikaretu. To this day the area is remembered as Te Akitanga-o-Rongomai. A rahui was laid over the fishing grounds for a long period, prohibiting people from harvesting the rich seafood in the area. To this day descendants of Rongomai still avoid eating the flesh of the araara and tamure.

It is said that as a result of this accident, some of Rongomai's children and others of the tribe returned to the north and settled at Rangaunu. The Mahuhu was hauled up a creek and left to decay; the exact spot is known as Te Wai-popo-o-Mahuhu and is still tapu. Soon after the Mahuhu-ki-te-rangi left for the north a great storm is said to have struck Taporapora and totally destoyed it, the only sign of the island's previous existence being sandbars which are visible at low tide.

JPS, Vol. 48, pp. 186–8.
Maori Art, p. 32.
Muriwhenua Fishing Report, p. 257.
Te Roroa, pp. 4, 10.

MAHUNU-AWATEA

Name variations: Mahunu, Awatea

The Mahunu-awatea was one of the waka that sailed with Whakatau when he travelled to Hawaiki to destroy the temple known as Te Uru-o-Manona. (*See* Hakirere.)

Maori Art, p. 37.

MAMARI

Ko Ruanui te tangata
Ko Mamari te waka
i uu mai ki Ripino

> Ruanui was the man
> Mamari was the waka
> that landed at Ripino

The Mamari, under Ruanui, was one of the earliest migration waka to journey to Aotearoa. It voyaged in the company of the waka Nga Toki-mata-wha-o-rua, whose captain was Nuku-tawhiti. Ruanui made careful preparations for the voyage and learnt the sailing directions directly from the famous navigator and explorer Kupe: 'When you go, lay the bow of the waka to the Cloud Pillar that lies south west. When night falls, steer towards the star, Atua-tahi. Hold to the left of Manga-roa (the Milky Way) and travel on. When day breaks, again sail towards the Cloud Pillar and continue on'.

Kupe arranged for a number of taniwha to swim with the two waka to protect them during the voyage. Those chosen to accompany the Mamari were named Arai-te-uru, Niua, Te Tohi-o-te-po and Kanapu-i-te-rangi. The god Tohi-nui-a-rangi, said to live in the Rising Moon, was also sent to watch over the waka as they sailed south to the new land. As a final word of advice to Ruanui before the departure, Kupe warned him not forget the karakia for the Sky Rope, nor that for the anchor.

The voyage of the Mamari was fairly uneventful, trouble occurring only when the taniwha of both waka managed to get caught in the nets of Kahukura. Papatara, the most powerful tohunga from Nga Toki-mata-wha-o-rua, chanted a karakia in an effort to break the giant nets, which soon fell away freeing the trapped deities.

Carefully following the Sky Rope and the details from the karakia of the anchor, Ruanui was able to sail the Mamari directly to Hokianga, the harbour from which Kupe left on his return to Hawaiki many years previously. As the Mamari approached the entrance to the harbour, the two most powerful taniwha, Arai-te-uru and Niua, smoothed the way over the bar, allowing the waka to land safely on the shore. (These two taniwha are said to still guard the entrance to the harbour, Niua living in a cave on the north side, and Arai-te-uru on the south.)

After staying at Hokianga, Ruanui and his crew decided to explore further down the west coast in the Mamari. Unfortunately, before they had sailed far they were caught in a storm and the waka was wrecked on Riripo Beach, thereafter named Omamari.

Those remembered to have sailed on the Mamari during the migration voyage are as follows (from *Tai Tokerau*):

Ruanui	*captain*
Hou-mai-tawhiti	*tohunga and grandson of Kupe*
Te Maru-o-te-huia	*son of Ruanui*
Ruatapu	*daughter of Ruanui*
Pehiriri	Whai-putuputu
Ngoingoi-ariki	Te Hou-o-te-rangi
Patari-kai-hau	Toka-tu-tahi
Te Toko-o-te-rangi	Tuki-te-Nga rangi
Tuaiahu	Te Ao-kai-tou
Haraki	Manawa-a-rangi
Kura-i-te-whatu	Kura-pounau
Papa-a-rangi	Tama-a-rongo
Matiti-ki-te-rangi	Tangaroa
Konuku-tau-rangi	Moehau
Te Hurinui	

It is often claimed in traditions recorded early on by such well-known collectors of Maori legends as S. Percy Smith and his contemporaries that the captain of the Mamari was Nuku-tawhiti. This is probably a confusion caused by the close relationship between Mamari and Nga Toki-mata-wha-o-rua and their crews.

Muriwhenua Fishing Report, p. 257.
Tai Tokerau, pp. 55–56, 108–109.

MAMARU

Name variation: Mamamaru

The Mamaru, with Te Parata as captain, was one of the earliest waka known to have landed on the east side of the Tai-Tokerau district. The waka had earlier voyaged to Aotearoa under the name Tinana, with Te Parata's uncle Tumoana as captain and landed near Ahipara on the west coast.

The Mamaru first sighted land at Karikari Peninsula (then known as Rangiawhia), before sailing to Otengi, just south of Taipa, where the crew finally completed their journey. From Otengi the crew split into three hapu: Te Korohuri, Patu Koraha and Te Whanau Moana, each hapu establishing themselves in the vicinity of Doubtless Bay and Rangaunu Harbour.

Muriwhenua Fishing Report, pp. 260–1.
Treasury of Maori Exploration, p. 265.

MANGARARA

According to information collected by Ngata, the Mangarara and its contemporary Tauira originated from the Cook Islands, with ancestors of both waka going on to inhabit lands about the East Cape. The captain of the Mangarara was Wheke-toro, and other chiefs accompanying him were Te Wai-o-po-tango, Tua-heke, Te Rau-ariki-ao and Tara-whata.

The waka is said to have carried a cargo of birds, lizards and insects. Included amongst the 'passengers' were the tuatara, weri (centipede), whee (caterpillar), weta, kekerengu (black beetle), teretere (brown gecko), kumukumu (lizard), moko-parae and moko-kakariki (both species of gecko), and birds such as the torea (pied oyster catcher) and the whai-o-io or whi-io (a sacred bird used in sacrifices to the gods).

The first landing place of the Mangarara was Whanga-o-kena (East Island), a small island just off East Cape. Here Wheke-toro offloaded the lizards, geckos, tuatara and some of the birds. To protect them he immediately proceeded to make the island tapu. First Wheke-toro chanted a karakia, then lit a sacred fire that he named Takuahi on the beach. Next he threw a stone from Takuahi at the beach-head, causing a landslide making it practically impossible for waka to land on the island. This part of the coastline he named Te Horo-roa. Lastly, Wheke-toro and Te Rau-ariki-ao each took a stone from the sacred fire and formed two fresh-water springs, naming them Whaka-au-ranga and Te Muri-wai respectively. With the ceremonies finally complete, the Mangarara was refloated and sailed towards the coast of Aotearoa.

On nearing land, Tarawhata's dog somehow managed to end up in the sea, and in the confusion that followed, the waka was swamped by the surf and began to drift towards Tokaroa (presumably the name of some rocks in the area). Te Rau-ariki-ao, aware of the imminent danger, called upon the remaining birds to take ropes and drag the waka to the safety of the beach. The Mangarara, totally waterlogged and badly damaged, was left where it lay, too heavy to move, and eventually it turned to stone.

The Ancient History of the Maori, Vol. 2, pp. 189–90.
Treasury of Maori Exploration, pp. 17–18.
Whakatane and District Historical Society Inc. Memoir #8, p. 1.

MANO
Chatham Islands

The only mention made of the Mano is of its being the second hull for the Moriori waka Poreitua. The relationship between Poreitua and other Moriori waka suggests that the double waka was sailing about the time of the first Moriori migration to the Chatham Islands.

JPS, Vol. 5, p. 17.

MANUKA
Name variation: Manuka-tai

The Manuka was the sister waka to Arai-te-uru, both waka being built from the same large totara tree that had been found stranded on a beach by Tua-kakariki. While Tua-kakariki was away rounding up a work party to help him move the log to a safe spot, Rongo-i-tua, a visitor, came across the same log, and seeing footprints in the sand knew he would be challenged if he claimed it for himself. Desperate to return to his homeland, Rongo-i-tua deposited excrement on the tree as part of a plan to claim the log, and then returned to the pa to listen as Tua-kakariki claimed the tree by right of first discovery. Once Tua-kakariki had finished, Rongo-i-tua stepped foward and challenged him on the grounds that there was a mark of his ownership on the log, and suggested they go to where the tree lay to establish once and for all who owned the totara. The tree was subsequently awarded to Rongo-i-tua, and as soon as the decision was made he went about organising a work party to construct two waka from the totara log. Rongo-i-tua had no trouble getting co-operation from the Kahui-tipua people he was living amongst, as he had introduced kao to them, a food made from kumara, and had promised to lead an expedition to acquire kumara from the island where it grew.

The Manuka was completed first, and was apparently named after the disgust felt by those who saw the excrement on the log. As soon as the waka was completed the Kahui-tipua appropriated it and set off for Hawaiki, so eager were they to gather the new food. When they reached Hawaiki they managed to obtain some kumara tubers, but to their great disappointment were unable to cultivate the crop successfully upon their return to Aotearoa.

In some South Island traditions it is the Manuka and the Horouta that feature in the voyage back to Hawaiki to seek the kumara. It is also interesting to note that the main storyline of this legend is very similar to the North Island tradition of Hoaki and Tau-kata, who built the waka Te Aratawhao to return to Hawaiki to procure kumara.

JPS, Vol. 24, p. 112.
Maori Place Names, p. 129.
Traditional Lifeways of the Southern Maori, p. 301.
Treasury of Maori Exploration, pp. 54–5.

MANUKA-TERE

Name variation: Manu-ka-rere

The captain of the Manuka-tere was Kahu-kura, and he is sometimes said to have lived at Upolu, Samoa, and to have voyaged widely about the Pacific from there. Among his many journeys in the Manuka-tere was a trip to Fiji, and another to 'the lands his father had visited, which were to the south, south-west, and west of Samoa. One of these Islands was named Nuku, which possibly may be intended for Nuku-roa, an old name for New Zealand'. From another reference, we learn that the Manu-ka-rere 'was hewed out of a tree in the forest of which Rata-i-te-wao was the guardian. The Rarotongans say the tree was a Maota-mea (which grows in Samoa), and that the tree was growing in the Island of Kuporu, i.e, Upolu of Samoa'.

To add another twist to the story, a Samoan legend declares that the original name of the Manu-ka-rere was Tarai-po (which in Maori legend was renamed the Kurahaupo), and the name change came about when Tane's birds of the forest transported the newly built Tarai-po to its waka shed. During the ceremony for the new waka, the second name of Pori-o-kare was bestowed upon it when the waka reached the paepae of the waka shed, and the final name, Pori-o-nou, was given when it entered the waka shed.

History and Traditions of the Taranaki Coast, p. 64.
JPS, Vol. 16, p. 180.
JPS, Vol. 21, p. 54.
JPS, Vol. 28, p. 219.

MANU-KAU-MOANA
Chatham Islands

The first inhabitants of the Chatham Islands had occupied the island for many generations when Kahu voyaged there from the North Island of Aotearoa in his waka Manu-kau-moana, with the intention of settling there. Unfortunately for Kahu and his crew, their crops would not grow in the cold and wet climate and they were forced to return to their homeland.

This story is exactly duplicated from another source with Tanewai (or a variation of that name) being the waka of Kahu. (*See also* Tanewai.)

Transactions of the New Zealand Institute, Vol. 32, p. 357.

MAPOURIKI
Chatham Islands

The Mapouriki is one of four waka said to have voyaged to the Chatham Islands directly from Rarotonga, the other three being Aotearoa, Rangi-ahua and Te Ririno.

Despite other legends associating the Aotearoa and Te Ririno to mainland Aotearoa, it is not impossible that they made separate trips to the Chatham Islands, although it is perhaps more probable that the passage of time has intertwined several waka into the one saga.

(The similarity between the name of this waka and that of another Moriori waka, Pouariki, should be noted.)

JPS, Vol. 23, p. 76.

MATAATUA

Name variation: Matatua

Much has been written about this waka, and much is still debated, with several major tribes descending from the crew of the Mataatua having their own versions of various incidents. Those tribes most closely associated with the Mataatua waka are Ngati Awa, Tuhoe and Whakatohea. Many other hapu also have affiliations with the waka, through ancestral links with individual crew members.

The Mataatua enters tradition as the waka used by the crew of the Aratawhao in which they returned to Aotearoa from Hawaiki. After the brothers Hoaki and Taukata had introduced kumara to the people of the Kapu-te-rangi (Tapu-te-rangi) pa, near present-day Whakatane, they were persuaded to return to Hawaiki to obtain a supply of kumara tubers for cultivation in Aotearoa. Hoaki and Taukata built the waka Aratawhao in which to make the return voyage to Hawaiki, and while Hoaki led the expedition, Taukata remained in Aotearoa. (*See* Aratawhao for a crew list.) At Hawaiki it was suggested that the Aratawhao was not seaworthy for the return journey to Aotearoa, and the crew transferred to the Mataatua.

Several people from Hawaiki joined the crew of the Aratawhao when they returned to Aotearoa in the Mataatua. One of them, Toroa, is generally accepted as having been the captain of the waka. Toroa's navigator for the voyage was Tama-ki-hikurangi, who had accompanied Hoaki in the Aratawhao during the original expedition seeking kumara. Others remembered among the original crew from Hawaiki are:

Muriwai	*Toroa's sister*
Weka-nui	*a wife*
Puha-rau-nui	*a wife*
Rake-piki-tua	*a wife*
Rahiri	*a son*
Ruaihonga	*a son*
Wairaka	*his daughter*
Puhi-kai-ariki	*his brother*
Taneatua	*his half brother*
Tahinga-o-te-ra	*a grandson*

Nuiho	Puharaunui	Kakepikitia

Taka	Tarawhata	Manu
Hinemataroa	Ruauru	Kaniora
Tuturiwhatu	Puhi-moana-ariki	

Immediately prior to the return voyage, Toroa's father, Irakewa, who had visited Aotearoa previously, described the landing place that Toroa should look for. He described a waterfall that cascades down a high cliff near the sea, a river mouth that provides a safe anchorage, and a cave that gives good shelter. He was in fact describing the Wairere waterfall, Whakatane River, and the cave later named Te Ana o Muriwai.

The following karakia has been attributed to Toroa, and is said to have been chanted by him during the ocean voyage. It was used to strengthen the waka for the last part of the voyage.

> Tutapa, tutapa, tutapa mai kawa,
> Ko te kawa nui, ko te kawa roa;
> Koruru mai heai tuku mai Pou?
> Pou hoki te aniwaniwa?
> Koia rutua ki te toi nuku.
> Koia rutua ki te toi rangi.
> Hamoa kua ruru taku rama.
> Ko te rama na wai?
> Ko te rama na Tu.
> Ka ruru ki hea?
> Ka ruru ki Waioriki,
> Ka ruru ki Waioraka.
> Kape ti. Kape ta.
> Kape mahuki te marangai tua.
> I aua kia eke,
> Eke, eke Tangaroa,
> Eke panuku.
> Ui — e! Taiki — e!

> Recite, recite, recite the ritual,
> The great ritual, the long ritual;
> Whence comes this overcast that descends on Pou?
> Is it not Pou by the rainbow?
> Therefore bind it to the summit of the sky,
> Now my torch is sheltered.

Whose torch is it?
It is the torch of Tu.
Where is it sheltered?
At Waioriki and Waioraka.
It moves this way and that way,
It rides the throbbing storm
And rises up on top.
Up! up Tangaroa!
Up! Move on!
Disengage! Taiki — e!

Little is remembered about the actual sailing of the Mataatua during its southern voyage, other than that it is said to have stopped at both Rarotonga and Rangitahua (possibly Sunday Island in the Kermadec group). While at Rangitahua, the waka Kurahaupo, Aotea and Te Ririno are also said to have made landfall. Near the island, Kurahaupo was badly damaged on rocks or a reef. Such was the extent of the damage that several of the Kurahaupo's crew abandoned the waka and joined the crews of the Aotea and Mataatua for the remainder of the voyage to Aotearoa. These included Te Moungaroa, Turu, Tukapua and Akuramatapu.

From Rangitahua, the waka was sailed to Aotearoa. Several places are claimed as its first landing place, including Whangara, Ahuahu, Muriwhenua, Takou and Whangaparaoa. Most traditions favour Whangara, with travel along the coast accounting for other places suggested.

Upon landfall at Whangara, an argument broke out between Te Moungaroa (who was originally from Kurahaupo) and Taneatua, over which of them had the right to offer the first karakia in Aotearoa. The argument was finally decided in Te Moungaroa's favour, because he proposed to remain at Whangara, while Taneatua presumably decided that he should explore some of the island before settling down.

Several other well-known events occurred during the coastal voyage of the Mataatua. It is claimed that at that time the Rangitaiki River entered the sea near the Matata lagoon. While sailing past the river mouth, Wairaka is said to have made a comment that was paraphrased to Te-awa-o-te-atua, the Maori name retained for the river to this day. Further along the coast the Mataatua arrived at the Whakatane River mouth. Wairaka is said to have become seasick due to the ocean swell, and thus the promontory now known as Kohi point was named. Soon after beaching the Mataatua in the mouth of the river (then known as Tamahine-a-Hinemataroa), the men from the crew went to make contact with the local inhabitants. While away, the waka started to drift in the river currents, and was in danger of being wrecked. It was Wairaka (or in Whakatohea tradition, Muriwai) who reacted first and, uttering the phrase 'Kia whakatane ake au i ahau' (Let me make a man of myself), managed to save the Mataatua. From Wairaka's chant, the river received its new name, Whakatane.

Immediately after this episode, Muriwai took the mawe, the sacred vessel used to protect the waka and crew during the voyage, and placed it in a cave, subsequently named Te Ana-o-Muriwai. (Tutaka also names the following places as depositories for the mawe: Te Atea, Purakau, Wharepapa, Aropaki, and Tahuarangi.) From Hawaiki, Muriwai's mother, Wairakewa, became aware of her daughter's actions through her supernatural powers. In an effort to protect her child from the consequences of her action, Wairakewa voyaged to Aotearoa on a manuka bush, and intervened by way of her extraordinary powers. Possibly because of her high position within the tribe, her relationship to Toroa, and no doubt Wairakewa's influence within the tribe, Muriwai got away with her serious breach of protocol. The ceremony would usually have been reserved for the captain of the waka, and certainly would not have been performed by a woman.

The next event undertaken by Toroa and his people was to build a tuaha (an altar) to the gods, which was named Makaka. The tuaha was built on the site of present-day Whakatane, and consisted of a manuka pole. Once the people had settled at Whakatane, the precious kumara was planted at a garden named Matire-rau. It is said that Taukata, brother of Hoaki, was sacrificed to ensure the spirit of the crop remained with the garden. In some versions of the event, the sacrifice followed instructions from Hoaki, given to Tama-ki-hikurangi prior to his return to Aotearoa. Toroa built the whare wananga Tupapaku-rau near the Whakatane River mouth, while Taneatua took the tauihu and feather ornaments of the Mataatua further up the river valley and built his whare, which he called Whare-ariki.

While the immigrants were living at Whakatane, Toroa's brother, Puhi-kai-ariki, chose to show his resentment at his brother's authority over the tribe by singing the following song of insult.

Korokoro iti, korokoro rahi,
Tu ana te manu i runga i nga puke rara.
Tenei te kai ka iri, he kai whakarere te kai;
He kai i pokaia noatia i runga i a Tu ka riri,
I a Tu ka ritarita.
E haere ana ki uta te tangata kainga kore
Ka pau te ki ona mata.
He nui kai maoa e tu ana i runga i a Turoa,
He nui kai, he mano te kai, he tutae taua
Ka kai tiko iho ki waenga.
He aha aku kai te pau noa ai?
Maku te tohenga ki te whitu, ki te waru,
Kite roa o te tau.
Waiho nei matau hei timokamoka kai
Mo te ngahuru;
Tangi ana te whakatopatopa o kai,
O kai mai he toroa, he taiko.

A bird with a small and large throat,
Sits on yonder hill.
For here is food abandoned
And strewn on Tu in anger.
A homeless man travels inland,
And he sees nothing.
There is an abundance of food on Turoa:
It is excreta of a war party
To be consumed in the wilderness.
But why should my supplies be exhausted?
I will provide for the seventh and eighth months
And for the rest of the year.
We will also have remnants of the food for the autumn.
I hear the planting chants resound,
But your food is toroa (albatross) and a taiko (black petrel).

Undaunted, Toroa composed a song of his own, in which he mocked Puhi-kai-ariki.

Te ko miti runga, miti raro, miti haha
Ka tupu te wai, ka ora te wai
Ko te wai na wai,

Ko te wai na Uru-mananawa
Ka tohi atu tama ki te ake rautangi
Te hekenga o Tu ki Tauaraia
E Puhi. E! Ngahoro. E!
Kai tai, kai tai, kai te whakarua koia e — e.
Te ko makauea ki runga o Maketu
Tatara mai i Hikurangi
Ko te ika moe tahuaroa
Ka piri te hono ko mau whakaarahia
Uru o Weka ki te tuku roa ki te wai puatea
Ka mahuta e Puhi, E!
Kai tai, kai tai, kai te whakarua koia — e
A — ha-ha!

The spade works above, below and aside:
The waters rise and all is well.
To whom does the water belong?
To Uru-mananawa.
It is struck and parted with the ake rautangi (a wooden
   weapon)
And Tu descended to Tauaraia
O Puhi! you are fallen!
The twice drinker of sea water!

Unfortunately Grace translates only the first part of the song in *Tuwharetoa*, but the verse continues on to degrade Puhi-kai-ariki.

At the conclusion of Toroa's verse, a fight broke out between the two brothers. Before Taneatua could intervene and break up the altercation, Toroa's grandson Tahinga-o-te-ra, who was still a child, took a swipe at Puhi-kai-ariki. This final insult was too much for Puhi, who soon took command of the Mataatua, which had been moored at the Orini canal, and sailed it north.

Those of the tribe remembered as having left with Puhi-kai-ariki are: Rahiri, Nuiho, Nuake, Tukapua, Waituhi, Wekanui and Akuramatapu.

Having successfully journeyed north, the waka was sailed to Matauri Bay, where a small stream named Takou runs into the sea. This stretch of water is given as the Mataatua's final resting place. The exact spot is said to be some five kilometres upstream from the stream mouth.

> ADDITIONAL INFORMATION

Crew

Akuramatapu, Mirupokai, Rongoitua, Ruauru and Toroa have all been named as captains of the Mataatua in various versions of the Mataatua story. The most probable explanation for the wealth of names put foward is that the waka was used for subsequent voyages along the coasts of Aotearoa as the immigrants either sought uninhabited lands, or explored their new homeland. Presumably, each of those named took command of the waka at one time or another.

The following crew lists are from A.C. Lyall's *The Mataatua Question*, and have been grouped together in settlement units. (It will be noted that some individuals are in more than one list).

People who stayed in vicinity of Whangara and Turanga-nui:
Awariki	Hamokiterangi	Hinehakitai
Hoihoitipua	Kanoa	Maia
Matuatiti	Matuatonga	Rongoitua
Tukaitangi	Uenuku Whakarongo	

People who arrived at Whakatane:
Hikaroa	Hinemataroa	Kakepikitea
Moungaroa	Muriwai	Puhi-kai-ariki
Rahiri	Ruaihonga	Taiaroa
Tahinga-o-te-ra	Tamakihikurangi	Taneatua
Tarawhata	Toroa	Wairaka
Whakapoi	Whare	

People who are presumed to have stayed at Whakatane:
Mu	Wekanui	Waituhi
Tukapua	Mahanga	Nuiho
Nuake	Akuramatapu	

People who travelled to the West Coast:
Akuramatapu	Te Moungaroa	Ruauru
Tukapua	Turu	

People who voyaged north after Puhi-kai-ariki and Toroa's fight:
Akuramatapu	Nuake	Nuiho
Taneatua	Waituhi	Wekanui
Mirupokai	Rahiri (ancestor of Ngati Rahiri)	

The family names, or perhaps hapu names, of some of the crew members were Te Puhi-matua, Te Puhi-mau, and Te Puhi-haere. Another spelling of Ruauru's name, as given in *Maori Lore*, is Kuru-auru.

The waka

According to one source recorded in *The Maori–Polynesian Comparative Dictionary*, it was the Mataatua, and not the Matahourua, that was the twin half of the Aotea. The same source claims the cargo of the waka was taro, rather than kumara, and that Ruaauru was the captain. In a passage recorded in the *Journal of the Polynesian Society*, volume 27, the name of the protecting karakia during the voyage was called Haere.

Landfall in Aotearoa

In one version, several waka including the Mataatua, Tainui and Te Arawa made first landfall at Ahuahu (Great Mercury Island). The Mataatua was guided to the island by two birds named Mumuhau and Takere-Tou (the birds were tieke, or saddlebacks, land birds). While at Ahuahu, Te Moungaroa is said to have had words with several of the chiefs of the other waka, claiming that the Kurahaupo had been bewitched by some or all of them. From Ahuahu the waka are said to have explored Aotearoa independently.

Another version, recorded by R.W. Halbert, suggests that the Mataatua first landed at Muriwhenua, then travelled south to Aotea (Great Barrier Island), Repanga (Cuvier Island) and Ahuahu. From Ahuahu the waka continued south, sailing through Cook Strait, before journeying up to Whangape and Herekino in the far north, where Mirupokai settled. After Mirupokai left the waka, the Mataatua returned to Taranaki under the command of Ruauru, where Te Moungaroa rejoined the crew. It was then sailed to Pokotakina on the East Coast.

An account furnished by Te Kahui Kararehe states that the Mataatua arrived at the East Coast, but that the land was fully occupied. The waka was then sailed to the Taranaki region, where Te Moungaroa and Turu settled. Akuramatapu and Tukapua subsequently returned to the East Coast.

Yet another claim, recorded by Judge Wilson, states that the 'true story is that Mataatua, after the meeting at Ahuahu, went north like Tainui and Arawa, but unlike them, she did not turn back south. She landed at Takou at the bottom of the first bay immediately north of the Bay of Islands. Here her immigrants settled and spread'. Later, according to Wilson, Nga Puhi forced the Mataatua people to abandon their land and travel to Whakatane under Muriwai.

While on another voyage that the Mataatua undertook within Aotearoa, it is recorded by Colonel T.W. Porter that the waka sailed through Raukawa (Cook Strait) and landed at Motutaputeranga, at Island Bay, Wellington. The Mataatua apparently stayed at Motutaputeranga for some time taking on provisions.

JPS, Vol. 7, p. 32.
JPS, Vol. 27, p. 143.
Maori Lore, p. 295.
The Maori-Polynesian Comparative Dictionary, p. 21.
Treasury of Maori Exploration, pp. 228, 229, 231, 232, 234.
Tuwharetoa, pp. 92–8.
Whakatane and District Historical Society Inc. Memoir #7, pp. 1, 4, 7, 9–12, 16, 17, 19–23, 25, 26, 30–5, 37, 38.

MATAHOURUA

Name variations: Kowhao-mata-rua, Mataharua, Matahoru, Matahorua, Matahoura, Mataorua, Matawhaoru, Matawhaorua

The tradition of Kupe and his voyage to Aotearoa has been extensively studied over the years, from which it has been concluded that there may have been as many as three men named Kupe, who at one time or another voyaged to Aotearoa. (For those wishing to pursue the debate further, Simmons has written a comprehensive chapter on Kupe in *The Great New Zealand Myth*, and other points of view are expressed in *Treasury of Maori Exploration*). The following versions of Kupe's story both feature Matahourua as his waka.

The Matahourua is famous in Maori tradition for being the first waka to voyage to Aotearoa (although there are other less well-known waka that challenge it for the right). Kupe was the commander of the Matahourua, and Reti (Rete) was his navigator. In an account of the Kupe tradition supplied by Himiona Kaamira and translated by Bruce Biggs, Kupe is said to have been commissioned by Toto to build two waka for his daughters, Rongorongo and Kura-maro-tini. A huge tree with twin trunks was located by the river Awa-nui-a-rangi and, after the appropriate ceremony, was felled. At that point it was decided by Toto to ask two other expert waka builders to assist in the project. Kauika and Turi-ua-nui were asked to build Rongorongo's waka, later named Aotea, while Kupe proceeded to build Matahourua for Kura-maro-tini.

Once the two waka were completed, Toto decided that it was time for his daughters to wed. Rongorongo agreed to marry Turi, while Kura-maro-tini chose a man named Hoturapa for her husband. The waka were to be captained by the women's husbands. It was soon apparent to Kupe, however, that Kura-maro-tini was attracted to him, and he set about forming a plan to eliminate Hoturapa. First he readied Kura-maro-tini's waka for an ocean voyage. Then he arranged a fishing expedition, with Hoturapa to be his only companion. Finally he instructed Kura-maro-tini to meet him on the beach that very night. As soon as Kupe's fishing waka was well out of the sight of land, Kupe lowered the anchor while Hoturapa busied himself preparing to fish. Once the anchor had been lowered, Kupe proceeded to recite a karakia that would ensure that it would be impossible to retrieve.

Later in the day, when it had been decided to return to shore, Kupe complained to Hoturapa that the anchor would not budge. Kupe then asked his companion to dive to the sea floor and free the anchor, which Hoturapa agreed to do. While Hoturapa was on the sea floor trying to free the anchor, the devious Kupe cut the anchor rope, and sailed off, abandoning Hoturapa as drowned. Fortunately for Hoturapa, Rangi-uru-hinga, one of the deities of the ocean, had seen the whole episode and decided to help him back to shore. Hoturapa was, however, too late to stop Kupe and Kura-maro-tini from eloping in the Matahourua.

Those said to have accompanied Kupe and Kura-maro-tini from Kupe's homeland of Hawaiki-rangi, were as follows.

Te Mauru	Wai-ehua	Tama-ki-hikurangi
Ripi-i-roa-iti	Te Rangi-pouri	Tamatea-uri-haere
Rua-rangi	Tupu-te-uru-roa	Pari-i-Taane
Tirairaka	Kahu-nui	Whauri
Te Tuhi-o-te-po	Rangi-riri	Matino
Makaro	Tuputupu-whenua	

Others picked up along the way at 'Nui-o-Whiti, which is a place called Pikopiko-i-Whiti or Nui-o-Wara', included Tutei, Karere,

Pou-poto, Karihi, Turehu and Pohe-te-ngu (Poho-te-ngu).

From *Treasury of Maori Exploration* we can add the following names to the list of crew members suggested as being involved in the voyage: Tutu-mai-ao, Pari-ka-rangaranga, Tunga, Weeta, Po-kohu, and Moko-roa.

During the voyage, the Matahourua was sailed in the path of the sun, until they reached a part of the ocean named Raro-poouriuri. It was here that Kupe noticed that the waka was being chased by Tupua-horo-nuku and Tai-horo-nuku-rangi — the nets of Kahukura. These were the men sent by Kiwa and Kama to pursue Kupe. Despite trying all the tricks that he knew, Kupe was unable to outrun the nets. In a last desperate attempt to avoid being caught he sacrificed two of his crew. Te Tuhi-o-te-po and Rangi-riri were thrown into the sea, and immediately became guiding taniwha for the Matahourua. Kupe was therefore able to evade the nets of Kahukura, by following the course set by the two taniwha.

Soon after the run-in with Kahukura and his nets, the Matahourua reached an island named Wawau-atea-nui. From Wawau-atea-nui, it was a brief three-day voyage to Aotearoa. In a short article discussing the landing place of Kupe, it is claimed that the Matahourua first made landfall at Whangaroa Harbour. The writer then goes on to explain that Whangaroa was one of the major arrival and departure points for voyaging waka. In the clear coastal waters of Whangaroa, a phenomenon called Te-au-kanapanapa was evident. (It has been suggested that Te-au-kanapanapa refers to a natural occurrence known throughout the Pacific by various names, and used as an aid to finding land. A detailed explanation of Te Lapa, an underwater flashing of phosphorescence, is recorded in *We, the Navigators*, pages 208–11).

Kupe's exploration of the newly discovered lands took him to most corners of the islands now known as New Zealand (there is a comprehensive collection of place names associated with this version of Kupe's journey throughout Aotearoa in the *Journal of the Polynesian Society*, volume 16, pages 155–9).

In the better-known version of the discovery of Aotearoa, Kupe in the Matahourua and Ngahue in the Tawirirangi are said to have pursued a giant octopus (wheke), known as Te Wheke-o-Muturangi, over vast distances of the Pacific. The reason for the chase was that the wheke had a habit of stealing bait off Kupe's fishing hooks while Kupe fished the oceans near his homeland. Despite Kupe warning Muturangi that he would be forced to kill his pet octopus if it wasn't restrained, Muturangi took no action to control it. The two crews followed the red glow of the wheke as it swam underwater, but were unable to corner it as it continued on its southern course into unfamiliar waters. It was as the two waka approached the coastal waters of Aotearoa that Kupe's wife, Hine-i-te-aparangi, first saw the clouds that are so often prevalent above Te Ika a Maui. From this first sighting of the land, tradition states the name Ao-tea-roa (Ao — cloud, tea — white, roa — long) was given to Te Ika a Maui.

Once the two waka had made landfall on the northern shores, and the crews had rested, it was agreed by Kupe and Ngahue to split up, with Ngahue following the wheke down the east coast, and Kupe sailing along the west coast. It was Ngahue that first caught up with the wheke, and he managed to corner it at Rangi-whakaoma (Castlepoint), in a cave known as Te Ana-o-te-wheke-o-Muturangi. Soon after, Kupe also arrived at Rangi-whakaoma, and immediately broke in to the cave. Fortune was on the wheke's side, however, and it escaped in the night, fleeing south towards Te Kawakawa (Cape Palliser). The two waka are said to have landed in Whanganui-a-Tara (Wellington harbour), where the crews rested, and many places were named after Kupe, or deeds carried out by his companions.

Among the places and landmarks associated with Kupe and the Matahourua expedition are the following.

> Matakitaki — a large rock on the east side of Palliser Bay, where Kupe stood looking at Te Wai Pounamu
> Nga-ra-o-Kupe — two triangular, light-coloured patches surrounded by green vegetation to the west of Cape Palliser
> Nga-waka-a-Kupe — a range of hills near Greytown; also a group of rocks in Admiralty Bay
> Te Kakau-o-te-toki-a-Kupe — a rock on Te-uira-ka-rapa point in Tory channel, opposite Moioio Island
> Taonui-o-Kupe — a spot at Jacksons Head, Queen Charlotte Sound
> Te Kupenga-a-Kupe — also in the vicinity of Jacksons Head
> Nga-tauari-a-Matahourua — a spot over six kilometres south-east of the mouth of the Wairau River, on the bluff called Pari-nui-a-whiti, and now known as White Bluff
> Te Ure-o-Kupe — one of the pointed rocks on Barretts Reef, at the entrance of Wellington harbour
> Te Tangihanga-a-Kupe — Barretts Reef

Te-ra-o-Matahourua — a place near Ohariu, on the coast west of Wellington; the sails are sometimes said to have been at Hataitai Beach or Lyall Bay

Te Punga-o-Matahourua — a spot near Paremata where the discarded anchor of the Matahourua was left

Toka-haere — a rock near Sinclairs Head

Mo-huia — also a rock in the vicinity of Sinclairs Head

Matiu — Somes Island

Makaro — Ward Island

Rangiora Point, Hokianga — where one of the waka's anchors is said to rest

Te Tou-o-Puraho — one of the Matahourua's bailers was turned to stone here

Te Kohukohu — another of the bailers is near this Hokianga landmark

Whirinaki river mouth — a rock there is said to be in the shape of one of Kupe's dogs

Te Whakarara-a-Kupe — at Tara-roto-rua, the site of a feast arranged by Kupe, between Kerikeri and Whangaroa

Wharo (Waro) — north of Hokianga on the coast; Kupe's footprints are said to be indented in rock

(For a full explanation of the naming of those places listed above, see the *Journal of the Polynesian Society*, volume 22, pages 124–7.)

Other places named in a similar manner to the preceding list are:

Te Kawakawa — Cape Palliser, where one of Kupe's daughters made a wreath of Kawakawa leaves

Te Rimurapa — where bull kelp was collected and made into bags for preserving food

Next the Matahourua was sailed to Porirua Harbour, where its anchor, Tatara-a-punga, was swapped for a stone found on the eastern shore. The new anchor was a kowhatu-hukatai (white stone), and was named either Hukatai or Hukamoa. From Porirua Kupe sailed his waka to Mana Island, where he left his wife and daughters (Matiu, Makaro, Mohuia, Hine-te-uru and one other). He then sailed south to the South Island and joined up with Ngahue.

By now the wheke had become aggressive, and was charging the waka. As the wheke approached, the captains widened the gap between the vessels and let it pass between the two of them, whereupon Tohirangi, from the Matahourua, and Ngahue, captain of the Tawirirangi, both threw spears at it. The wheke then grabbed hold of both waka with its huge tentacles. Kupe immediately began to hack at the tentacles with his adze, Ranga-tu-whenua. Despite losing several tentacles, the wheke would not let go. Kupe then ordered Po-heuea to cast some calabashes at the monster, which was distracted into attacking them. Kupe then took his chance, and with one fierce blow of his adze, killed the wheke.

After the battle, a karakia was said and the waka departed. The Matahourua and Tawirirangi were then sailed down the west coast of the South Island, to Arahura, where pounamu was found. From Arahura, the two waka travelled further south and rounded the bottom of the South Island. After exploring the east coast, the waka voyaged back across Cook Strait. Kupe returned to Mana Island and picked up his family, and the waka continued on up the west coast. Landfall was made at Whanganui, where Kupe and his people stayed for a while. There they named the area Kaihau-o-Kupe, because of the strong winds that battered the land. Further north at Patea, Kupe stopped to smell the soil, and judged it to be very good for growing crops. From Taranaki, the expedition continued up the coast, before Kupe and his people settled at Hoki-anga-nui (now known as Hokianga).

It was not long before Kupe's desire to return to his homeland was too strong to suppress, and he decided he wanted to see out his days among the familiar landmarks of Hawaiki. Before his journey home, Kupe is said to have cast a hirihiri (a type of spell) over his son, Tuputupu-whenua, and sacrificed him in the spring Te Puna-i-te-ao-marama. It is supposed that this sacrifice was to appease the gods and ensure a safe voyage. After Kupe returned to Hawaiki, he was asked if he would ever return to Aotearoa. His reply 'E hoki Kupe?' has since become famous, and is still used to politely say no.

ADDITIONAL INFORMATION

In most traditions, it is claimed that none of the crew from either waka remained in Aotearoa, although there are some contradicting claims. Tribes such as Mua-upoko, and Nga Puhi hapu Mahurehure, are said to claim that they have ancestors among the crew. In a version of the Kupe tradition collected by the Reverend Richard Taylor from Whanganui, it is claimed that Kura-maro-tini was originally Kupe's wife, and that Kupe was forced to chase his brother Hoturapa to reclaim his abducted wife.

It is usually said that Kupe saw no evidence of inhabitants during the entire circumnavigation of Aotearoa. There are, however, one or two claims to the contrary. In *The Story of Aotea*, it is said that Kupe visited Taikehu and his people at Patea, while other sources claim that the Tiwaiwaka and Kokako seen by Kupe during his voyage were actually men, rather than birds. It is also remembered that the waka Matahourua was later re-adzed and renamed Nga Toki-mata-wha-o-rua, for a subsequent voyage to Aotearoa, with Kupe's grandson Nukutawhiti the commander of the vessel.

Another story related to the legend of Kupe is that of his slave Po-whe-tu-ngu. In some traditions, Po-whe-tu-ngu was instructed to remain in Aotearoa when Kupe returned to Hawaiki. (*See* Rewa-atu.)

The Ancient History of the Maori, Vol. 2, p. 179.
Forest Lore of the Maori, p. 358.
JPS, Vol. 22, pp. 122–30.
JPS, Vol. 66, pp. 232–5.
Maori and English Dictionary, p. 70.
Maori Art, p. 33.
Maori Religion, Vol. 2, p. 204.
The Peopling of the North, p. 15.
Tai Tokerau, p. 108.
Te Ika a Maui, p. 291.
Thames and the Coromandel Peninsula 2000 Years, p. 15.
Treasury of Maori Exploration, pp. 22, 39.
We the Navigators, pp. 208–11.

MATA-O-TE-TOA

The Mata-o-te-toa was one of thirteen waka in Te Heke-o-Naia (the migration of Naia) from Hawaiki to Iva, then on to Tahiti and from there to Rarotonga. Five waka stayed to colonise Rarotonga: Arorangi, Rangiatea, Ngaia, Tumuwhenua and Te Mata-o-te-toa. The remaining eight, comprising Tainui, Te Arawa, Tokomaru, Mataatua, Kurahaupo, Takitimu, Okutura and Muri-whenua, sailed on to Aotearoa. The recollection of the last two lesser-known waka in this legend would suggest that they too successfully reached their destination, and for one reason or another have dropped out of popular recognition. (It is doubtful whether the above-named waka that continued south actually sailed together, it being generally accepted that the majority of them voyaged to Aotearoa independently).

JPS, Vol. 11, p. 252.

MATA-RANGI

Chatham Islands

The Mata-rangi is remembered through its karakia, which was taken by the Rauru people when they migrated to the Chatham Islands. The waka itself was left behind when the people voyaged on the Rangihoua and Rangimata. (There is an obvious similarity between the last-named waka and the Mata-rangi, but the text the information was taken from quite clearly states that they are different waka.)

JPS, Vol. 5, p. 18.

MATITI

It is recorded that the ancestors of the Waitaha tribe of the South Island journeyed to Aotearoa in the waka Matiti.

Te Arawa, p. 492.

MOANA-WAIWAI

Name variations: Moana-waewae, Ronawaiwai, Roua-waewae

Owned by Karangahape of Te Tini-o-Toi, the Moana-waiwai was the waka in which Tama-ahua returned to Hawaiki after having been insulted by his wives Tauranga and Kau-whanga-roa. In one account, Tama-ahua lived at Oakura in a house named Whakamoe-ariki. Unaccustomed to the practice of circumcision in their Ngati Ruatamore and Ngati Maruiwi tribes, his wives laughed when the waist cloth Tauhere being worn by Tama-ahua fell to the ground in daylight. Enraged by their reaction, Tama-ahua departed with the following message: 'when you see the glow of redness from the sun from sunrise to sunset, you will know I have reached my destination'. As he commenced his voyage, Tama-ahua called upon a pod of whales to guide him to Hawaiki, and when he arrived at his destination, he caused an apparition to appear on the Pouakai Ranges, thus signalling to his wives his safe arrival. (*See also* Otauira.)

JPS, Vol. 24, p. 54.
JPS, Vol. 29, p. 216.
JPS, Vol. 34, pp. 293–4.

MOE-KAKARA

Name variations: Moetekakara, Riuhakara, Riukakara, Tuwhenua (*see* second entry under Tuwhenua.)

The Moe-kakara made land just north of Cape Rodney at a small bay named Te-waka-tu-whenua. The unfortunate crew are said to have been afflicted with leprosy, and the majority of them died from the disease. A few did manage to survive and they became ancestors of Ngai Tahuhu, Te Kawerau, Te Waiohua and Ngati Rongo tribes.

In one account, the crew of the Mahuhu came across the survivors of the Moe-kakara on the coast near the Waitakere ranges, and they stayed clear of them because of the leprosy. It is also remembered that many of the dead were buried at the mouth of the Waitakere River, a spot not visited by anyone aware of the associations. The Riukakara is usually given as an alternative name for the Moe-karara, but its tradititional landing spot is named as Whangaroa, in Northland.

The Great New Zealand Myth, p. 232.
The Peopling of the North, pp. 12–13.
Treasury of Maori Exploration, p. 253.

MOTUMOTUAHI

Name variation: Motumotu

Puatautahi is credited with being the captain of the Motumotuahi, and the ancestors of the Nga Rauru and Ngati Ruanui tribes are said to have made up the crew.

Maori Lore, p. 296.

MUA-KI-A, TE

Name variations: Ru-nakia, Runga-ki-a, Ru-ngakia

This waka belonged to Rukutia, wife of Tama-nui-a-raki. No other information has been recorded. (*See also* Whaka-teretere-te-uru-rangi.)

Ancient History of the Maori, Vol. 2, p. 37.
Maori Art, p. 34.

MURI-WHENUA

Name variation: Muri-enua

According to Rarotongan tradition, the Muri-whenua was part of the great migration fleet known as Te Heke-o-Naia. The voyage took them from Hawaiki to Iva, from there on to Tahiti, and then on to Rarotonga.

At Rarotonga five waka are said to have stayed, the crews preferring to colonise that lush island rather than hazard the voyage on to Aotearoa. Among the waka which sailed on with Muri-whenua were the Tainui, Te Arawa, Tokomaru, Mataatua, Kurahaupo, Takitimu and Okutura. The Muri-whenua and Okotura were both described as fighting vessels.

(Note: It is extremely doubtful whether the waka named in this legend actually ever sailed together, or in fact were even active during the same century.)

Hawaiki, p. 265.
JPS, Vol. 11, p. 252.

NGAENGAEMOKO

Name variation: Naenaemoko

Nothing but the name is remembered, although the Ngaengaemoko was thought to be an ancestral waka belonging to one of the northern tribes.

Maori Art, p. 34.
The Great New Zealand Myth, p. 217.

NGAIA

Name variation: Ngaio

This waka was also part of the Heke-o-Naia (*see* Te Mata-o-te-toa), but stayed on at Rarotonga when the majority of the fleet sailed on to Aotearoa.

Hawaiki, p. 265.
JPS, Vol. 11, p. 252.

NGA PUA-ARIKI

Nga Pua-ariki is primarily remembered as a Cook Island ancestral waka, and Ru is attributed with having been its captain when it sailed from Hawaiki to Aitutaki. The kiato (cross-beams for connecting the outriggers to the waka hull) were named, from front to back, Tane-mai-tai, Te-pou-o-Tangaroa and Rima-auru. There is one unsubstantiated tradition that has Ru and his brothers voyaging to Aotearoa with Kupe in Nga Pua-ariki, and naming Araura (Arahura?) after the Araura in Aitutaki.

JPS, Vol. 64, p. 194.
Legends of the Maori, Vol. 2, p. 79.

NGA TOKI-MATA-WHA-O-RUA

This waka has its main descent lines to Nga Puhi and Te Rarawa of Northland. The captain of the waka was Nukutawhiti, grandson of Kupe, and it was in fact from Kupe's waka, Matawhaorua, that the Nga Toki-mata-wha-o-rua was remodelled. In *Tai Tokerau* it is recorded that Kupe and his good friend Tokaakuaku, grandfather of Ruanui, used their famous adzes Ngapakitua and Tauira-ata respectively to complete the re-adzing work of Matawhaorua. Work was commenced on the fourteenth day of the moon in accordance with the custom pertaining to this work, and as each part of the work was completed a karakia was chanted over it. Finally the entire waka was finished and a ceremony held to bless the 'new' waka and to transfer the mana of the waka from Kupe to Nukutawhiti. The popular tradition states that it was from this second adzing of the Matawhaorua that the prefix Nga Toki (the adzes) was added to the original name.

It was agreed that the Mamari, captained by Ruanui, would accompany Nga Toki-mata-wha-o-rua on its voyage to Aotearoa, and each waka was accorded several taniwha to look after it. For Nukutawiti's waka, Puhi-moana-ariki, Rangi-uru-hinga, Te Hiko-o-te-rangi and Mahere-tu-ki-te-rangi were assigned, and for Mamari, Te Arai-te-uru and Niua.

As the time for departure neared, Kupe gave his grandson final instructions for how to reach Hokianga, where he had sacrificed his son Tuputupu-whenua in a freshwater spring called Te Puna-i-te-ao-marama when he returned to Hawaiki.

Soon after Nga Toki-mata-wha-o-rua and Mamari had taken to the sea, Nuku-tawhiti commenced a sacred karakia to summon Ngaru-nui, the great wave, to support the two waka and speed them on their way. With the taniwha at the side of their vessels, the expedition sped on and on across Te Moana Nui o Kiwa for three days and nights towards Aotearoa. On the fourth day, with the strength of Nuku-tawhiti's karakia weakening, the taniwha Puhi-moana-ariki called to him that it and all of the other taniwha had been caught in the nets of Kahu-kura, and that the karakia would have to be strengthened to break through. To assist him, Nuku-tawhiti called upon the assistance of the Papatara, a tohunga with much mana, to chant his most powerful incantation. The combined power of Nuku-tawhiti and Papatara was soon able to destroy the net, opening the way for the two waka and their taniwha to continue their voyage.

Before long, land-based seabirds and the distant outline of land were seen, telling the travellers they would soon reach their destination, the shores of the Hokianga Harbour. As the two waka approached the harbour mouth, Nuku-tawhiti recited another karakia to make safe the entrance and land fall.

> Swim on the sea, swim on the sea,
> swim now, O Tane.
> Split the foamy waves of Mare-rei-ao
> Ascend the sacred current of Taotao-rangi.
> The foam of Tangaroa is standing in crests
> Is descending on the sacred plumes of my waka.
> I look down on the inner and outer rows of surf,
> The handle of the paddle is lifted to the sky.
> The head of my waka is pulled foward
> On the skin of mother earth lying there
> With the sacred head of Tane standing above.
> The paddle of Poupoto breaks in two
> And the paddle of Kura is taken.

After safely paddling the two waka into the harbour, Nuku-tawhiti himself went ashore and took eight rimu shoots. He gave one each to the four taniwha that had assisted Nga Toki-mata-wha-o-rua and asked that they take them back to Kupe to let him know of their safe arrival in Aotearoa. To the two strongest taniwha that had accompanied Mamari, Te Arai-te-uru and Niua, he also gave a shoot each, but their task was to stay at Hokianga as a token of remembrance for himself. The last two rimu shoots were planted on shore as a whakapuna-a-waru, to preserve his mana as chief.

Before long the newcomers were able to make contact with those who had stayed behind when Kupe returned to Hawaiki and a great feast was held. There was at least one reunion of crew members from the original voyage of the Matawhaorua when Tirairaka, who had remained in Aotearoa, and Poupoto, who returned as an elder on Nga Toki-mata-wha-o-rua, were reunited after many years' separation. After the newcomers had made a home for themselves in their new land, Nga Toki-mata-wha-o-rua was dragged to a cave by the crew, where it remains to this day, in a fossilised form.

In an interesting variation on how the waka was given its name, one legend says that Kupe was out searching for a suitable tree from which to build a new waka. He selected a tree high on a cliff, and cut a scarf in it to mark his intention to use it. Later Kupe apparently found a more appropriate tree and abandoned the first. Some time after this, Nuku-tawhiti came across the tree, still standing high on the cliff, and proceeded to complete the job of felling it. From the use of the two sets of adzes is said to originate the name Nga Toki-mata-wha-o-rua. It is also interesting to note that Nuku-tawhiti is sometimes claimed as the captain of Mamari, the passage of time obviously confusing the two histories.

Tai Tokerau, pp. 51–5.
Tainui Sexcentenial Waka Celebration, p. 6.

NUKUTAIMARORO

The Nukutaimaroro is mentioned briefly in the following chant, and no further information has been found about it. Its place in Maori history is not clear, although the reference to the waka beating down waves may suggest that it was an early explorer of 'uncharted waters'.

> I have mounted upon the great
> Foaming girdle of Tanga-roa,
> The waves beaten down by the waka Nukutaimaroro.
> O Nukutaimaroro, I am as Hine-tu-a-hoanga,
> Searching for the descendants of Rata,
> Slain at the river Pikopiko-i-whiti.

Treasury of Maori Exploration, p. 100.

NUKUTAWHITI

This is possibly the waka in which Tuputupu-whenua and Kui voyaged to Aotearoa during the earliest period of discovery and migration. These two figures are often associated with Maui, and are sometimes named as the guardians Maui left behind to look after Aotearoa when he returned to Hawaiki. Both Nuku-tawhiti and Tuputupu-whenua feature in the legend of Nga Toki-mata-wha-o-rua, Nuku-tawhiti as the grandson of Kupe and captain of the waka, and Tuputupu-whenua as Kupe's son who was left behind at the spring Puna-i-te-marama when Kupe returned to his homeland in the Matawhaorua. It is possible that the tradition as recorded above has been confused over time.

Treasury of Maori Folklore, p. 138.
Tai Tokerau, pp. 51–5.

NUKUTERE

Sources conflict over who the captain of Nukutere was, with several candidates being put foward. Tauturangi is named by members of Te Whakatohea (although sometimes his son Ngatorohaka is substituted), while in some parts Whironui is claimed to have been captain. The following quote from a Ngati Porou legend backs up the call for Whironui to be recognised as captain, and at the same time gives an interesting insight.

> *Nukutere was the waka in which Porou-rangi came to these islands from Hawaiki — that is, Whironui and his wife Arai-ara came in the waka Nukutere, and Porourangi is descended from Whironui and Arai-ara; therefore Porourangi also came in her, though at the time he was not born.*
>
> *There were many learned men who came in that waka. The names of two of them are these: Takataka-pu-tonga and Marere-o-tonga, with a number of other people.*

A Ngati Awa tradition recorded in *Ancient Polynesian Migrants* by Best states:

> *Nukutere made land at Waiaua, and that among the crew were seven persons bearing the name Tamatea. Also that one Roau came by that waka, and brought hither the Karaka, Ti, taro, the*

> two latter being known as Te Huri a Roau. The name of the Ti was Whakaruru-matangi; it was planted at Pokerekere. The Karaka was cultivated at Wai-o-weka.
>
> Tamatea-nukuroa appears to have been the chief man of Nukutere. His children were Roau, Rangiwaka, and Nga Tai-e-rua. One Tunamu is also said to have come in Nukutere from Hawaiki, but a genealogy given of him by Manihera Maiki does not support the statement.

To add to the above list of candidates we have Tao-tu-rangi, who is named as captain of the Nukutere in a tradition collected by Gudgeon.

> Tao-tu-rangi is alleged to have been the chief of Nukutere, and from him and his wife, Rangi-haka, are descended the ancient tribe once known as Te Wakanui and afterwards called Te Pane-nehu, who are now represented by the Whakatohea of Opotiki.
>
> Rawiri Tuahine, the most learned man of the tribe in question, is of the opinion that the following persons came in Nukutere: Nga-toro-haka, Nga-tora-rere, Nga-toro-puehu, Nga-toro-mango, Nga-toro-taita, Te Piki-o-te-rangi, Te Tao, and Te Matata, and he makes Tao-tu-rangi a son of Nga-toro-haka.

The Nukutere made landfall in the eastern Bay of Plenty at Opape, the then mouth of the Waiaua River. In one version of the landing, the exact spot has been named as Te Ko Tukutuku, while another claims that 'Along the Opape rocks to Awaawakino was the landing place of Nukutere, the exact entrance being known as Te Rangi, so named after Tauaterangi, wife of Tauturangi, captain of Nukutere; on the Awaawakino beach and well sheltered from all winds'.

Another source suggests that the Nukutere arrived some eight months before the flood known as Te Tai-a-Ruatapu hit Aotearoa, while another states that the crew brought with it the god Tama-i-waho who 'took possession of the sacred place then known as Te Kapurangi'.

The Ancient History of the Maori, Vol. 3, p. 41.
JPS, Vol. 12, p. 120.
Maori Lore, p. 298.
Transactions of the New Zealand Institute, Vol. 37, p. 126.
Whakatane and District Historical Society Inc. Memoir # 8, pp. 1–3.

OKAHU
Chatham Islands

This waka is one of five in which the tribes of Rongomaitere and Rongomaiwhenua voyaged to Chatham Island from the villages of Tahurimanuka and Wharepapa in Hawaiki. The captain of Okahu is remembered as Kahu.

Transactions of the New Zealand Institute, Vol. 22, p. 76.

OKOKI

The Okoki, the Kahukura and the Tai-korea are said to have landed at Ngamotu, Taranaki, after voyaging directly from Horanui-a-tau and Haupapa-nui-a-tau (two unknown places, presumably situated in the midst of the Polynesian Islands), soon after the discovery of Aotearoa. Tai-ta-waro is credited with being the captain of Okoki, whose crew members gradually spread throughout Taranaki.

The Maori, p. 42.
Treasury of Maori Exploration, p. 48.

OKOTURA
Name variation: Okoturu

The Okotura, along with the Muri-whenua and eleven other waka, is credited with being part of the Heke-o-Naia that travelled through the Pacific on its way to Aotearoa. Despite being named alongside Tainui, Te Arawa and other well-known waka in Rarotongan traditions, nothing is remembered of the waka's arrival in Aotearoa. There is a suggestion that both the Muri-whenua and Okotura were fighting vessels rather than migration waka.

Hawaiki, p. 265.
JPS, Vol. 11, p. 252.
Whakatane and Districts Historical Society Inc. Memoir #7, p. 19.

OROPUKE
Chatham Islands

This waka, captained by Moe (in one account Mohi), grandson of either Pohokura or Horopapa of the Rauru tribe, voyaged to the

Chatham Islands at some time within one generation of the main migration in the Rangimata and Rangihoua waka. This is known because Moe was a boy when the two waka left Hawaiki, the crews fleeing a vicious and bloody war. The only detailed account of the arrival of Oropuke at the Chatham Islands says that the waka was 'Wrecked at the cliffs of Chatham Island, in Pitt's Strait, so giving the name to all that part of the cliffs and up to trig station L, about a mile inland. The crew landed safely'. It is suggested that there were 80 crew on Oropuke, the same number as for Rangimata, and that Moe, a fearless warrior, introduced cannibalism to the Chatham Islands.

JPS, Vol. 5, pp. 28–30.
Transactions of the New Zealand Institute, Vol. 9, p. 18.

OTAUIRA

The story of Otauira and its two contemporary waka, Potaka and Te Whatupu-rangi, is mirrored in the tradition of Moanawaiwai. Tama-ahua, of the Kurahaupo, organised the construction of the three waka while he was in Taranaki for a return voyage to Hawaiki. Tama-ahua himself captained the Otauira and first journeyed south to Arahura to collect pounamu before commencing the long passage home. On his arrival in Hawaiki, Tama-ahua caused a Kura-hau-awa-tea (red glow of the rising sun) to signal to those who stayed behind in Aotearoa the safe arrival of the three waka. (*See also* Moana-wai-wai.)

How the Maoris Came to Aotearoa, p. 36.
Treasury of Maori Exploration, pp. 63–4.

OTUREREAO

Name variations: Otu-rere-roa, Turereao

The most authoritative account of this waka has been recorded from Rakuraku of Te Waimana, who was a descendant of the captain of Oturereao, Tairongo, and was an important chief at the time of his death. He stated that the Oturereao made land at Ohiwa in the Bay of Plenty and brought with it the aute (paper mulberry) to Aotearoa. Rakuraku also asserted that the Tairongo tribe of the Ohiwa area derived their name from the captain of the Oturereao.

From a second source comes the claim that Tai-kehu was the captain of the Oturereao, and that Tairongo and the Hapu-oneone people were established at Ohiwa when the waka arrived. (Note: Tai-kehu has been tied into the traditions of several waka, and his exact place in the order of things is confused to say the least.)

JPS, Vol. 12, pp. 130, 166.
Transactions of the New Zealand Institute, Vol. 37, pp. 125–6.

OUMATINI

From traditions collected in the Cook Islands comes the following.

The learned men of Mangaia, one of the Cook Island Group, believe that Toi went from that place to Aotearoa, but they are quite certain that he returned from the latter place in the Oumatini waka, and en route landed at Nuku-te-Varovaro (Rarotonga). That on his return to Ahuahu (Mangaia) Toi was known as Pau-te-anua, and his marae as Taumatini.

JPS, Vol. 12, p. 172.

PAEPAE-KI-RAROTONGA

The Paepae-ki-Rarotonga appears in two distinct legends passed down by Maori orators. One legend claims that Toi-te-tuatahi voyaged the seas searching for his grandson Whatonga and his companion Tu-rahui (who is sometimes said to have been a grandson of Toi as well), the pair having been swept before a storm in their waka Te Wao. During the search, Toi-te-tuatahi sailed first to Rarotonga, then on to Samoa and from there south to the Chatham Islands. From the Chathams Toi journeyed to the Tamaki Isthmus, where news of his grandson still eluded him. It was here at Tamaki that Toi's niece, Pare-ira, married a man of the tangata whenua and settled in the Henderson Valley, where her name was given to a stream now known as the Wai-pare-ira stream. The Paepae-ki-Rarotonga was next sailed to Aotea (Great Barrier Island) and then to Tuhua before stopping at Whakatane, where the crew built a pa named Kapu-te-rangi and settled. It was while Toi-te-tuatahi was living at Kapu-te-rangi that Whatonga was reunited with him after an epic voyage of his own.

In the other tradition, Waitaha-ariki-kore is named as the captain of Paepae-ki-Rarotonga, and it is stated that the waka made land at Tara-o-Muturangi near Matata, some time before the arrival of the Mataatua.

It is interesting to note that there is also a Rarotongan legend featuring a waka named Paepae-o-Rarotonga.

Treasury of Maori Exploration, pp. 64–5.
Tuhoe: Children of the Mist, pp. 686–7.

PAHIKO

Very little is remembered about the Pahiko, other than that it returned to Hawaiki from the East Coast.

Treasury of Maori Exploration, p. 266.

PAHI-TONOA

The Pahi-tonoa, captained by Rauru, was chosen to accompany the Hakirere on a voyage to Te Wairuangangana to collect taro, a food not grown in Hawaiki at that time. During the outward voyage disaster struck the Pahi-tonoa and it was wrecked. Fortunately for Rauru and his crew, they were rescued by the Hakirere and despite the disaster the expedition continued and the taro was procured. In a second reference that seems to at least in part support the above statement, Hetaraka Tautahi claims the Pahi-tonoa to be an ancestral waka of the Nga Rauru people.

JPS, Vol. 9, p. 213.
Maori Agriculture, p. 235.

PAKIHI-KURA

The Ngariki people voyaged to Aotearoa in this waka, landing first at Ohiwa Harbour and then sailing along the coast to Opotiki, where the bar at the Opotiki River still carries the shortened name Pakihi. It was at Opotiki that the Ngariki people lived until they were driven out by the tangata whenua. The survivors apparently made their way to the Whanau-a-Apanui tribal lands where they were allowed to settle peacefully.

The Pakihi-Kura is said to have been one of the earlier waka to voyage to Aotearoa, although the above story obviously precludes it from being the first.

Whakatane and Districts Historical Society Inc. Memoir, #8, p. 15.

PANGATORU
Name variations: Papakatoro, Papakatoru, Pongatoru

The captain of this waka was Rakewanangaora (Raka-wananga-a-ru, or Rakei-wananga-ora).

Most accounts of the Pangatoru have the crew either met by hostile tangata whenua and not permitted to land, or staying only for a short while before returning to Hawaiki.

According to an entry in *Te Ika a Maui*, ancestors of the Ngati Ruanui and Nga Rauru came in the Pangatoru, which would seem to support the tradition of the crew landing and staying for a while at least.

JPS, Vol. 16, p. 190.
Maori Art, p. 34.
Maori Lore, p. 296.
Te Ika a Maui, p. 290.

PAPAHUAKINA

The Papahuakina is mentioned in notes following a Ngati Kahungunu waiata recorded in *Nga Moteatea* as having landed at Nukutaurua, Mahia, with the principal person on board named as Whiringatau.

In another tradition, Hau-nui-a-nanaia was forced to stow away on the Papahuakina for the voyage to Aotearoa, after having returned to Hawaiki from Aotearoa for adventure. During his stay in Hawaiki, Hau-nui-a-nanaia learnt that his wife Wai-raka had been abducted in Aotearoa. Despite a passionate plea to his brothers, who were about to voyage to his home in their waka Papahuakina, they refused his request to accompany them. With no alternative available, Hau-nui-a-nanaia stowed away aboard the waka, and it wasn't until well into the voyage that he was discovered. Certain to be killed by his murderous brothers, Hau-nui-a-nanaia jumped out of the waka and was astonishingly conveyed to the Taranaki coast by a shoal of fish. When his brothers finally arrived in their waka,

Hau-nui-a-nanaia sought revenge for the treatment he had received from them and without mercy killed them all.

Nga Moteatea, Vol. 2, p. 39.
Treasury of Maori Exploration, pp. 96–7.

PARIRAU-O-TE-TARA, TE

According to tradition supplied by Te Tahuna Herangi, Raka-taura voyaged to Aotearoa in Te Parirau-o-te-tara. Raka-taura is also often credited with having been the overseer during the construction of the Tainui, and having been one of the Tainui's crew. Some accounts, however, state that Raka-taura was left behind in Rarotonga when the Tainui sailed for Aotearoa, leaving the possibility open that he did in fact voyage to Aotearoa in this waka.

Nga Iwi o Tainui, p. 28.

PAUIRARAIRA

Name variations: Pauiraira, Pauiriraira, Pauiriraiira

This waka, under the command of Raka-taura, is claimed by some to have been the very first to voyage to Aotearoa. According to tradition, it first made land at Tuhua (named as Flat Island, Bay of Plenty), and from there voyaged to Moehau, Te-upoko-ta-marimari, Manukau, Hikurangi, Whangaparaoa, Waikato, Whaingaroa, Kawhia, Marokopa, Awakino, Mokau, Ngamotu, Patea, Whanganui, Whangaehu, Turakina, Rangitikei, Manawatu, Kapiti, Whanganui-a-Tara, Kaikoura (where a man and woman were put ashore) and then back to Tuhua. During the entire journey not one sign of human life was seen by the crew of the Pauiriraira. Convinced he had found an uninhabited island, Raka-taura returned to Hawaiki where he is said to have passed on the sailing directions to the famous Kupe.

Maori Art, p. 34.
The Ancient History of the Maori, Vol. 2, pp. 188–9.
Treasury of Maori Exploration, p. 266.

PIOPIOTAHI

The Piopiotahi was captained by Kahotea, and Tangiwai was one of the crew. It landed at a spot in what is now called Milford Sound.

The area was originally called Piopiotahi, named after the waka, and both the above-mentioned crew members have been remembered in the names of pounamu.

JPS, Vol. 28, p. 49.

POREITUA
Chatham Islands

The Moriori waka Poreitua was a double waka, of similar design to its contemporary Pouariki. The only other information remembered is that the second, smaller hull was named Mano.

JPS, Vol. 5, p. 17.

POTAKA

One of three waka built under the command of Tama-ahua for a return voyage to Hawaiki during his stay at Taranaki, the Potaka, along with the Otauira and Whatupu-rangi, sailed to Arahura to pick up pounamu before commencing the challenging voyage north into the Pacific.

How the Maoris Came to Aotearoa, pp. 36–7.
Treasury of Maori Exploration, p. 64.

POU-ARIKI
Chatham Islands

Details of the voyages of this waka are largely forgotten, although it is remembered that the Pou-ariki sailed in the company of Poreitua about the same time that Rangimata and Rangihoua were voyaging to the Chatham Islands. It has been said the Pou-ariki was a large top-sided double waka, with the the second hull named as Katoko.

JPS, Vol. 5, p. 16.
JPS, Vol. 23, p. 77.

POUTINI

The Poutini was originally the waka of Tama, tohunga of the Tainui. Tama, having been persuaded by Hoturoa to join his crew on board the Tainui, handed command of his waka to a contemporary whose name has long been forgotten. Some time after his arrival in Aotearoa Tama found out that his waka had also successfully made the voyage, and had made land in the Tamaki area. Later during the Tainui's voyages, Tama was able to rejoin the crew of Poutini at Tamaki, where he settled.

How the Maoris Came to Aotearoa, pp. 78, 80.
Treasury of Maori Exploration, p. 167.

PUHI-TANIWHA

Little information other than the name of this waka is remembered. It is, however, suggested in one account that Nga Puhi derive their tribal name from this waka.

Sketches of Ancient Maori Life and History, p. 38.

PUKEATEAWAINUI

Name variations: Pukateawainui, Pukatewainui, Pukeatuawainui, Puketeawainui, Pukanui

Only one waka other than Te Arawa is said to have landed in the vicinity of Maketu, according to the tradition of Te Arawa people, and that was Pukeateawainui. The story behind the voyage of Pukeateawainui, whose commander was Ruaeo, follows.

As the crew of Te Arawa readied to leave Hawaiki on its voyage to Aotearoa, Tama-te-kapua asked Ruaeo to return to their village to retrieve a sacred adze that he had supposedly left behind. While Ruaeo was searching for the non-existent adze, Tama ordered Te Arawa to set sail, carrying all of Ruaeo's possessions and his wife Whaka-oti-rangi. During the voyage, the treacherous Tama took Whaka-oti-rangi as his wife, believing he was beyond the reach of Ruaeo's revenge. Ruaeo however quickly gathered a crew and prepared the voyaging waka Pukeateawainui to chase Te Arawa and to gain the revenge he so desperately wanted.

After an apparently uneventful voyage, the Pukeateawainui made land during the night close to where Te Arawa had been beached. As Tama-te-kapua and his people slept, Ruaeo and his men silently surrounded the sleeping crew and with a slap of a taiaha on the waka hull, woke the startled travellers. Ruaeo immediately challenged

Tama-te-kapua to a fight, which was accepted. After an epic fight, Ruaeo was able to beat down Tama-te-kapua and pin him to the ground. Ruaeo then produced a handful of vermin and proceeded to rub it into Tama's face and hair, thereby gaining his revenge. In a last act of protocol, Ruaeo gave his wife to Tama-te-kapua as payment for the final insult he had forced upon him.

The Coming of the Maori, p. 56.
How the Maoris Came to Aotearoa, pp. 66–7.
JPS, Vol. 12, p. 128.
The Maori Waka, p. 415.
Te Arawa, pp. 18–19.
Treasury of Maori Exploration, p. 266.

PUNGARANGI

Name variation: Whatu-purangi

Tradition usually tells of the Pungarangi and Te Whatu-ranganuku travelling from Hawaiki and landing in the Wairarapa (although in one account the Pungarangi is said to have landed at Aotea). During the voyage the Pungarangi also made land at Rurima. The waka is associated with Maori of the Nelson region.

JPS, Vol. 10, p. 135.
The Story of Te Waharoa, p. 252.
Treasury of Maori Exploration, p. 266.
Whakatane and Districts Historical Society Inc. Memoir 8 #1, p. 15.

PUWHENUA, TE

The history of this waka is confused, with most accounts claiming Puwhenua to have been the original name of the Takitimu. Occasionally, however, it is the Horouta which is said to have been given the name at the conclusion of a waka race held in Hawaiki. Either way, the tree used to build this waka was called Puwhenua, and those asked to build the waka were Rua-wharo, Tai-kehu, Rongo-tawhao, Tupai, Kohu-para and Pawa (or Paoa), all expert waka builders from the tribe of the chief Tamatea-ariki-nui. The adzes used by the craftsmen were Hui-te-rangiora, Te Rakuraku-o-Tawhaki, Kaukau and Wharau-rangi.

After the tree had been felled, it was placed in a ditch, covered and left to season, a precaution taken to avoid splitting when the shaping of the waka proper commenced. As soon as the log was ready to be worked, it was taken from the ditch and the skilled craftsmen adzed the hull. After this long and strenuous process, the adzemen handed over the waka to those responsible for finishing touches. This included fitting the washboards, the tauihu and taurapa (bow and stern pieces) and the many other jobs associated with completing a new waka.

The initial project completed, the tohunga decided to build a second waka to join the Puwhenua for the launching ceremonies. With their combined skill and ability, the second vessel was quickly completed and the two waka launched with the appropriate karakia at the lagoon named Pikopiko-i-whiti. After the launch of the Puwhenua and its companion they are said to have been joined by the likes of Te Arawa, Tainui and Mataatua for trial races in front of the massed inhabitants of Hawaiki, who eagerly watched the contest from the hill Pukehapopo. The Puwhenua easily out-raced all of its competitors and left them well in its wake, to the delight of many of the spectators.

At the finish of this race the Puwhenua was renamed Takitimu by its crew, and the other waka built by the builders of Tamatea was named Horouta, reportedly because when the speed of the Puwhenua was seen by the people on land, someone commented that it was so fast that it looked as if it was speeding past or eating the land (horo — speed or eat, uta — land). The words were overheard and relayed to the crews as they returned to shore. Those onboard the un-named waka liked the name so much that they adopted it for their waka, and thus Horouta was named.

The episode of the speed of the Puwhenua (subsequently named Takitimu) prompting the name of the Horouta, has been one reason suggested for the confusion that exists in the relationship between the respective waka. There are however many other points of comparison that add to the perplexity of the Takitimu and Horouta traditions.

JPS, Vol. 23, pp. 199–202, 205.
Transactions of the New Zealand Institute, Vol. 48, p. 451.
Treasury of Maori Exploration, pp. 190–1.

RAKAUTAPU

All that is remembered of Rakautapu is that it landed at Whakatane.

The Story of Te Waharoa, p. 252.

RANGARANGA

During an interview with Te Neke in 1860, it was claimed that the Rangaranga and the Kapakapa-nui were ancestral waka belonging to Te Ati Awa. Apparently no other information about the two vessels was forthcoming.

JPS, Vol. 16, p. 189.

RANGIAHUA
Chatham Islands

There is virtually no information recorded about this waka, other than a claim that it voyaged directly to the Chatham Islands from Rarotonga.

JPS, Vol. 19, p. 212.

RANGI-AMIO

The Rangi-amio is briefly mentioned in a waiata recorded as part of a transcript relating to the Aotea waka:

Noku te tipuna i whiti ki rawahi
Ko Torokaha, Ko Te Rangi-amio, te waka, a, i.

No other information has been found relating to the waka.

JPS, Vol. 9, p. 231.

RANGIATEA

The Rangiatea is talked of in traditions of the Heke-o-Naia as having been a contemporary of well-known vessels such as Tainui, Te Arawa and Tokomaru. The waka is said to have remained in Rarotonga, where its crew settled, while the majority of the other waka in the Heke-o-Naia voyaged on to Aotearoa. (For a full list of the fleet, *see* Te Mata-o-te-toa.)

JPS, Vol. 11, p. 252.

RANGIHOUA
Chatham Islands
Name variation: Rangihoana

The Rangihoua was captained by Te Rakiroa, and the tohunga is remembered as Te Honeke (in one version Kawanga Koneke), who worshiped the atua Rongomaiwhiti. Having been soundly beaten at war by the Nga Rauru tribe, the Wheteina people (said to have been closely related to their conquerors) fled their homes in Hawaiki, seeking refuge at the Chatham Islands. The two waka they are said to have voyaged in were Rangihoua and Rangimata. The decision to leave Hawaiki was so sudden that they were forced to use the Rangihoua despite the fact that it had not been completely finished, and therefore would not have received the final blessings to ensure its safety at sea.

In one account, the voyage commenced on the night named Orongo-nui in the eighth month (August 27th), while another claims the two waka reached the Chathams on Te Whitu o Rongo (June 7th), in the season of rough seas. Nothing is known of the voyage to the Chatham Islands, but it is evident from the description of the landing that it must have been a long and arduous journey. Tradition tells that the Rangihoua was wrecked at Okahu on the northern coast while the crew tried to beach their waka. The crew were apparently so weak from lack of food and water that they were unable to control the Rangihoua as it neared the beach and many of them, including Te Raki-roa and Te Honeke, drowned. Of the few that survived the ordeal, only Taupo, Tarere-moana and Tunanga are remembered by name.

JPS, Vol. 5, pp. 16–18.
JPS, Vol. 23, p. 78.
Transactions of the New Zealand Institute, Vol. 22, p. 76.

RANGI-KEKERO

Rangi-kekero and Rangi-totohu were two of several waka mentioned in 'The Lament of Te Rangi-mauri', a waiata tangi sung for Tonga-awhikau of the Ara-ukuuku and Okahu tribes. It is suggested in this waiata that the Rangi-kekero belonged to Ngangana. Both of the waka named here are also included in a fleet of ancestral waka listed by Hetaraka Tautahi of the Nga Rauru during a discussion with S. Percy Smith in 1900. (*See also* Takere-o-Toitahi.)

JPS, Vol. 2, p. 112.
JPS, Vol. 9, p. 213.
Nga Moteatea, Vol. 3, p. 435.

RANGIMATA
Chatham Islands
Name variation: Rangi-mata-wai

It is usually stated that the Rangimata was captained by Mihiti of the Wheteina tribe, although in some accounts his son Mawake is named. It was after the Wheteina had lost a decisive battle under the command of Tumoana at the beach named Whanga-patiki, that the survivors are said to have fled to the Chatham Islands in the Rangimata and the Rangihoua.

Those remembered from the voyage of the Rangimata are: Mahiti and his wife Kimi; their three sons Mawete, Tama-te-kahia and Mawake; Mawake's wife Wairaka; and the following crew members: Nunuku, Pehe, Mihi-toro, Tarewa, Tokoraro, Kauitia, Hapa, Kakatai, Maruroa, Kauanga, Tehu-te-ngana and Matarangi.

The exact time of year the two waka voyaged is in question, with one tradition claiming they left on the night Orongo-nui in the eight month (August 27th), and another stating the waka made landfall on Te Whitu o Rongo (June 7th) during the rough weather season. Despite the urgency of the voyage, it is remembered that the brothers Maruroa and Kauanga had

> *travelled to the land of Tahiri, Irea and Momori (prior to the migration), who told them of Rekohu, or the Chathams, and taught them many things. The place they went to was called Hukarangi.*

As the two waka left the shore, the voice of Tumoana's sister Kirika was heard reciting a karakia that refered to Tumoana's maro. It is possible that this karakia was recited to place the two waka under the protection of Tumoana during the voyage.

From other karakia (several are recorded in the *Journal of the*

Polynesian Society, volume 5, pages 19–26), it is evident that the crews must have suffered greatly during the voyage from contrary winds and a lack of food and water. Traditions recall the journey as 'the Kimi (searching) and Waipu (immensity of water, ocean only)'. Finally the Rangimata and the Rangihoua reached the shores of the Chathams. As the Rangihoua attempted to land, disaster overtook it and many of the crew drowned.

Those on the Rangimata were more fortunate, however, and the waka made landfall on the northern coast without mishap. The first spot the waka landed at was called Wairarapa, near Te Ika-rewa at Te Umumoki. Here the crew planted a karaka tree and a creeper named marautara.

From Wairarapa they sailed to the north-east corner of the island to a place called Te Whakuuru. Here Maruroa, Kauanga and others from the crew went ashore and met with the local inhabitants. Following on from this stop, the Rangimata voyaged to Okawa (or in some versions at an unidentified beach to the south), where it was nearly wrecked on rocks. Fortunately the waka was saved due to the skill of the crew.

Finally, the waka made landfall at Te Awapatiki. As the Rangimata was dragged up the beach that formed a low breakwater between the ocean and the Whanga lagoon, it caused a channel to form in the sand. The overflowing waters of the lagoon soon forced their way down the thin channel, and catching the Rangimata in the increasing torrents, virtually destroyed it.

It is possibly after this disaster that Mahiti erected two posts as a sign that he and his people intended to occupy land in the vicinity of Te Awapatiki and Poretu on the eastern coast. An image of their god Heuoro was also erected at each of these sights. The Kau Te Hamata people soon discovered Mahiti's plan, and are said to have pulled the posts up and made it clear that they opposed his intentions. No mention is made of hostilities arising from this exchange and the migrants moved on to Rangitira. The crew are said to have named several spots along the way including; Nukutaurua, Nukutaotao, Mana-aotea and Moreroa.

In an interesting tradition collected by Captain Mair, it is claimed that the ancestors of the Moriori voyaged to the Chathams in five waka: Rangitane, Rangihoua, Rangimata, Ruapuke and Okahu. The fleet set out from the villages of Tahurimanuka and Wharepapa in Hawaiki, and their tribes were known as Rongomaitere and

Rongomaiwhenua. Mararoa was the chief of the Rangimata in this version.

The Coming of the Maori, p. 15.
JPS, Vol. 5, pp. 17–21, 26–7.
JPS, Vol. 23, p. 77.
Transactions of the New Zealand Institute, Vol. 22, p. 76.
Transactions of the New Zealand Institute, Vol. 32, p. 356.
Transactions of the New Zealand Institute, Vol. 37, p. 158.

RANGIMATORU, TE

Name variations: Rangimatoro, Ringamatoro, Ringamatoru

The Rangimatoru landed at Ohiwa, and in most versions was captained by Hape-ki-tu-matangi-o-te-rangi or Hape-ki-tu-manui-o-te-rangi (although in one text Rangiwhakaia is named as captain and the protecting deity of the waka was Tu-kai-te-uru). Other chiefs on board were Tau-ira-a-rangi and Puhi-moenga-ariki, and two of the crew remembered by name were Te Hoka-o-te-rangi and Tikitiki-o-te-rangi. Tribes credited amongst the descendants of the crew are Te Hapu-oneone, Ngai Turanga, Ngariki and Ngati Rangi.

The actual story of the waka itself is interesting, with one tradition recorded from Te Arawa sources suggesting the Rangimatoru was originally known as Kurahaupo, and was renamed after the vessel had been abandoned either before the voyage to Aotearoa or en route at Rangitahua. The waka was later repaired by those who found her, and was successfully sailed on to Aotearoa under the new name Rangimatoru.

How the Maoris Came to Aotearoa, p. 105.
JPS, Vol. 1, p. 217.
JPS, Vol. 3, p. 71.
The Peopling of the North, p. 15.
Transactions of the New Zealand Institute, Vol. 37, p. 124.
Treasury of Maori Exploration, p. 246.
Tuhoe: Children of the Mist, p. 687.

RANGI-PAE-NONO

Rangi-pae-nono is remembered as the waka of Tawhaki. No other details are given.

Maori Art, p. 35.

RANGI-TAKO

The waka Rangi-tako was used by Ihenga, Rongomai and their companions to return to Hawaiki. Ihenga and Rongomai had taken their war party to the house of learning Te-tatau-o-te-po in the underworld to learn from Miru rituals, karakia and any other useful knowledge he could teach them. They had descended to Miru's realm on a flax rope, named Tukutuku-o-te-rangi, made from flax stolen from Tau's garden.

When Tau learnt that his flax had been used without consent he informed Miru, who at once severed the flax rope, leaving his guests trapped in the underworld. After much fighting — which saw the deaths of Ngo and Kewa — Ihenga and Rongomai were able to defeat Miru's men and raze Te-tatau-o-te-po to the ground with Miru inside it.

The victors searched continuously for a way to return to their homes, finally coming across the home of Hahuia and Matatiro-ta in a land of plentiful forests. It was here that Aio-rangi and Ngangana of the survivors built two waka: one named Rangi-tako, built by Aio-rangi, and another whose name is now forgotten, built by Ngangana.

Ihenga and Rongomai successfully returned to their homeland in Rangi-tako, while Ngangana and his waka were lost at sea in the first light.

Rangi-tako is also mentioned as part of a fleet of waka (*see* Takere-o-toitaha) in Hetaraka Tautahi's version of the migration of the Aotea.

JPS, Vol. 7, p. 62.
JPS, Vol. 9, p. 213.
Nga Moteatea, Vol. 3, p. 431.

RANGI-TAKOU

The Rangi-takou is one of six ancestral waka named in a waiata tangi sung by Te Rangi-mauri for Tonga-awhikau of the Ara-ukuuku and Okahu tribes. In the waiata it is said that Tonga-awhikau should let his bones 'rest on Rangi-takou, the waka most expressly consecrated with mighty power'.

JPS, Vol. 5, p. 113.

RANGI-TANE
Chatham Islands

This waka is named as one of five in traditions of the migration that carried the Moriori to the Chatham Islands, as collected by Captain Mair. The fleet set out from the villages of Tahurimanuka and Wharepapa in Hawaiki and the immigrants were of the Rongomaitere and Rongomaiwhenua tribes.

Transactions of the New Zealand Institute, Vol. 22, p. 76.

RANGI-TOTOHU

It was recorded in one text that the Rangi-totohu belonged to Uru, and was described as a waka containing death. In a second reference, it was listed as an ancestral waka belonging to the Nga Rauru tribe. No other details were recorded. (*See also* Takere-o-Toitahi.)

JPS, Vol. 5, p. 112.
JPS, Vol. 9, p. 213.
Nga Moteatea, Vol. 3, p. 435.

RANGI-TU-MAKOHAKOHA, TE
Chatham Islands

Te Rangi-tu-makohakoha is mentioned in the legends of *The Moriori People of the Chatham Islands* along with the Turore as a waka of witchcraft (e waka makutu). No other information was collected.

JPS, Vol. 5, pp. 17–18.

RANGIUAMUTU
Name variations: Rangi-ua-mate, Rangi-mutu, Rangi-na-mutu, Ringauamotu, Ringauamutu, Tairea

Tamatea Rokai (or Kokai) was the captain of the Rangiuamutu, and the crew are claimed as the ancestors of Ngati Ruanui and Ngati Awa tribes of the west coast. The waka landed at Rangatapu, near the Waingongoro River, Taranaki, where the crew are said to have seen ovens, stone flint knives and numerous moa bones.

In a footnote at the end of a report by Haast on moa and moa sites, he states that during an expedition to Rangatapu, 'I also discovered a large quantity of the bones of the Dinornis. The stones were the stone flakes used as knives, which are still there found by the side of the ancient ovens, a proof of their having belonged to a more ancient race than the Polynesian'.

In another account, the Rangiuamutu is said to have had a second name, the Tairea, although it is usually said that this was a different waka. Furthermore, in an alternative and unsubstantiated statement found in *Treasury of Maori Exploration*, it is claimed that Ringauamutu was the name given to the Matahourua after it had been reconstructed. (It is widely accepted that the new name was Nga Toki-mata-wha-o-rua.)

Maori Art, p. 35.
The Morioris of the South Island, p. 39.
Tainui Sexcentennial Waka Celebrations, pp. 2, 5.
Transactions of the New Zealand Institute, Vol. 4, p. 94.
Transactions of the New Zealand Institute, Vol. 7, p. 91.
Treasury of Maori Exploration, p. 266.

RANGIWHAKAOMA

The Rangiwhakaoma is named in a Ngati Hau tradition as having been built by Kupe during a waka building contest with Ngake. Kupe was able to build his waka in the time between dusk and midnight, and easily won the contest. He named his waka after the spot where the two waka were built, Rangiwhakaoma, and Ngake named his waka Kapui-rangi when he finally completed it.

The Ancient History of the Maori, Vol. 3, p. 93.

RARO-TUA-MAHENI

Kia mate ia nei koe, e hika,
Ko Atamira te waka, ko Hotutaihirangi
Ko Tai-o-puapua, ko te Raro-tua-maheni,
Ko Araiteuru, ko Nukutaimemeha;
Ko te waka i hiia ai te whenua nui nei.

You are gone indeed, dear one,
(for your) waka there are Atamira, Hotutaihirangi,

Tai-o-puapua, Te Raro-tua-maheni,
Araiteuru, and Nukutaimemeha;
The waka which fished up this widespread land.

This verse from a Ngati Porou apakura (lament) lists five, perhaps six, ancestral waka (it is claimed that Atamira 'is a figure of speech, the reference is to the place upon which the dead were placed called an atamira, a stage or platform used as a bier'). In the notes following the lament it says that no other information is remembered about Te Raro-tua-maheni other than the name.

Nga Moteatea, Vol. 2, pp. 6–7.

REPEREPE-TAUTINI-A-TINIRAU

The following information was collected by J. Herries Beattie from an old man at Otago Heads. He was very clear in explaining that he did not know the entire story or how it ended but was sure of the following.

Hineteiwaiwa was chasing after the handsome Tinirau. She met several fish during her chase and asked each of them whether or not they had seen Tinirau. Hineteiwaiwa received insulting replies from each of the fish and punished them accordingly: she flattened the kutuhori (sole); she trampled the moeanu (sand fish) into the sand, where it lives to this day; she scratched the humpbacked whale, Paikea, and those corrugations are still visible down its front; and finally Hineteiwaiwa threw her maro (waist cloth) over the nose of the mako-repe (elephant fish) and formed the elongated nose it still carries.

Finally she caught up with Tinirau, but he was able to elude Hineteiwaiwa in his waka Te-repe-repe-tautini-a-Tinirau (now the name of a type of jelly fish).

Traditional Lifeways of the Southern Maori, pp. 561–2.

REWAREWA

Name variation: Utupawa

The waka Rewarewa was used by Kui-wai and Haunga-roa, two sisters of Ngatoroirangi, when they fled their husband Manaia and voyaged to Aotearoa. The only other person remembered from this voyage was Tane-whakaraka. The sisters carried the gods Maru, Iho-o-te-rangi, Rongomai, Itupawa, Hangaroa and in some accounts Kahukura with them during the voyage. Their first landing place in Aotearoa was Tawhiuwhiu on Whakaari (White Island).

Maori Art, p. 35.
Treasury of Maori Exploration, p. 126.
Treasury of Maori Folklore, pp. 191, 194.

REWA-ATU

After the well-known Kupe had finished circumnavigating Aotearoa in his waka Matahourua and was preparing to return to Hawaiki, he ordered one of his slaves, Po-whe-tu-ngu, to remain at Aotea (or Patea) and 'look after his land' as a way to stake a claim to it. Po-whe-tu-ngu was apparently less than enthusiastic with this arrangement because of the hostility of the tangata whenua. (Although, contrary to this, most traditions state the land was uninhabited when Kupe arrived.)

No sooner had Kupe left on his return voyage to Hawaiki, than Po-whe-tu-ngu began to construct his own waka to follow in the wake of the Matahourua. Once Po-whe-tu-ngu's waka had been constructed, and provisioned with food and water, Po and his crew prepared to leave. Unbeknown to Po, however, Kupe had suspected that he might disregard his order and had recited a kawa (ceremonial incantation) to prevent him from leaving the harbour. As Po's waka, the Rewa-atu, passed out of Aotea harbour, the seas unexpectedly grew and fierce winds blew, causing the waka to capsize with total loss of life. The waka was instantly turned into a reef, and it is said it can still be seen at the Wahapu-o-Aotea (the harbour entrance of Aotea). In another version of this story, the Rewa-atu is to be seen as a reef at the mouth of the Patea River in the Taranaki district.

JPS, Vol. 28, p. 112.
Treasury of Maori Exploration, p. 38.

RIMA-RAPA

Name variation: Rimu-rapa

This waka is only named in passing in a legend that talks of Kupe passing on the sailing directions to the people of Hawaiki, soon after he returned from his epic voyage of discovery. The Rima-rapa was one of the first waka to follow in Kupe's wake and journey to Aotearoa.

Maori Art, p. 25.
Te Ika a Maui, p. 291.

RIRINO, TE

The Ririno is another waka that has a history full of conflicting information. The chiefs Po-turu and Po-rua are named as being on the waka, with most accounts stating that Po-turu was the captain. As well as a full crew, several dogs also travelled on the waka. It is generally agreed that Ririno met up with the Aotea at an island thought to have been in the Kermadec chain when it was forced to repair storm damage during its voyage. The name of the island is usually given as either Rangi-tahua or Rangi-tawhi (Sunday Island).

As part of the voyaging customs observed by the crew of Ririno, two of the dogs, named Whaka-papa-tuakura and Tanga-kakariki, were sacrificed to the gods to ensure a safe arrival in Aotearoa. Some say that Po-turu made a mistake during the ceremony and because of this his mind was affected. Whatever the reason, there developed a heated argument between Po-turu and Turi of the Aotea as to the correct sailing directions for the remainder of the voyage. According to legend, Po-turu sailed a westward course from the island, while Turi in the Aotea headed off in an easterly direction.

The final destination of Ririno is also shrouded in mystery and contradiction. Most legends state that it was wrecked on a reef or boulder bank. The exact spot that Ririno made landfall has been variously given as Tapu-tapu-atea reef, Te Au-miti (French Pass), or the boulder bank at Nelson, named either Te Rangaatamatea or Tama-i-ea. The following from *Maori Life in Old Taranaki* backs up this last claim:

> Thou camest on board Te Ririno,
> The waka that caused dissensions in Turi's fleet,
> And Poturu was cast ashore in Raukawa current,
> Landing on the bank at O-Tama-i-ea.

To add to the list of possible destinations we can include the Chatham Islands. One legend from a Moriori source has Ririno land at Rangi-kapua, with the chiefs Tahua-roa and Kapohau remembered from the crew. Although unsupported, the Reverend T.G. Hammond states that 'the Taranaki people have some knowledge that "Te Ririno" did go to the Chathams'.

JPS, Vol. 2, p. 121.
JPS, Vol. 19, p. 212.
JPS, Vol. 23, p. 205.
Maori Life in Old Taranaki, p. 24.
Maori Lore, p. 297.
Polynesian Mythology, p. 134.
Sir Apirana Ngata Memorial Tribute, p. 76.

RU, TE

Little information has been recorded about this waka, other than that it landed at Matata.

Maori Art, p. 35.

RUAKAPANGA

In the legend of the introduction of the kumara to Aotearoa, Pou-ranga-hua is often credited with flying on the back of the giant bird Te Manu-nui-a-rua-kapanga, with two baskets of kumara and some tools to cultivate the earth. Despite instructions to the contrary from Tane-nui-a-rangi (the bird's owner), Pou-ranga-hua delayed the return of the bird to its master by insisting it fly the extra distance from the agreed drop-off point on the coast to his garden at Manawaru, somewhere in the vicinity of Turanganui. It was during the return flight that the ogre Tama-i-waho seized the bird as it flew past its lair on Hikurangi and devoured it.

Following the legend is an explanation suggesting that Pou-ranga-hua actually made the journey to Hawaiki and back in a waka named Ruakapanga.

Treasury of Maori Exploration, pp. 71–3.

RUAKARAMEA

Name variation: Riukaramea

According to traditions recorded in *The Tail of the Fish*, Mirupokai was the chief of the Ruakaramea, although other sources claim that Te

Uri-paraoa and Te Papa-wi shared the captaincy of the waka with him. It made land at Mangonui and a stone now commemorates the feat.

In a second legend, it is recorded that the chiefs Paoa and Po-huri-hanga journeyed in a waka named Riukaramea and landed at Mangonui about the same time that the Mamaru waka arrived at Otengi, just south of Taipa. The Riukaramea had a very large shark protecting it during its voyage, and the Mangonui Harbour is said to have been named after this taniwha (mango — shark, nui — big).

Maori Art, p. 35.
Muriwhenua Fishing Report, p. 261.
Treasury of Maori Exploration, p. 266.

RUAPUKE
Chatham Islands

The Ruapuke is one of several waka recorded by Captain Mair as having transported the Moriori to the Chatham Islands, where they defeated the original inhabitants, the Hiti. The other waka in the migration fleet were the Rangitane, Rangihoua, Rangimata and Okahu. The fleet set out from Tahurimanuka and Wharepapa in Hawaiki, and the immigrants were of the Rongomaitere and Rongomaiwhenua tribes.

Transactions of the New Zealand Institute, Vol. 22, p. 76.

TAHATUNA
Name variation: Tahatura

The captain of this waka was Manaia, borne out in the following abstract from a Ngati Ruanui lament sung for Tonga-awhikau by Te Rangi-mauri.

E iri E papa! i runga o Tahatuna,
Te waka o Manaia

Recline O sir on Tahatuna
The waka of Manaia.

There is considerable confusion over the exact identity of the captain of the Tahatuna, with some sources claiming that the Manaia named above was from the Tokomaru waka, and others claiming

TAHUUPOKO

The Tahuupoko was captained by a man named Kupe, who lived many generations after the better-known Kupe of the waka Matahourua. Little is known, although the Tahuupoko is said to have been left by Kupe at Waikaremoana, where it still lies in the lake in the form of a rock.

Transactions of the New Zealand Institute, Vol. 37, p. 127.
Tuhoe: Children of the Mist, p. 684.

TAIKORIA

Name variation: Taikorea

This waka was commanded by Ruatamore, and voyaged to Aotearoa in the company of the Kahutara and the Okoki, landing at Ngamotu on the Taranaki coast. It is said that the crews of these waka were the first inhabitants of Aotearoa and that their homelands were Horanuiatau and Haupapanuiatau, two large and very hot lands.

The Coming of the Maori, p. 10.
Treasury of Maori Exploration, p. 48.

TAINUI

The following version of the Tainui tradition follows that recorded in *Nga Iwi o Tainui*. It is stated that the reason for the migration was the continuing famine caused by a long-standing war between the chiefs Heta and Uenuku.

After suffering continuously over the years, it was decided by Hoturoa and his fellow tribesmen to build a voyaging waka to escape the endless wars and subsequent food shortages. Hoturoa's wife, Whakaotirangi, approached her father, Memeha-o-te-rangi, to provide a skilled waka builder to oversee the project. Memeha-o-te-rangi agreed to his daughter's request, and called on Raka-taura to assist with the construction. Raka-taura is said to have been an expert waka builder, and to have owned three adzes: Hahau-te-po, an adze for felling trees; Paopao-te-rangi, an adze for splitting timber; and Manu-tawhio-rangi, an adze for shaping waka.

The tree chosen stood at the summit of a mountain called Maunga-roa. It was said to have grown from the spot where the foetus of a deformed child, named Tainui, was buried. (According to some versions, the child was born with a body, arms and a head, but nothing from the waist down.) Before Raka-taura began cutting down the tree, he is said to have visited an old woman by the name of Mahu-rangi (also known as Maruanuku), to ask how he should fashion the waka. Mahu-rangi told him to look at the new moon, and build the waka in its likeness, with a raised stern and bow.

In this version of the legend, it is suggested that after the tree had been cut down by Raka-taura, the birds of the forest re-erected it each night for three consecutive nights, forcing Raka-taura to hide on the third night to try to discover why the tree stood as if untouched each morning. Having witnessed the work of the porihawa and hokioi, Raka-taura returned to Mahu-rangi for advice. She instructed him to fell the tree once more, and then to lay grated kumara on the topped end of the tree (in one version, Raka-taura is told to place Mahu-rangi's menses on the stump). Next, she provided Raka-taura with a karakia to chant over the fallen tree.

The next day, Raka-taura returned to the tree. After felling the giant of the forest, and carefully following Mahu-rangi's instructions over the fallen log, he retired to his whare for the night. The following morning Raka-taura returned to the forest to find the tree as he had left it the previous evening, lying prone and silent. (This part of the tradition is remarkably similar to the legend of Rata and his waka-building exploits.)

Although there were seven workmen who helped Raka-taura build the Tainui, only Kohiti-nui is remembered by name. It is also recorded that Kohiti-nui was a particularly lazy and deceitful man, who was in the habit of placing dust and chips of wood about his person to look as if he had had a particularly industrious day. To top this off, he was also in the habit of taking the choicest food at meal time, whether it was placed in front of him or not. It wasn't long before Raka-taura could no longer contain his anger at Kohiti-nui, and in a fit of rage killed him. Raka-taura then buried the body among the wood chips of the waka.

When finally the waka was finished, the tribesmen were assembled to drag it to the ocean. At first it could not be moved, even though the canoe-hauling karakia was being chanted.

Tikina ki te wao-tapu
Totokia mai ai te whatu
Matakataka tu mai,
Oroia ki te toki!
Aitu, aitu!

E tapu takahu, e tapu takahu.
Koia te whetu, te whetu
Te marama, te marama!
Tangaroa, puta i te whana-putuputu!
Tautika, tau tonu to ara,
E Tane, ki a Papa-te-rangi.
Ka kau tu, ka kau tu,
Ka kau horo, ka kau horo,
Te mate o koutou, e-e.

Ka wheuru, ka riro ki te uru
No Rangi-tu-mai me ana hara.
Takitakina te waka,
Ka tere — hi ha! ka tere te waka.
Ka tere na tai.

Tutaki ake i te heke nui no Tukurangi,
Waiho kia kau ana
Waiho Kiore kia kau ana,
Ka mawhetewhete i te whiwhi,
Ka mataratara i te hara
I te whakarotu o Tane.
I eke ai te whita.

Koukou mai te manu ki raro mea
Ka tatai aromea me he oromea.
Te rukutia ki pou mua o taku manawa
Kaore ra, ko au e tatari atu ana
Kia murimuri awa te here
A nga tangata i te maire tauhua.
Kura nui! Kura nui! Kura nui!
Awheawhe taku kura,
Whakaapa ki Tahatu-o-te-rangi!

Taku tama ka uaia e te ua,
Ka rotua e te matangi.
Tena e Rata, kei uta, kei tai;
Kei te whata o te matuku,
E tau ana i Whanga-marino.
Piki ake au ki runga o Tarawera,
Ka tatai poko;
Ka huaia, ka huaia, ka huaia
Ka reretia, ka reretia!
Whano! Whano! Hare mai te toki!
Haumi e-e, Hui e-e, Taiki e-e!

Next, Hoturoa stood and commenced a karakia, and as he did so, a fly is said to have flown from the place Kohiti-nui was buried, directly to the ocean.

Hiaroa! Hiaroa
Tapotu ana te ngaru ki tatahi.
Ma wai e to?
Ma te whakarongo ake e whakarongo nei
Ki te taha o te rangi
He tarawai nuku, he tarawai rangi.
Puhia te ahi e-e,
Nau mai, e Tane,
Ka kau taua i te wai,
Kia matakitakina taua
E te tini, e te mano.
Miroi, e Tane,
Koakoa, e Tane.

Ka turuturu haere te wai
O te hika o Mahu-rangi.
Patua ana mai
E te komuri hau
Na runga ana mai
O Wai-hihi, o Wai-haha!
Turuki, turuki! Paneke, paneke!

At the conclusion of the karakia, the haulers tried once again to move the waka, and this time they succeeded in dragging the Tainui to the sea.

Soon after the waka reached the sea, the naming ceremony was performed, and the following karakia, which is very similar to the preceding one, was recited.

Toia, Tainui!
Tapotu ki te moana.
Ma wai e to?
Maku e to, ma Whakatau e to.
Whakarongo ake au
Ki te taha o te rangi
He tarawai nuku,
He tarawai rangi;
Puhia te ahi, e-e.
Nau mai, e Tane!
Ka kau taua i te awa
I Pikopiko-i-whiti,
Kia matakitakina koe
E te tini, e te mano.
Naku koe i tiki atu
Ki te Wao-nui-a-Tane;
Miroi, e Tane,
Koakoa, e Tane.

Turuturu haere ana te wai
O te hika o Maru-a-nuku:
E patua ana mai
E te komuri hau;
Na runga ana mai
O Wai-hihi, o Wai-haha!
Te iringa tena o Tainui
Ura te ra, wewero te ra;
Nga tangata i whakaririka,
Mamau ki te taura;
Kia tu mata-torohia atu
Taku tu mata-toro:
Ihu o waka
Turuki, turuki!
Paneke, paneke!

(Note: translations for the karakia recorded above are given in *Nga Iwi o Tainui*.)

As the waka sat in the tide, Marama-kiko-hura, one of Hoturoa's wives, noticed that it did not ride well in the water, and suggested to her husband that the hull be re-adzed. The waka was accordingly dragged ashore, and after the workmen had thinned it down, returned to the ocean where it floated well.

It is estimated that the Tainui was 21 metres long (the distance between the two stone pillars that mark the prow and stern of the waka at its resting place at Kawhia), and had an ama, or smaller secondary hull, which was named Takere-aotea.

Those remembered from the crew by Biggs and Jones's informants include the following.

Amonga	Hairoa	Ha-popo
Hautai	He-ara	Hine-puanga-nui-a-rangi
Hinewai	Horo-iwi	Hotu-ope
Hotu-awhio	Hotu-nui	Hoturoa
Kahu-keke	Kahungunu	Kahu-tairoa
Kearoa	Kopuwai	Marama-kiko-hura
Maru-kopiri	Mate-ora	Ngatoroirangi
Okaroa	Pou-tukeka	Raka-taura
Rangi-whakairi-ao	Riu-ki-uta	Rotu
Tai-haua	Taikehu	Taiki
Tai-ninihi	Takahi-roa	Tane-whakatia
Taranga	Tari-toronga	Taunga-ki-te-marangi
Te Huaki-o-te-rangi	Te Kite-ana-taua	Torere
Uhenga	Waihare	Whaene-muru-tio
Whakaotirangi		

When the Tainui left the sands of Hawaiki, it was immediately hindered by rough seas as it tried to pass through the gap in the reef that surrounded Pikopiko-i-whiti lagoon. It wasn't until Ngatoroirangi chanted an ancient karakia to calm the seas that the waka was able to make any progress, and it soon reached open ocean. After sailing for a number of days, the Tainui stopped over at Rarotonga, where Ngatoroirangi and his wife Kearoa were kidnapped by Tama-te-kapua of the Te Arawa (see Te Arawa).

After Ngatoroirangi's untimely departure, Riu-ki-uta was appointed navigator, and he immediately summoned the children of Tangaroa to accompany the waka for the remainder of the voyage. The leader of the fish is remembered as Mawake-nui-o-rangi.

Pane-iraira is said to have broken the waves for the Tainui as it sped onwards, and garfish and thresher shark are said to have swum on the flanks. In all there were eighty fish surrounding the waka. During the voyage Taikehu is credited with speeding the waka along, by way of a karakia over the paddles. Closer to land, when the first land birds were sighted, another karakia was chanted, this time by Rotu, who asked for favourable assistance from the winds.

The first landfall the Tainui made was at Cape Runaway, where the crew of the Tainui were captivated by the sight of the pohutukawa in full bloom (in some accounts, it is said to have been the flower of the rata that deceived the crew). As the Tainui approached the shore, Tai-ninihi and Hapopo are said to have discarded their red feather ornaments, thinking that the red flowers were birds in the trees that they could make new head-dresses with. Later, the ornaments were washed up on the beach, and found by Mahina and Ma-ihiihi, who despite an impassioned plea, refused to return them to the previous owners. Further along the coast, while the crew were busy watching for signs of life on shore, the Tainui was caught in a strong current, and dashed against rocks covered with mussel shells. Fortunately, the waka was grounded on the inland side of the rocks, and the ocean swell soon lifted the vessel free, and the crew was able to paddle the waka clear.

As one of the final ceremonies for the voyage, the tohunga (sometimes named as Taikehu) entered the tide, and having taken a number of hairs from his head and body, threw them into the sea. This at once freed the numerous fish and taniwha that had accompanied the waka of their responsibilities, and they left the Tainui.

It was soon evident that several other waka had arrived in the vicinity of Whangaparaoa prior to the Tainui, which Hoturoa objected to (the main reason was probably that the waka that arrived before him would have first call to the land). Hoturoa immediately went about building an altar from timber he had disguised to make look old (by singeing it with fire), and had the anchor rope of the Tainui secretly placed under those of the other waka. In this way, Hoturoa was able to show to the other crews that he and the Tainui were in fact the first of the several waka to land at Whangaparaoa.

From Whangaparaoa, the Tainui voyaged to Ahuahu (Great Mercury Island) in the company of Te Arawa, where after a meeting of the chiefs, the two waka parted company.

As the Tainui sailed along the coast near Taumata-apanui Point, one of the women, Torere, secretly jumped overboard, and swam to shore. Despite Raka-taura searching for her the next morning, she was not found. Eventually Torere married a local man by the name Manaki-ao. Further on, Tari-toronga is said to have left the Tainui at Ha-wai, near Opotiki, and gone on to settle at Motu.

The next place of note the waka called at was Whitianga. Here one of the sails was left by a cliff, now known as Te Ra-o-Tainui. From Whitianga, the waka was sailed to Wharenga, where the sacred stone altar named Kohatu-whakairi was built. Tikapa, Tararu and Wai-whakapukuhanga were all visited during the coastal voyage, an anchor being left at the latter. Whare-kawa, on the west side of Hauraki Gulf, was the next place the waka stopped. It was here that the people of the Tainui learnt from the local tribe that another sea lay to the west. It was decided that Marama-kiko-hura would lead a party overland, and meet the Tainui at Otahuhu. As the waka made its way north, Taikehu named the island Motu-tapu, and later the Tainui landed at Te Kurae-a-Tura, now known as Tura's Point, Devonport. The Tamaki River (then known as Wai-o-Taiki) was the next ara-moana for Hoturoa and his waka. Several of the crew are said to have stayed at Tamaki. Among those remembered as having settled in the vicinity were: Te Kete-ana-taua (and probably her son Tai-haua) at Taurere; Horo-iwi at the mouth of the Tamaki River; Riu-ki-uta at Three Kings; and Pou-tukeka, Ha-popo, Te Uhenga, and Hautai nearby as well.

Marama-kiko-hura and her group rejoined the Tainui at Whangai-makau, near Otahuhu, as arranged. All seemed well until Hoturoa ordered the waka to be dragged across the portage between Tamaki and the Manukau Harbour. Despite the use of several neke (rollers), the waka could not be moved, and after much effort and discussion, it was decided that for such a misfortune to fall upon the waka, Marama-kiko-hura must have had a relationship with someone other than her husband. Marama was accused of having slept with her slave, Okaroa, during the overland journey, and the unfortunate man was immediately put to death. After the appropriate karakia had been effected, the waka was successfully moved to the Manukau Harbour.

Hoturoa's younger brother, Hotunui, was now given charge of the vessel's navigation, Riu-ki-uta having left the waka. As the Tainui sailed along the harbour coast, several places were named, including Rarotonga (Mount Smart), Wai-hihi, and Wai-haha. From the Manukau Harbour, the Tainui was sailed south along the treacherous west coast. While still out at sea near Te Karaka, one of the bailers was swept overboard. It still stands where it was washed up, as a rock on the beach. Next the waka was landed at the mouth of the river Mimi, where Hoturoa visited his relations from the Tokomaru waka. He is said to have planted a pohutukawa tree near the river mouth, where it stood until less than 100 years ago.

From Mimi, the waka was sailed back to the Mokau River, where three stakes were set up to moor the vessel. The three stakes are said to have turned to stone over the centuries, while it is also remembered that one of the waka's anchors was also left at Mokau. The Tainui was left at Mokau by Hoturoa and his crew, who explored inland for some distance. During the journey, Hoturoa and Raka-taura were reunited, and put aside their differences. It was decided that the two of them would continue overland to Kawhia, while the remainder of the crew would return to Mokau, and paddle the waka along the coast. When the Tainui finally reached Kawhia, it was hauled ashore, below the altar named Ahurei, which had earlier been built by Raka-taura. Two further altars were constructed for the occasion; Hoturoa named his Puna-whakatupu-tangata, while Raka-taura named his Hani.

ADDITIONAL INFORMATION

In Hawaiki

The main reason suggested for the migration to Aotearoa was the ongoing feud between neighbouring tribes over the gardens Tawaruarangi and Tawaruararo. In one version of the tradition, the person killed by Raka-taura and buried among the wood chips was Kowhiti-nui, and was a child of either Manaia or Rakataua. Another account claims that the murder was committed by Hoturoa, and that he killed a boy in a fit of rage with his adze. Apparently the child had laughed at his work when he was lashing the topsides of the Tainui. A further tradition of the building of the Tainui, recorded in Graham's *The Account of Kupe and Tainui*, states that the builder of the Tainui was Rata-o-Wahie-roa.

The following karakia was performed before the tree was cut down, and is stated by sources used for Kelly's *Tainui* as having been chanted by Whakatau-potiki.

No whea te waka?
No uta te waka,
No te nehenehe nui.

I kimihia, i hahautia.
Koia ra ka kitea
Nga rau nuku o te whenua.
Ka riri hoki au
Ki a Tane-i-te-wao.
Kei te kotikoti au
I nga uaua o Papatuanuku,
I nga taero o Tainui,
I nga tau rori o Hinekura,
Ka hinga i te whenako
Ka whatu petia
Ka takoto i te tapairu ariki
Ki o tu taia
Whatiwhati ana iwi.

Another karakia recorded in *Tainui* follows. This karakia was chanted when the waka was dragged from the forest to the shore.

Kotia te pu, ka waiho i uta,
Kotia te kauru, ka waiho i tai,
E ai ra ko te umutuhi
Kihai i tae ki nga pukenga,
Ki nga wananga, ki nga tauira.
He kura! He kura!
He kura te winiwini!
He kura te wanawana!
Ki tua o Rehia
Ki tua o Rena.
Ki taku whainga makau e-e.
Keke! Keke! Ana mai te keke!
Hara mai te toki,
Haumi e-e!
Hui e-e!
Taiki e-e!

Before the Tainui departed Hawaiki, Whakaotirangi is said to have asked her father for the mauri Puanga. It is suggested that this is in some way connected to the knowledge of, or a guardian for, cultivating kumara. In some accounts, Whakaotirangi is the daughter of Uenuku. It should be noted that Whakaotirangi is claimed by the descendants of the crews of both the Tainui, and the Te Arawa as having migrated on their respective waka.

The karakia that Ngatoroirangi is said to have chanted as the Tainui tried to leave the lagoon Pikopiko-i-whiti is remembered as follows.

>Ka hura tangata uta te tiaki atu ki tangata a tai,
>Ka hura tangata tai te tiaki atu ki tangata a uta.
>Pera hoki ra te korepe nui, te korepe roa,
>Te wahi awa, te totoe awa.
>Whakamoe Tama i araia te awa
>Ko Tu, ko Rongo, ko Tama i araia te awa
>Kauraka Tama e uhia.
>Tukua atu Tama kia puta i waho i te tawhangawhanga,
>He putanga ariki no Rongo ki te ata.
>Tauira mai, ea mai, ea mai, ea mai, ea mai te tapua,
>Mai ea mai te tawhito, i hara mai koe i whea?
>I te whakaotinuku, i te whakaotirangi?
>Whakahotu to manawa!
>Ko taku manawa e Tane, ka irihia.
>Whano! Whano!
>Hara mai te toki!
>Haumi e!
>Hui e!
>Taiki e!

The crew

Other ancestors claimed to have been among the crew of Tainui include:

Ao-o-rangi	Hiaora	Hotumatapu
Houmea	Huaki-o-terangi	Kahurere
Kokotangi-ki-raukawa	Kuo	Mahia
Manio-o-rangi	Motai	Oho-mai-rangi
Rua-moe-ngara	Ruamuturangi	Tama
Tama-te-Marangai	Tarawa	Tari-tarona
Te Peri	Te Taura-waho	

Te Peri, who was the sister of the deformed child Tainui, is said to have been a kapehu, or guiding god, and sat in the bow of the waka.

As well as giving instructions for the navigation of the Tainui, she was also expected to ward off any evil directed at the vessel. Marama-kiko-hura, or Marama-hahake, was originally named Marama, but was given the additions to her name after her exposure as an adulteress.

Tribes claiming descent from the Tainui include: Ngati Haua, Ngati Maru, Ngati Maniapoto, Waikato, Ngati Tuwharetoa, Ngati Raukawa, Ngati Apakura, Nga Puhi, Ngati Toa, Ngati Mahuta, Ngati Tai, Ngati Paoa and Ngati Awa.

The voyage

It is remembered that the Tainui left Hawaiki in the season of Tatau-uruora, on the day known as Orongonui (28th day), with the corresponding moon phase Tama-tea. This was a time when there were constant gales and continuous bad weather at sea. Hoturoa was only able to ensure a safe voyage by way of his sacred karakia, which calmed the ocean. Even so, it is sometimes said that the Tainui tried three times before it successfully reached the open ocean. On both of the first two attempts to leave Hawaiki, Hoturoa was warned of impending danger by the toroa (oyster catcher).

Taikehu was in charge of the paddle Hauhauterangi, which features in the following paddling chant, said to have been performed by Riukiuta during the southern voyage.

> Taku hoe tapu nei ko Hauhauterangi!
> Taku hoe tapu nei ko Hauhauterangi!
> Whaia Te Arawa me kore e rokohina,
> Me kore e rokohina.
> Ka riro ia i te tarawa putuputu.
> Whakapoi ake te kakau o te hoe
> Ko Maninitua, ko Maniniaro.
> Ka tangi te kura, ka tangi wawana!
> Ka tangi te kura, ka tangi wiwini!
> E hiki e Rata! Nau mai!
> Te haria, te kawea a Tane ki uta,
> Na Io te wai kei te pae o Maruaonui.
> Waimimiti, waipakora.
> Na Rangi-nui-a-Io,
> Taia te wai.

Mimiti! Pakora!

Other paddles remembered were named Maninitua, the steering paddle for the bow, and Maniniaro, the steering paddle for the stern.

There were nine karakia used during the voyage to ensure a safe passage. The following is a list remembered by Te Ao-te-rangi, and recorded in *Tainui*.

A karakia for the gods to disclose danger.
A karakia for the gods to give favourable winds.
A karakia for the gods to clear the skies of cloud.
A karakia for the gods to form the clouds into a barrier on
    the horizon, thus blocking off any unfavourable winds.
A karakia to ask the sea creatures to assist the waka.
A karakia for the gods, asking for strength.
A karakia to assist in bailing.
A karakia for the paddles.
A karakia to the birds (to assist in direction-finding).

The following karakia is said to have been chanted when there was a need to call upon the assistance of birds, and is recorded in *Tainui*.

Te manu nui a Ruakapanga e,
Nau mai! Kawea au ki uta.
He aha ra te manu nana i takahi te tauru awatea
I roki ai taku manu.
Ko nga manu kai takiwa a Rangi
Nana i takahi te tauru awatea
I roki ai taku manu.
E hiki e Rata! Nau mai!
Te haria, te kawea a Tane ki uta.

It is claimed in some versions of the Tainui legend that Raka-taura was left behind at Rarotonga when the Tainui sailed on to Aotearoa. The reason he was left at Rarotonga is said to have been his 'thievish' habits. Another tradition says Raka-taura turned himself into a rat, and stowed away on the Tainui; while in a third version, Raka-taura was conveyed ahead of the Tainui and reached Aotearoa on the back of a whale. A further discussion of the above claim that Raka-taura was left behind at Rarotonga, recorded in *Tainui*, suggests that Rakatauru may have been left behind at Rarotonga,

Mount Smart, rather than the Rarotonga in the Cook Islands.

During a break in the voyage to Aotearoa, the cross beams of the Tainui are said to have been strengthened by timber from the house Marua-a-nui (Maruaonui), in Rarotonga.

It is claimed in some traditions that after Ngatoroirangi had been abducted by the crew of Te Arawa, Hoturoa persuaded another tohunga to join his crew. Tama was the man's name, and he gave up command of his waka, the Poutini, to voyage on the Tainui. The Poutini sailed to Aotearoa without Tama, who eventually rejoined the crew at Tamaki.

In Aotearoa

The following notes are from a narrated account of the coastal voyage of Tainui, by Maihi te Kapua te Hinaki, of Ngati Paoa and Ngati Whatua.

After reaching Whangara the Tainui journeyed north, but was unable to round North Cape because of contrary winds. The waka returned to Tekapamoana (Hauraki Gulf), stopping at Waihihi. Due to adverse weather conditions, it sailed to Waitemata to seek shelter. The Maraetai passage was successfully navigated, and the waka made landfall at Te Haukapua (Torpedo Bay). After a short stay at Te Haukapua, the Tainui was sailed to Rangitoto, where it met up with Te Arawa. Hoturoa and Tama-te-kapua are said to have fought over Tama-te-kapua's desire for Hoturoa's senior wife, Whakaotirangi. Tama-te-kapua is said to have been badly beaten by Hoturoa, and lost a lot of blood. The island now commonly known as Rangitoto was given the name Te Rangitoto-o-Tama-te-kapua to commemorate this event.

From Rangitoto the waka was sailed up the Wai-o-Taiki, and moored inside Tamaki West Head, at Waiarohe. Here Horoiwi left the waka, marrying a local woman and naming his pa Te Pane o Horoiwi. It was while Taikehu was exploring the district that he saw in the distance the Manukau Harbour. It is said that Te Arawa was nearby when Tainui was in the Wai-o-Taiki, but soon left, no doubt because of the animosity between the two chiefs. The Tainui was poled (poutai) up to the portage, where Marama's indiscretion was discovered when the waka could not be dragged, even with the help of skids. It was Raka-taura who, by way of his second sight, disclosed Marama's secret. The slave, Okaroa, was immediately killed, and strung up on a karaka tree, and Marama was purified and cleansed in a sacred ceremony.

After the cleansing ceremony was complete, Marama chanted the following chant as she stood on the Tainui.

He tarawai — nuku,
He tarawai — rangi.
Pu-nui-e teina ma!
Kumea!

Turuturu haere ana —
Heke ana te wai
O te hika o Marama.

E takina-mai ana
E te komuri hau,
No runga o Waihihi,
No runga o Waihaha.

Turuki! Turuki!
Paneke! Paneke!
Ihu o te waka — E!

The Tainui was successfully dragged across the portage and was relaunched at Te Inuwai o Tainui. Further ceremonies were performed for the waka, because of its introduction to new waters in the Manukau. The tale ends with the Tainui sailing from the Manukau to Kawhia and on to Waimimi. At length, the Tainui returned to Kawhia, where it rests.

In at least one account of the Tainui's landfall in Aotearoa, it is said to have landed first at Te Mahia before sailing on to Whangaparaoa. Sometimes it is said that the Tainui was the first waka to come across the carcass of the whale at Whangaparaoa when the waka first reached Aotearoa, and that it was Tama-te-kapua who tricked Hoturoa out of the valuable food supply. It is also claimed that when the Tainui left Whangaparaoa, several crew members remained. Those named as having stayed were Rua-moe-ngara, Mahia, Taikehu and Kokotangi-ki-raukawa. There were others whose names have been forgotten.

One account claims that Taikehu was purposely left behind at Whangaparaoa so that Hoturoa could marry Torere, Taikehu's wife.

In an effort to escape Hoturoa's unwanted attention, Torere is said to have secretly jumped overboard near Taumata-apanui Point. (The exact place was named after her.) Other versions state that it was Raka-taura rather than Hoturoa that Torere left the waka to escape, or that Torere left the Tainui near Opotiki because of her menstruation. One reason given for Hoturoa's dislike of Raka-taura was the latter's desires for Hoturoa's daughter, Kahurere. It wasn't until Hoturoa and Raka-taura were reunited inland from the west coast that the two settled their differences, and as a reconciliatory gesture Raka-taura and Kahurere were married.

Tradition recorded in *Maori Lore* states that during the voyage along the coast of Aotearoa, the Tainui met up with several other waka, including Te Arawa, Mataatua, Kurahaupo, and Tokomaru. It is further claimed that the Tokomaru also passed over the portage between Tamaki and Manukau. Other accounts claim the Tainui was not transported across the Tamaki–Manukau portage, but was sailed north to the cape and down the west coast. A reference in *Nga Iwi o Tainui* quotes Ao-te-rangi as saying the waka 'rounded North Cape, but on being unable to cross the Hokianga bar, it turned round and came back to the Hauraki Gulf'. After Raka-taura left the crew, he and his sister, Hiaroa, followed the waka along the west coast, initially impeding the waka from entering several harbours, including Manukau, Raglan, Aotea and Kawhia, by way of karakia.

According to tradition given in *Tainui*, those that stayed behind when Raka-tauru left the Tainui at Otahuhu were Hiaroa, Marukopiri, Taranga, Tane-whakatia, Taunga-ki-te-marangai, Waihare, Rotu, Te Huaki-o-te-rangi and Hine-puanga-nui-a-rangi.

The karakia chanted to move Tainui across the Tamaki–Manukau portage is recorded in *Tainui* as follows.

Tapatapa hau!
Tapatapa hau!
Kawea e Tangaroa ma tupua.
Ka kau takawini
Ka kau takawawa
Ki tua o Rehia
Ki tua o Reao
He kiore kai tahora nui.
Toia, toia Tainui
Tapotu ki te moana.
Ma wai e to?

Ma te whakatau e rangona ake ana.
He tarawa i nuku
He tarawa i rangi
Punui teina.
Tinia! Monoa!
Nau mai, nau mai ra e Tane!
Ka kau taua i te wai
Kia matakitakina koe
E te tini e te mano.
Naku koe i tiki atu
Ki te Wao-nui-a-Tane
Tane mingoi!
Tane rangahau!
Takoto atu ana te ara ki tatahi.
Turuturu haere ana
Haere ana te wai
O te hika o Marama
E takina ana mai e te komuri hau
Na runga o Waihihi o Waihaha.
Turuki! Turuki!
Paneke! Paneke!
Ihu o waka.

Places named by the crew of the Tainui while they stayed in the Manukau Harbour are Te Tapotu-o-Tainui (a spot near Westfield, where the waka was relaunched), and two small islands in the vicinity, which were named Nga Rango-e-rua-o-Tainui. One explanation for the naming of Manukau harbour suggests that the harbour was originally named Te Manukau o Hoturoa, or the anxiety of Hoturoa, referring to Hoturoa's concern for the waka's safety as it crossed the Manukau bar. One place stopped at during the voyage down the west coast was Oeunuku, where several sharks are said to have been caught and thrown on to the shore.

The ama of the Tainui, a smaller waka named Takere-aotea, was abandoned at Kawa, where it had been taken up a stream to collect fresh drinking water. Those given the responsibility of collecting the water are said to have deserted the Takere-aotea, and probably taken up with a local tribe. From another source it is claimed that some time after the Tainui landed at Kawhia it was sailed on to Taranaki. While the waka was at Taranaki, Kopuwai married a local woman who was named Hine-moana-te-waiwai. Kopuwai then changed his name to Tara-pounamu, after receiving a greenstone barb (for skewering birds) from his wife. In later life, Tara-pounamu used the Tainui to further explore Aotearoa. He first visited Mokau, where he left several trees and an anchor. Next he stopped off at Te Wai-iti near present-day New Plymouth, before sailing to Mimi and visiting the people of the Tokomaru. After staying at Mimi for some time, he returned to Te Wai-iti, where the Tainui was dragged ashore and thoroughly neglected. When Hoturoa heard of the condition of the Tainui, he sent his people to retrieve the waka, and it was returned to Kawhia, where it remained among the people it had conveyed to Aotearoa.

In the *Maori–Polynesian Comparative Dictionary* it is claimed that the Tainui ended its days at a place named Paringatai.

Among the cargo in the hold of the Tainui was a variety of kumara known as anurangi.

An interesting story recorded in the *Journal of the Polynesian Society*, volume 46, says the anchor of the Tainui remained unmoved at Mokau for several centuries, until the captain of a cutter stole it one night from its resting place. Naturally enough it wasn't long before the treasure was missed, and suspicion immediately fell on the owner of the cutter. The tribe organised one of the chiefs, Te Horo, to visit the local inspector of police, who was told of the theft and whom the tribe suspected to be the perpetrator. It wasn't long before the inspector visited the cutter owner. The anchor was duly found in the back-yard, and the boat owner sensibly returned the anchor to Mokau, to the great relief of the local inhabitants. To complete the story, Buck states that the anchor's final resting place was on the grave of Tamati Kingi te Wetere, in the Awakino cemetery.

The plantation where Whakaotirangi and Marama-kiko-hura grew their seeds was called Te Papa-o-karewa. The seeds of Whakaotirangi were said to have grown strongly, while those of Marama-kiko-hura are said to have been affected by her offence with the slave Okaroa: kumara seeds grew as po-hue, hue seeds grew as mawhai, aute grew as whau, and para seeds grew as korokio.

Finally, the following version of the Tainui tradition was collected in 1950 from Jeffery Henry of Ureia, Cook Islands.

It is remembered that Tai-taraka built an outrigger voyaging waka from a tree growing from the grave of his stillborn brother, Rara-pakoro. The waka was subsequently named Karaea-kura, and sailed to Taiti-iva-nui, where Tai-taraka married and had a family. In later years, one of Tai-taraka's grandchildren, Tai-te-atai-nui-o-Taiti-iva-nui, visited him, and persuaded him to assist with the preparation of a voyaging waka in which to explore the vast oceans. The old man agreed, and called for Tama-te-kapua and Ngatoroirangi, two expert waka builders. The two craftsmen were asked to prepare the old waka Karaea-kura for one more ocean voyage.

Once the waka was completed it was given a new name, I-tere, and was soon on its way to Taiti, where the parents of Tai-te-atai-nui-o-Taiti-iva-nui lived beside the river Vairoa. During the voyage, two foreign waka were encountered: Te Ra-tu-mai-tonga from the Tuamotus, under the command of Takoto, and an un-named waka under the command of Maio. After a mid-ocean discussion, the three captains decided to sail in convoy to Taiti, where they could rest and reprovision their waka before going on to explore together. It was not long before the three crews were sufficiently rested, and the time came to leave Taiti. Unfortunately, soon after recommencing their voyage of discovery, the convoy was caught in a fierce storm, and the vessels were separated. It is remembered that the I-tere was blown as far as Araura (Aitutaki), while Te Ra-tu-mai-tonga ended up in Tonga, and Maio's waka landed at Manuae.

Ngatoroirangi and Tama-te-kapua voyaged alongside Tai-te-atai-nui-o-Taiti-iva-nui, and his brother Tai-te-nio-veri on the I-tere. Ill-chosen words by Tai-te-nio-veri before the voyage began caused tension throughout the journey. The problem came to a head when Tama-te-kapua tried to pass the blame of an illicit liaison with the wife of either Ngatoroirangi or Tai-te-pakopako on to Tai-te-nio-veri. Only the intervention of Tai-te-atai-nui-o-Taiti-iva-nui kept a murder from being committed. The insults were not forgotten, and while the waka was being landed at Araura, using the trunks of pandanus trees as skids, Tama-te-kapua and Ngatoroirangi tripped Tai-te-nio-veri, causing him to be crushed beneath the hull of the I-tere. Tai-te-atai-nui-o-Taiti-iva-nui seems to have been helpless to punish the two murderers, and could only arrange for them to be transferred to the waka Te Arava (Te Arawa). In return, Oturoa (Hoturoa) joined the I-tere (then renamed Tainui) as captain.

Those remembered as having been in the crew are as follows.

Ineuru	Kurei	Rongo-mai-te-auru-rangi
Tai-kai-vao	Tai-kura-vero	Tai-manawa-po-atu
Tai-mata-kino-tangata	Tainui	Tai-pakupaku

THE WAKA

Tai-roa	Tai-te-iiri	Tai-te-tara
Tai-tu-taua-rangi	Tai-uenuku	Tai-vai-to-taki
Tama-o-tea	Tao-paenga	Taua-i-kavai
Te Aovavana	Te Rangi-ua-take	Te Verovero
Torere-nui-a-rua	Tu-rangi-nini	Tu-te-auru
Vire-nui-ariki		

(*See also* Te Mahanga-a-Tuamatua for a discussion of Ngata's suggestion that Te Arawa and Tainui were two hulls of the one double waka.)

The Coming of the Maori, pp. 47, 52.
Echoes of the Pa, p. 117.
JPS, Vol. 1, pp. 216, 224.
JPS, Vol. 12, pp. 56, 57.
JPS, Vol. 14, pp. 97–8.
JPS, Vol. 28, pp. 112–13.
JPS, Vol. 46, pp. 83, 84.
JPS, Vol. 60, pp. 81–5.
JPS, Vol. 64, pp. 192–5.
Kahungunu, October 1992, p. 23.
Maori Lore, pp. 233–8, 302.
The Maori–Polynesian Comparative Dictionary, p. 21.
Nga Iwi O Tainui, pp. 16–50
The Peopling of the North, p. 33.
Tainui, pp. 34–7, 40, 44–8, 50–3, 56–8.
Treasury of Maori Exploration, pp. 165–9, 175, 177, 180.
Treasury of Maori Folklore, pp. 371, 404.
Tuwharetoa, p. 56.
Whakatane and District Historical Society Inc. Memoir #4, p. 5.

TAI-O-PUAPUA

This waka is named in a Ngati Porou apakura (lament) along with other waka that are known to have been early visitors to Aotearoa. Nothing else is known.

Nga Moteatea, Vol. 2, pp. 6–7.

TAIPARAEROA

It was from this waka that replacement paddles were taken for the Aotea, when it was discovered that those provided for it were made of huhoe, a wood unsuitable for paddles. No other mention of this waka is made, so it is doubtful that it actually voyaged to Aotearoa.

Treasury of Maori Exploration, p. 79.

TAIREA

The Tairea, captained by Tama (variously Tama-ki-te-rangi, Tama-taku-ariki, Tama-ahua or Tamatea), features in ancient South Island legends associated with pounamu. No description of the waka has been passed down, although some of the crew are remembered through their names being given to different types of pounamu.

In the tradition retold to Herries Beattie by Teone Taare Tikao, Tama was a very early visitor to the South Island. Despite managing to cross Te Moana-nui-a-Kiwa without any major mishap, the Tairea was wrecked on the coast at Westland due to an incorrect karakia. The remnants of the vessel were then carried inland up the Arahura River by a great wave to a place called Hohonu where it still lies as an immovable block of pounamu. Most of the crew were also turned to pounamu, with a different type named after each of them. Those remembered are Kawakawa, Kahurangi, Auhunga, Inanga Koko-tangiwai, Mata-kirikiri and Aotea. Tama managed to avoid the fate of his companions, and features in other traditions.

It is recorded that an explorer by the name of Tama-ki-te-rangi named at least two landmarks on the Kaikoura Coast (Te Ahi-kai-koura-a-Tama-ki-te-rangi in full): Te Rae-o-Tawhiti (the headland of Tahiti), the high precipitous cape which bounds the South Bay to the east; and Atiu, another headland on the Kaikoura peninsular to the north-east. (Atiu is also the name of an island in the Cook group.)

There is an unrelated North Island tradition that features a waka by the name of Tairea, but it is usually considered a different waka, and is often said to be a second name for the Rangi-ua-mutu. Finally there is a South Island tradition collected by Cowan that states that the poroporo fruit 'was brought to Aotearoa by Tunui-raki, the captain of the Tairea waka, and planted in the North Island'. No further information is available.

JPS, Vol. 14, pp. 45–6.
JPS, Vol. 29, pp. 162–3.
The Morioris of the South Island, p. 39.
Tikao Talks, p. 60.
Treasury of Maori Folklore, pp. 356–8.

TAKERE-AOTEA

Name variations: Takare-aotea, Takare-atea

> The Takere-aotea was the second waka and outrigger for the famous double-hulled Tainui. In a second reference, the Takere-aotea is also supposed to have voyaged to Aotearoa under the navigator Takere-ao independently, having been told the sailing instructions for the journey by Kupe.
>
> *The Ancient History of the Maori*, Vol. 2, p. 189.
> *Treasury of Maori Exploration*, p. 266.

TAKERE-O-TOITAHA

> In Hetaraka Tautahi's telling of the migration of the Aotea, mention is made of several other ancestral waka including the Takere-o-Toitaha. The others named were the Rangi-tako, Hakirere, Karamu-raunui, Tata-taiore, Whakarewarewa, Rangi-totohu, Rangi kekero and Pahi-tonoa (which was the waka of Rauru). No final destination of any of the waka is given in the interview, although several turn up in other legends where their exploits are expanded upon.
>
> *JPS*, Vol. 9, p. 213.

TAKE-ROA-OTEA

> It is recorded that the Take-roa-otea was captained by Take-reto, a contemporary of the famous explorer Kupe. It was on Kupe's return to Hawaiki that he gave Take-reto the sailing directions to Aotearoa, which were promptly tested during the long voyage south.
>
> *Maori Lore*, p. 298.

TAKITIMU

Name variation: Takitumu

> The Takitimu is remembered as being perhaps the most tapu of all waka to voyage to Aotearoa. Only specially selected chiefs and tribal gods were fit to embark on the Takitimu, and no cooked food could be carried on it for the voyage.
> Tradition sourced by Mitchell for his book *Takitimu* states that the

chief Tamatea-ariki-nui ordered a new waka to be built by the craftsmen Ruawharo, Tupai and Te Rongo-putahi in Hawaiki. The adzes used were named Te Awhiorangi (which was only used for ceremonial purposes), Te-whiro-nui, Rakuraku-o-Tawhaki, Matangirei and Hui-te-Rangiora. The types of stone used for the adzes were known as kohurau, ka-ra, anewa and pounamu. Tribesmen from the villages Whangara, Pakarae, and Rehuroa, all under the influence of Tamatea-ariki-nui, assisted in the construction of the waka. The names of the individual tribes were Ngati Huka-moana, Ngati Hukaturi, and Ngati Tutaka-hinahina.

Because the waka was so tapu, it was constructed in a special cordoned-off enclosure, which no one but those who underwent specific ceremonies were permitted to enter, or leave. After the initial shaping was completed at the hill known as Titirangi, the waka was completed at Tamatea's village of Whangara. Here were added: 'the rauawa (top sides), haumi (fore and aft pieces), taumanu (thwarts), karaho or rahoraho (flooring platform), tauihu (figurehead), rapa (sternposts), whitikotuku (parts of awning frame), tira (masts), puhi (ornaments of feathers), karewa and hoe (paddles)'. Six steering paddles were made, and they were named Rapanga-i-te-ati-nuku, Rapanga-i-te-rangi, Maninikura, Maniniaro, Tangi-wiwini and Tangi-wawana. The first two belonged to Tamatea-ariki-nui, while Ruawharo and Tupai were each issued with two. The names of the two bailers, Tipua-horo-nuku and Tipua-horo-rangi, have also been remembered.

During construction of the waka, a special compartment was built in front of Ruawharo's bow seat, reserved for the housing of the sacred articles personifying the gods. The gods named by Mitchell's informant were Rangi and Papa, Tawhirimatea, Tane-nui-a-rangi, Tangaroa, Rongo-marae-roa, Haumia, and Tumatauenga.

It is claimed that the following chant was used by Tamatea-ariki-nui to consecrate the finished waka.

Ko wai te waka e takoto nei i,
Ko Takitimu, ko Takitimu.
Pa atu ra taku hoe,
Ki te riu tapu nui o te waka e takoto nei,
Rei kura, rei ora.
Rei ora te mauri-e.
Ka turuturua, ka poupoua,
Ki tawhito o te ranai-e.

Rurukutia,
Rurukutia te waka e takoto nei.
Rurukutia te kei Matapupuni,
Rurukutia te ihu matapupuni a Tane.
Rurukutia i te kowhao tapu a Tane,
Rurukutia i te mata tapu a Tane.
Rurukutia i te rauawa tapu a Tane,
O te waka e takoto nei.

After the ceremony had been concluded, the Takitimu was launched with the help of four neke (rollers). The rollers were named Te Tahuri, Mounukuhia, Mouhapainga and Manutawhiorangi — the last two possessing supernatural powers.

The waka itself, having successfully completed its sea trials at Pikopiko-i-whiti, was taken to Te-whetu-matarau, where by moonlight Ruawharo recited incantations to protect the waka. The following chant is said to have been used in that particular ceremony.

Tu mai awa, tu mai moana
Ko koe takahia noa tia e au
Tupe aunuku tupe aurangi
Whati ki runga, whati ki raro
Urumarangaranga,
Perahoki ra taku manu-nui na Tane
Ka tatau atu ki roto o Nuku-ngaere
Maia whiwhia, maia rawea
Maia whakatakaia.
Ka taka te huki rawea
Koro i runga koro i raro
Koro i Tawhirimatea.
Ki kora hoki koe tu mai ai
Ka hura te Tamatea nunui
Ka hura te Tamatea roroa.
Te Kauaka nuku, te kauaka rangi
Te ai a nuku, te ai a rangi.
Te kura mai hukihuki
Te kaweau tetere.
Kawea a nuku kawea a tai
Oi! Tumata kokiriritia!
Hoatu waka ki waho.
Hoatu waka ki uta.

Ngaruhinga atu, ngaruhinga mai.
Irunga te mata wahine
I raro te mata Tane
Huki nawenawe.
Tenei te waka ka whakairia,
Ko Takitimu te waka ee,
Ko Tamatea ariki te tangata.

Little information has been recorded of the departure of the Takitimu, but all seems to have gone well until the food ran out. Thankfully, the priests on board Takitimu were able to call upon the gods Tangaroa and Tane to provide them with fish and sea birds to sustain them for the remainder of the voyage.

When the waka finally made landfall in Aotearoa, it was at Awanui, at the south end of Ninety Mile Beach. A number of the crew decided to settle at Kaitaia, a short distance from the beach. It wasn't long before those who wished to continue exploring relaunched their waka, and after rounding North Cape, sailed south along the eastern coastline. During the voyage south, several places were named, including Whangara, the river Pararae, and the hill Titirangi, which overlooks Gisborne. Tamatea was the next to leave the Takitimu, when he settled at present-day Tauranga. After Tamatea's departure, the captaincy was handed over to Tahu-potiki, who promised Tamatea he would sail south to search for a source of pounamu, which apparently was one of the major objectives of the voyage.

After Tauranga, the next stop was at Nukutaurua (Mahia Peninsula), where Ruawharo settled at a spot named Te Papa (said to be near present-day Oraka). Next Waikawa (Portland Island) was visited, and an altar built. The waka was then sailed to Te Wairoa, and up the Wairoa River to Makeakea. It was here that one of the neke fell into the river, and is said to have turned into a taniwha.

(Details of the southern section of the journey will be completed by reference to the version of the tradition published in *Kahungunu*.)

During the voyage south in search of pounamu, the Takitimu visited Ahuriri, and the mouths of the Ngaruroro, Te Awanga and Waimarama rivers, where men were put ashore. Karotimutimu went ashore at Te Awanga, and Taewha-ki-te-rangi and three un-named companions disembarked at Waimarama. It is also recorded that the waka's skids and two of its anchors were left behind with Taewha-ki-te-rangi, although no reason is given. The skids now feature as the

Kuku Rocks, while one of the anchors, named Taupunga, is a small rock in the bay, and the other is represented by Capstan Rock.

The next landfall was along the Wairarapa coast, where Tupai, the last of the three high-priests, along with some of the crew, disembarked to settle near the Waikare river mouth. Presumably with a much-depleted crew, Tahu-potiki is said to have continued on to the South Island in search of pounamu, successfully reaching the river Arahura, where the precious pounamu lay in abundance.

Another version of the Takitimu tradition, collected by Andersen for his *Maori Place Names*, claims that the Takitimu originally belonged to three tribes: Ngati Kopeka, Ngati Parauriuri and Ngati Pukohukohu. Having been badly beaten in war, they decided to build a large voyaging waka from a tree (named Te Puwhenua), set aside for this very purpose by ancestors of one of the tribes. It was discovered, however, that no one among the three tribes possessed the skill to build such a large waka, and a neighbouring tribe, the Ngati Wai-mahuehue, were approached to provide expert craftsmen to assist. It was soon obvious, though, that the Ngati Wai-mahuehue were more intent on preparing for war than helping build the waka, so it was decided to ask Tamatea-ariki-nui for assistance.

Tamatea-ariki-nui, a powerful chief, agreed to the request, and immediately sent for the expert waka builders Ruawharo and Tupai, who lived at the village of Whangara. After inspecting the tree Te Puwhenua, and declaring its suitability, Ruawharo and Tupai sent for their fellow craftsmen. Those chosen to help were Tai-kehu, Rongo-tawhao, Kohu-para, and Pawa. Ruawharo carried his adze Hui-te-Rangiora, Tai-kehu took Te Rakuraku-o-tawhaki, and Pawa and Tupai carried Kaukau and Wharau-rangi respectively.

As soon as the karakia had been chanted over the workmen, their tools and the tree, work commenced in earnest. After the waka was finally shaped, it was laid in a trench and buried to season. While this progressed, the fixtures, such as top stakes and masts, were crafted.

When all the work had been completed, but before the waka hull was ready to be taken from its trench, Pawa obtained permission to build a second voyaging waka. While Pawa's waka was still under construction, the Takitimu was taken from its resting place and dragged towards Pae-kawa, the village of its owners. It was soon evident that those charged with the responsibility of pulling the great waka to Pae-kawa were in need of expert help. Tamatea-ariki-nui once again agreed to help the three tribes, but only as far as the fork in the track that branched off to the village of Te Pakaroa or to the village of

Pae-kawa. While helping with the dragging, Ruawharo is said to have placed two magic skids among those used to drag the waka, each having been chanted over with a karakia to exhaust the workers, and delay the waka's progress.

Having reached the fork in the path, it was suggested by Ruawharo that the waka be dragged to Tamatea-ariki-nui's village, which was considerably closer, and an easier route, and then sailed around the coast to Pae-kawa. Despite feelings of unease on the part of the owners, the plan was agreed to, and the shorter route was taken. Ruawharo then fashioned two new skids to ease the effort required for the remainder of the hauling, which he named Te Manu-tawhio-rau and Te Manu-ka-tiu. Once the waka was at the seashore, Tamatea-ariki-nui suggested that it be left with his workmen for the final lashing of the top stakes, stern and bow, and other essential pieces. This also was agreed to, and while the work progressed, the owners cooked a huge feast to celebrate the completion of the Takitimu.

It was not long before the Takitimu, still in the hands of Tamatea-ariki-nui, was ready for sea trials, which were held alongside Te Arawa, Mataatua and other well-known waka at Pikopiko-i-whiti. The waka was so fast that it was said to swallow the land (swallow — horo, land — uta), and was renamed Horouta. (It is usually said that the Takitimu and the Horouta were totally separate waka, although some suggest that the Takitimu was re-named Horouta for a second voyage, when the crew members were perhaps less tapu.)

Soon after the trials on Pikopiko-i-whiti the majority of the waka sailed for Aotearoa, leaving the Takitimu as the last voyaging waka at Hawaiki. Soon the owners of the waka called for a meeting with Tamatea-ariki-nui, and it was decided that members from all of the tribes involved in the construction and hauling of the Takitimu would sail on her. It was also agreed that, once the waka had reached Aotearoa, Tu-takahinahina would return to Hawaiki to pick up those that couldn't be accommodated in the first voyage.

Andersen lists the names of the thwarts allocated in the waka. Starting from the stern, the following thwarts are remembered, along with those assigned to them.

Te Ra-kura	Te Rongo-patahi, Ruawharo and Tupai, each a navigator; close by to them were deposited the representations of the gods

Pae-rangi	no details
Pae-tahi	Tamatea-ariki-nui and his family
Kahu-tua-nui	Hope-hi-tua-rangi
Rakau-amoamo	Taikehu
Rakau-whatawhata	no details
Pia-tangi-rere	Tamatea-kota
Maire-kura	Tu-ai-te-rangi
(un-named)	Kohu-para, Mokinokino and their families
Te Ata-kura and Manu-tahi	Jointly with the following thwart, was occupied by Tu-taka-hinahina, Puhi-whakaawe, Rau-tahi, Mokomoko, and families
Maire-hau	Rongo-mahae-ata and family
Te Puwhenua	also occupied by Puhi-whakaawe, Tu-tokahinahina and families
Pae-kawa	Te Rau-tahi, Moko-nui-a-rangi and families
Riri-moana	Hau-tu-te-rangi and family
Tiritiri-o-te-moana	Te Rongo-patahi, Ruawharo and families
Ruku-moana	Rerehu-rangi and family
Aotea	Tu-ai-te-rangi and family
Horo-nuku-otea	Te Rangi-ka-tatau and family
Horo-nuku-rangi	Ira-kai-putahi and family
Ahuahu	no details
Maui-taha	no details
Maui-pae	no details

(Information relating to three further thwarts has been forgotten.) Several other parts of the waka are remembered by name as well.

Te Haeatu-o-te-rangi	aft sail
Pari-nui-te-re	front sail
Tangaengae and Takerekere	braces for the aft sail
Toko-ahuru	yard for the aft sail
Te Aka-rinorino	brace for front sail (the second was forgotten)
Pae-taku	yard for the front sail
Horu-moana	main anchor
Marohi and Mawake	ropes for main anchor

The waka left Hawaiki in the month known as Patoki-nui-o-tau (March), with the taniwha Ruamano, Arai-te-uru, Tu-tara-kauika and Te Wehenga-kauki all acting as guardians during the voyage. Arai-te-uru is said to have followed in the waka's wake, called Tahiti-nui or Harua-tai. Later, as the waka sailed on, it was joined by the tipua (goblins, in this case whales) Hine-kotea, Hine-makehu, Hine-korito and Hine-huruhuru. During the voyage the god Kahukura (in the form of a solar rainbow) was sent ahead by day to guide the waka, while Hine-korako (in the form of a lunar rainbow) was sent at night. The winds Para-wera-nui (the south wind) and Tahu-makeka-nui (warm west wind) were called upon by Ruawharo and Te Rongo-patahi to assist the waka during the voyage.

The only difficulty the Takitimu seems to have come across occurred at the part of the ocean known as Tuahiwi-nui-o-Hine-moana, where the waves are said to grow to an enormous size. The adze Te Awhio-rangi was taken out of its storage compartment Ahuahu-te-rangi, and while Te Rongo-putahi and Tupai chanted their karakia it was brought to bear down upon the waves to calm the sea. The area in the vicinity of this action was given four names: Tai-wawa, Tai-haro, Tai-wiwi, and Tai-whakahuka.

After surviving Tuahiwi-nui-o-Hine-moana, the waka is said to have landed at Rarotonga, before sailing on to Aotearoa and landing at Whangaparaoa. From Whangaparaoa it was sailed north to Muriwhenua (North Cape), where, after it had been beached, it was rolled on its side by high winds. Next the Takitimu was sailed down the west coast to Hokianga, where the taniwha Arai-te-uru was left to protect the harbour. The waka was then turned north, and after rounding North Cape a second time, proceeded south along the east coast.

Other places visited by the Takitimu included Te Mawahi, Tapuae-o-Rongo-kako, Nuku-taurua (where Ruawharo and his younger brother Tupai left the waka, taking with them the god figure Kahukura, carefully wrapped in the dogskin cloak Tawhiri-rangi), and Whanganui-a-Tara; and in the South Island, Tama-totea (near Lyttelton) and the Waiau River. While approaching the Waiau River, the Takitimu is said to have gone aground on a shoal, but was saved by Te Rongo-patahi who called upon the waves Tai-ahu-puke and Tai-ahuahu to lift the waka clear. The waka was then taken ashore, where it was left on the summit of a hill overlooking a nearby lake. (Andersen also mentions a slight variation on this legend, in which the Takitimu was wrecked at Te Waewae Bay).

Also listed are several places in the south that have names associated with the Takitimu and its crew.

Nga-ra-o-Takitimu	Waimeha Plains
Waimeha stream	a mast of the waka
Otamatea stream	a second mast of the waka
Hokanui hills	flotsam from the wreckage
Otamete or Otamita stream	was originally Otamatea stream

From the *Story of the Takitimu Canoe*, we learn from Tuta Nihoniho, one-time principal rangatira of Ngati Porou, the following details from his tribe's version of the legend. The Takitimu originally belonged to several tribes. Those named were Tini-o-te-Hakuturi, Kopeka-a-rangi, Whakarau-o-Tupa, Tu-taka-hinahina and Te Mangamanga-i-atua. Among the chiefs of these tribes were Whaiuru, Whaiato and Uenuku-kai-tangata. The adze used to fashion the waka was Hui-te-Rangiora, which belonged to Ruawharo and Tupai.

Once the waka had been built, and the adze Hui-te-Rangiora had been returned to its owners, Ruawharo and Tupai were asked to provide men to help drag the great waka from the forest to the shore. This was consented to, and Ruawharo tied his ropes to the inside of the waka, leaving the owners to tie their hauling ropes to the outside. All went to plan during the haul, until the waka reached a steep incline in the path at a point named Te Wiwi. Here Ruawharo was forced to place Manu-tawhio-rangi, the first of his five magic skids, under the waka to assist its progress. The Takitimu was easily moved along the path, because of the skid's magic. Once the waka had been dragged up to the summit of a hill known as Hiwi-ki-Matatera, Ruawharo and Tupai placed four more skids under the hull of the waka. These four skids, named Te Tahuri, Te Take, Hau-puritia, and Maukita, were also magic, and stopped the waka dead in its tracks. No matter how hard the men pulled on the ropes, the waka would not move. It wasn't until Ruawharo and his men turned the waka towards their village that any progress was made. Again the waka was turned towards the village of the Tini-o-te-Hakutari, and for a second time the waka stuck fast.

This second time, the moment the haulers of the Tini-o-te-Hakutari took the full strain of their waka on their ropes, Ruawharo severed the outside ropes with the adze Hui-te-Rangiora, sending them sprawling down the hill. The Takitimu was immediately turned to

Ruawharo's village and dragged effortlessly, with the skid Manu-tawhio-rangi conveying the waka.

Once Takitimu had been launched, it was evident that it was a fine vessel, and preparations were made for an ocean voyage. Ruawharo and Tupai first went to the cave of Ututangi (Timu-whakairia) to acquire the rituals needed for the voyage. There were many rituals to be learnt, and each was used to interact with specific guardians or gods. The following is a list of gods and guardians for whom rituals were known.

atua or gods	Io and Ha (the most superior of the atua); Kahukura, Tama-i-waho, Motipua, Tu-nui-o-te-ika, Tu-korako, Te Po-tua-tini and Hine-pukohu-rangi (lesser atua)
divinities of earth	Ruaumoko, Ruamano, Houmea, Hakikino, Te Oi, Te Ririo and Tara-kumukumu
divinities of ocean	Ruamano, Arai-te-uru, Tutara-kauika, Houmea, Te Petipeti, Te Ranga-hua, Tai-mounu and Tane Rakahia

Paddles were made, and each was given a name: Rapanga-te-ati-nuku, Rapanga-te-ati-rangi, Manini-kura, Manini-aro, Tangi-wiwini and Tangi-wawana. Bailers were also fashioned, including Tipua-horonuku and Tipua-hororangi. Finally, two feather plumes were attached to the stern piece. The higher of the two was named Puhi-kai-ariki, and the one that touched the water was named Puhi-moana-ariki.

It is claimed in some traditions, collected both in Aotearoa and Rarotonga, that the Takitimu returned to Hawaiki shortly after the first southern voyage. As the Takitimu was being prepared for the journey to Aotearoa, Puhi-whanake promised his younger brother Puhi-whakaawe that he would return in the Takitimu to take him on the great southern voyage. Although, according to this version, Puhi-whanake managed to return to Hawaiki from Waiau, he was unable to keep his promise, and the waka never returned to Aotearoa.

ADDITIONAL INFORMATION

The crew

The following ancestors' names have been collected from several sources, and are all said to have voyaged on the Takitimu.

Tamatea-ariki-nui, Tamatea-huatahi-nuku-roa, Tamatea-mai-tawhiti, and in Rarotongan traditions Tamatea-takapini-enua.

Rongokako *Tamatea's father*

Hau-tu-te-rangi	Hine-kau-i-rangi	Hope-hi-tua-rangi
Ira-kai-putahi	Kaewa	Kahu-tua-nui
Karotimutimu	Kiwa	Kohu-para
Manu-tawhio-rangi	Mareao	Matua-iti
Matua-tonga	Mokinokino	Mokomoko
Moko-nui-a-rangi	Ngarangiteremauri	Ngutoro
Puhi-whakaawe	Puhi-whanake	Rau-tahi
Rerehu-rangi	Rongo-mahae-ata	Ruawharo
Taewha-ki-te-rangi	Tahu-potiki	Taikehu
Tamatea-kai-matamua	Tamatea-kota	Tamatea-nui
Tamatea-roa	Tangaroa	Te Aonoanoa
Te Iri-angi	Te Kauru-o-te-rangi	Te Rangi-ka-tatau
Te Rongo-patahi	Te Whakawiringa	Tohi-te-uruangi
Tokitoki-whakaone-tangata		Tua
Tu-ai-te-rangi	Tupai	Tutakahinahina
Uhengapuanaki	Whakaroao	Whatuira

Kohupara and Tupai are said to have been experts at steering voyaging waka. Puhi-whanake and Whatuira were skilled at predicting the weather from the stars at night, and in observing the sun and moon to ensure the waka stayed on track. Mokinokino was given the important task of 'quartermaster', looking after the distribution of food to the priests. Te Rongo-patahi and Ruawharo were the two tohunga given the honour of contacting the gods when their assistance was needed during the voyage. Finally, Kaewa (possibly Taewha-ki-te-rangi) was the bearer of the firesticks.

Tutakahinahina was on board Takitimu, and he disembarked at the Bay of Plenty. It is said that Tamatea did not like Tutakahinahina, and was happy to see him leave the waka.

In a traditon of the Kurahaupo waka, given in *The Coming of the Maori*, it is stated that Taneroroa, daughter of the Aotea waka's Turi, married Uhengapuanaki (Uhenga-ariki, Uwhenga-ariki, Uhenga-pua-nake), who voyaged to Aotearoa on the Takitimu. A legend collected from Wi Pere claims that the Takitimu voyaged from Hawaiki to Tawhiti-nuku, on to Tawhiti-rangi, to Tawhiti-pa-mamao, and to Rarotonga, before finally reaching Aotearoa. Pere goes on to name

Kiwa as the captain of the waka, with other crew remembered being Kahu-tua-nui, Matua-iti, Matua-tonga, and Ruawharo (who owned the waka). In some traditions, Kiwa is claimed to have been the captain of the vessel, although he is more often than not associated with the Horouta.

Kai-heraki is named as one of Tamatea's party in *Treasury of Maori Folklore*. While in the vicinity of the South Island range subsequently named Takitimu, she is said to have wandered off, and was never seen again. Ngati Porou sources quoted by Gudgeon claim the following to have been members of the crew: Te Ariki-whakaroau, Ngarangi-tere-mauri, Tohi-te-ururangi, Te Irirangi, Te Aonoanoa, Te Whakawhiringa, Te Kauru-o-te-rangi, Te Manu-tawhio-rangi and Ruawharo.

Tribes claiming descent from Takitimu include Ngati Kahungunu, Rongowhakaata, Aitanga-a-Mahaki and Ngai Tahu.

According to a version of the tradition supplied to Gudgeon by Rawiri Makaua, the primary occupants of the Takitimu were the gods Tahaia, Tukopiri, Te Whanuapo, Tu-nui-o-te-ika, Tara-kumuku-mu, Poro-hinaki and Tama-i-waho. One of the crew, Tokitoki-whakaone-tangata, left the Takatimu at Tauranga, after which the waka voyaged south to Kaikoura. From the same source, we learn that live eels were also transported on the Takitimu. Tradition says that the eels were released into the Whakatane River.

Ngai Tahu tradition, as given in *The Maoris of the South Island*, states that Tamatea was the captain of Takitimu, and others among the crew were his sons, Ranginui and Kahungunu (although Kahungunu is usually said to have been born in Aotearoa), and the tohunga Ruawharo, Te Rongopatahi and Tupai. Having first dropped people off at Poverty Bay and Hawke's Bay, the waka was sailed south to Whanganui-a-Tara, where Tamatea met Whatonga's son Tara. Next the Takitimu continued south to Murihiku (the Southland region), where the waka struck a reef at the entrance to the Waiau River and was wrecked.

From the book *The Peopling of the North* we learn from Eratara, of Ngati Whatua, that important ancestors of his people migrated to Aotearoa in the Takitimu. Those he claimed to have direct links to the tribe from the Takitimu were Tangaroa, Mareao, and Tua. Other Ngati Whatua sources claim that Mareao brought the toheroa with him, and that he planted the shell-fish on the west coast of the North Island.

The waka

According to one source, prior to leaving Hawaiki the Takitimu was placed under the protection of the gods Kahukura, Tama-i-waho, Tunui-o-te-ika, Hine-korako, Rongomai, Tuhinapo and Ruamano. The seven gods were said to have resided in the cave known as Te Kohurau, and each was assigned a wooden vessel for the voyage. Those responsible for the welfare of the gods during the voyage were Te Rongopatahi, Ruawharo, Tupai, Kohupara, Kaewa, Puhi-whanake, Mokinokino and Whatuira.

The following birds are stated in part two of *Maori Religion and Mythology* as having helped pull the Takitimu to the coast after its construction in the forest: koko, kaka, kereru, tieke, koropio, hore, tititi-pounamu and kakariki.

Ngata suggested the possibility that the Takitimu and the Horouta were in fact double hulls of the one waka. He pointed out that if the two waka were one double waka, it would explain the numerous crew members claimed by both waka. He also stated that he had collected a tradition from the Cook Islands, claiming that the Horouta and the Takitimu had left the Islands as a double canoe. A reference recorded in *Cook Island Origin of the Maori* states that the Takitimu was a vaka purua (double canoe), and that when it sailed to Aotearoa, her captain was Tamatea-takapini-enua.

In one tradition, the Takitimu was built to escape fighting over two cultivations remembered as Tawarua-a-raro and Tawarua-a-rangi.

The following awa-moana chant is recorded in *The Maori Canoe*, and has been credited to the Takitimu.

> Ko wai taku waka?
> Ko Te Puwhenua pea taku waka.
> Ko wai taku waka?
> Ko te ara moana taku waka.
> Ko wai taku waka?
> Ko Uruhau taku waka.
> Ko wai taku waka?
> Ko te take o te rangi taku waka.
> Ko wai taku waka?
> Ko te timu o te rangi taku waka.
> He waka kautere nui, he waka kautere rangi.
> He waka atua no nga rangi taku waka.

He waka tapu taku waka no nga apa rangi.
No nga poutiriao taku waka.
He waka tapu taku waka.
No nga tawhito taku waka.
He waka tapu taku waka.
No Kahukura taku waka.
Ko wai taku waka?
Ko Takitimu taku waka.
He waka no Hine-korako taku waka.
No wai taku waka?
No Tama-i-waho taku waka.
No wai taku waka?
No Maru taku waka.
No wai taku waka?
No Tunui-o-te-ika taku waka.
He waka atua taku waka.
No te ihonga nuku, no te ihonga rangi.
No takere nuku, no takere haea te piere nui.
Haea te piere moana, haea taku ara.
Ko te ara o wai?
Ko te ara o nga apa a rangi.
Haea taku ara, ko te ara o nga tawhito.
Haea taku ara, ko te ara o nga wehenga kauki.
Whakahoru noa ra i te moana waipu
Haea taku ara, ko te ara o Tutara kauika.
Taku ara ko te ara o Ruamano taku ara.
No wai taku ara?
No Arai-te-uru taku ara.
Waerea, wawrea taku ara.
Takoto, takoto te ihu o taku waka nei.
Ki roto i te awa moana o takere nui, o takereroa.
Ka takoto te ihu o taku waka.
I roto i te awa tai heke.
Heke te tai nui, heke te tai roa.
Heke te au kume, heke te au rona.
Heke te au taiparipari ki whea.
Pari ki tawhiti ki tiritiri o te moana tuauriuri . . . e . . . i.
Ka ea, ka ea taku waka i te ihi moana.
Ka ea, ka ea taku waka i te tai nui, i te tai roa.
Ka ea, ka ea taku waka i te ngaru tu, i te ngaru wharewhare.
Ka ea, ka ea taku waka i te tai wharewhare i te tai maranga.

Ka ea, ka ea ki te ihu whenua, ki te tai uru, ki te tai marangai . . .
    e . . . i.
Ka whakaea, ka whakaea taku waka.
Tenei to tapuwae ko te manu ka roha, ko te manu ka tiu.
Ko te manu ka whakaangi ki te ihu whenua.
Ka tau taku waka, ka tau ki take whenua . . . e . . . i.
Ka tere, ka tere tenei waka, he waka no nga pia.
He waka no nga taura, he waka no nga tauir.
He waka no nga ariki, he waka no nga tamaroa.
Ka takoto i runga i te au kume, i te au rona.
I te au whakaea ki tawhiti.
Ki tiritiri o te moana ki te ihu whenua.
Amohia, amohia taku waka e nga kauika o Hinemoana.
Awhitia, awhitia mai nga papa o taku waka e Tutara kauika.
Awhitia mai nga papa o taku waka e te wehenga kauki . . . e.
Takoto, takoto taku ika taki ko Ruamano i taku waka.
Takoto, takoto, e taku ika.
Waerea, waerea te ara moana o taku waka.
Ko koe, e Arai-te-uru, ki roto ki te awa o taku waka o Awarua.
Tahia te au moana, tahia te kare moana.
Tahia te huka moana ki tawhiti muri.
Ki tawhiti whakaaweawe ki te hiku o taku waka.

It is remembered in Rarotongan tradition that a waka called Takitimu transported immigrants to Rarotonga from an unknown homeland. Subsequently a district was named Takitimu in Rarotonga. It is believed that this migration occurred several centuries prior to the migration to Aotearoa.

The following chant was recorded in the magazine *Kahungunu*, and is said to be Te kawa o Takitimu (an incantation to ensure a safe voyage).

Tau ake au ki te tau nei
Ko rua tipua, ko rua tawhito
Ngarua i runga, ngarua i raro
Ngarua i te ihu o Tane, te ihu o Tane
Ko taku waka ko Takitimu
Rere mai te maramara
Ko ihi nui, ko ihu roa, ko te awhiorangi
E ko wai kei runga nei, e tu pawahaiake
E ko au ko Uenuku, e tu pawhaiake

E Rata, e Rata, he aha tau hanga e tu pawhaiake
Inumia te kawa, inumia te takina te kawa
Te kawa o Takitimu
Inumia te waka o tirari
Inumia te waka o tirara
Inumia te waka o Rongokako
Inumia te waka o Tamatea-mai-tawhiti
Haramai te toki
Haumi e
Hui e
Taiki e

The voyage

From *Tikao Talks*, we are told that the Takitimu was accompanied by the waka Arai-te-uru during its southern voyage to Aotearoa. While the Arai-te-uru was wrecked at Matakaea, the Takitimu reached Foveaux Strait, where she went aground at Te Waewae Bay. Those named as being on board the waka include Tamatea (later named Tamatea-pokai-whenua after circumnavigating the land); three of his sons, Tamatea-nui, Tamatea-roa and Tamatea-kai-matamua; and another chief, named Tutakahinahina.

In another version of the southern voyage recorded in *Treasury of Maori Exploration*, it is said that the Takitimu was accompanied by the waka Te Karaerae, whose captain was Te Ahu-ruru. It is also stated in this particular account that the Takitimu was a single-hulled waka.

It is sometimes claimed that when the food ran out during the voyage to Aotearoa, it was decided to sacrifice Ruawharo to feed the starving crew. It is not clear whether Ruawharo was singled out because he was a navigator for the trip, and therefore responsible for the longer than expected voyage, or whether he was unlucky enough to lose a ballot. In either case, it was only his ability to summon assistance from Tangaroa, who provided seafood for the crew, that saved his life.

In ancient lore recorded from a Maori living in Waimate (in the South Island) by J. Herries Beattie, it is claimed that some of the stars used by the tohunga for navigating the Takitimu to Aotearoa were Matariki, Puaka, Meremere and Autahi.

In Best's *The Astronomical Knowledge of the Maori*, we are given the following list of guiding stars: Autahi (Canopus), Tautoru (Orion's Belt), Puanga (Rigel), Karewa (?), Takurua (Sirius), Tawera (Venus as Morning Star), Meremere (Venus as Evening Star), Matariki (Pleiades), Tama-rereti (Tail of Scorpion) and Te Ikaroa (the Galaxy).

Landfall in Aotearoa

In a statement recorded from Matiu Kapa of Kaikohe, and referred to by Best in *Tuhoe: Children of the Mist*, it is said that after the crew of the Takitimu had been unsuccessful at procuring land at Rangaunu, the first landfall, the waka was sailed south, stopping at Aurere on the way. Another source has the Takitimu stopping at Te Mawhai before sailing on to Tapuwae o Rongokako. While at Te Mawhai, it was suggested by Hautu (possibly Hau-tu-te-rangi) that they stay and catch fish. The exact spot was named Toka-ahuru.

From a referrence to the Takitimu in an article from the *Journal of the Polynesian Society*, it is claimed that at one time Tamatea lived at Tarahaukapiti, at the foot of Mount Takitimu.

The Astronomical Knowledge of the Maori, p. 35
The Coming of the Maori, pp. 39, 48, 55, 58.
Fishing Methods and Devises of the Maori, p. 80.
JPS, Vol. 7, p. 111.
JPS, Vol. 12, pp. 52–3.
JPS, Vol. 16, pp. 220, 223.
JPS, Vol. 17, pp. 99–103.
JPS, Vol. 21, p. 26.
JPS, Vol. 24, p. 43.
JPS, Vol. 28, p. 49.
JPS, Vol. 64, p. 189.
Kahungunu, November/December 1992, pp. 16–17.
Maori Art, p. 36.
Maori Lore, pp. 295, 297.
Maori Place Names, pp. 172–84.
Maori Religion and Mythology, part 1, pp. 216–17.
Maori Religion and Mythology, part 2, pp. 116, 548, 574, 594.
The Maori Canoe, pp. 223–5.
The Maoris of the South Island, p. 19.
Nga Moteatea, Vol. 2, p. 269.
Nga Waka, p. 11.
The Peopling of the North, pp. 53–4.
Takitimu, pp. 30–3, 35, 40–4.
Te Ika a Maui, p. 290.
Tikao Talks, pp. 63, 77, 112, 114.
Traditional Lifeways of the Southern Maori, pp. 202, 442.

Transactions of the New Zealand Institute, Vol. 48, p. 453.
Treasury of Maori Exploration, pp. 57, 190, 192, 259.
Treasury of Maori Folklore, p. 224.
Tuhoe: Children of the Mist, p. 688.
Tuwharetoa, p. 55.
Whakatane and District Historical Society, Vol. 4, pp. 16.

TAKOTO

According to Cook Island traditition, the Takoto was encountered by the waka I-tere (later renamed Tainui) during its voyages of the Pacific. Little information is given about the Takoto other than that its captain was Te Ra-tu-iva-iti and that it was voyaging from the Tuamotu Archipelago.

JPS, Vol. 64, p. 193.

TAMA-KORORO
Chatham Islands

The Tama-kororo was one of seven waka left behind in Hawaiki by the Nga Rauru people when they migrated to the Chatham Islands. Only the karakia of these seven waka were taken to the Chathams by Nga Rauru.

JPS, Vol. 5, p. 18.

TANEWAI
Chatham Islands
Name variations: Tane, Tane-kaha, Tanetewa

Built by Akaaroroa from a kauri log found washed up on a beach, the Tanewai is usually acknowledged as being the waka in which Kahu (Kahu-koka) discovered the Chatham Islands. The tradition tells that Kahu's son, Tamauri, dreamt that some logs cut down beside the Rangitikei River to build a waka had drifted out to sea, and after a long journey had washed up on a beach somewhere to the south-east. When Kahu heard of Tamauri's dream, he was sure that it had been a message from the gods telling him to search for land, and arrangements were made. As well as Kahu, the crew consisted of his daughter Hinetewaiwai, Tamauri and several unnamed tribesmen.

The voyage seems to have been uneventful, and the waka successfully landed at a spot they named Kaingaroa, after a place in their homeland. Soon after landing and building shelter, the expedition prepared a garden they hoped would be able to sustain them in the period ahead. Fern seed from a calabash named Te Awhenga, kumara seed from a totara-bark vessel named Rangiuru, and taro were all sown in the soil. However, nothing would grow in the wet, cold climate of the Chathams. Disappointed by their lack of success, several of the migrants, including Kahu and his daughter, turned their backs on the desolate island and chose to return to Aotearoa.

In a short reference to the Tanetewa it is claimed that 'all those who came first in the Tanetewa waka were well skilled in carving'.

JPS, Vol. 23, pp. 75, 81.
The Coming of the Maori, pp. 15–16.
Transactions of the New Zealand Institute, Vol. 1, p. 446.
Treasury of Maori Exploration, pp. 50–1.

TANGIAPAKURA

This was one of three waka in which Nuku-tama-roro and his companions chased Manaia as he fled to Aotearoa in the waka Tokomaru. Along with the outrigger waka Te Houama, the two double waka Waimate and Tangiapakura pursued Manaia from Hawaiki, stopping en route at Rarotonga to take on supplies and water.

With no sighting of the Tokomaru during the voyage south to Aotearoa, the three waka first landed at Arapawa Island in Cook Strait during their relentless seach. It wasn't until Nuku-tama-roro's fleet had ventured north near Mana Island that they finally caught up with the Tokomaru and the speedy outrigger waka Te Houama headed it off until the two double waka could catch up.

The opposing sides engaged in a savage sea battle that lasted well into the late afternoon, at which time it was agreed by Manaia and Nuku-tama-roro to rest for the night and allow their forces enough time to recover from their arduous voyaging and fierce fighting. It was agreed that Manaia and his men would rest ashore, while Nuku-tama-roro and his force would recuperate at anchor in their waka. Special attention was given to Nuku-tama-roro during the night, as he had been wounded in the thigh during the fighting. His tohunga were well aware that he was not only the chief, but the main navigator for their fleet and would be needed for the return voyage home. During the night, while Manaia and most of his exhausted men slept, the tohunga from the Tokomaru, Te Ao-whainga-roa, succeeded in calling up a terrible storm that battered Nuku-tama-roro and his men severely, giving them no chance to rest as they fought the huge seas and driving winds to save their waka from being smashed upon the rocky shoreline.

In the morning Nuku-tama-roro was forced to sue for peace, with his men in no position to recommence the hostilities of the previous day, and he himself still badly wounded. Manaia accepted the proposal for a truce, and an uneasy peace was entered into by the former enemies.

Nuku-tama-roro was well aware of the vulnerability of his men and immediately ordered the two double waka to be dismantled and each converted into two single outrigger waka for the return voyage. After gathering what provisions they could, the crews of the five waka solemnly headed back to Hawaiki.

JPS, Vol. 23, p. 13.
Treasury of Maori Exploration, pp. 44–5.

TAPATAPA-HUKARERE

Name variation: Tapatapa-nukarere

This was one of the waka that Whakatau and his kinsmen sailed in to avenge the murder of Whakatau's brother. (*See* Hakirere.)

Maori Art, p. 37.
Polynesian Mythology, p. 62.

TAPUAE-PUTUPUTU

Tapuae-putuputu is said to have been a name given to Kupe's waka (usually it is recorded as the Matahourua), and it is claimed that rats and a species of fern root that grows at Ohuri in the Hokianga were part of its cargo.

The Peopling of the North, p. 15.

TARAI-PO

The Tarai-po is commonly regarded as the original name of the Kurahaupo waka in Maori tradition. References to the Tarai-po in

Rarotongan and Samoan legends say the waka was built by Orokeu and Oro-inano, brothers of Atonga (Whatonga in Aotearoa-Maori), or by Atonga-atua (Whatonga-atua) himself, respectively. In both legends the storyline follows that of the Aotearoa Maori legend of Rata and the felling of the tree.

In a further note from the Samoan tradition, the Tarai-po was given three additional names: Manu-ka-rere, after birds had transported the newly completed waka from the forest to the front of the waka shed; Pori-o-kare, when it reached the paepae of the waka shed; and finally Te Pori-o-nou, when it had entered the waka shed.

JPS, Vol. 19, p. 142.
JPS, Vol. 21, p. 54.

TATA-TAIORE

Name variation: Tatataeore

The Tata-taiore is often spoken of in oratory as a waka of death, used to convey the souls of the dead to their final resting place. The orator begins by describing the preparation of the waka, including the lashing on of the tauihu (bow-piece) and the placement of white albatross feather streamers on the taurapa (stern). After this has been done the orator will call upon the Tata-taiore to come to collect the soul and take it to Hawaiki, where the ancestors will greet it. The Tata-taiore is also one of several ancestral waka named by Hetaraka Tautahi of Nga Rauru during an interview in 1900 with S. Percy Smith.

The Coming of the Maori, p. 61.
JPS, Vol. 9, p. 213.

TAUIRA

It is claimed that the Tauira made land at Whangaparaoa after voyaging directly from one of the islands in the Cook group. The captain is remembered as Motatau-mai-tawhiti, and other chiefs on board were Rakiroa, Maru-papa-nui and possibly another chief by the name of Tauira. From this waka came the ancestors for the Pane-nehu tribe of Opape, near Opotiki, and of Te Whanau-a-Apanui.

JPS, Vol. 12, pp. 128–9.
Maori Art, p. 36.
Treasury of Maori Exploration, p. 50.

TAWHITI

Although unsubstantiated, it is suggested that the well-known Whiro voyaged to Aotearoa in the Tawhiti. He supposedly made landfall at Oakura on the Taranaki Coast, not far from the spot known as Waipiropiro-a-Whiro.

Whakatane and District Historical Society Inc. Memoir #1, p. 71.

TAWAWAO

Name variation: Tawaowao

Nothing is known about this vessel other than it was very ancient.

A Leaf from the Natural History of New Zealand, p. 49.
Maori Art, p. 36.

TAWIRIRANGI

Name variations: Tahirirangi, Taiwirirangi, Tawhiri-kura, Tawhiri-rangi, Tawhitirangi

The Tawirirangi, with Ngahue (Ngake) as captain, and the Matahourua, under the famous navigator Kupe, were the two waka that chased Te Wheke-o-Muturangi from Hawaiki to Aotearoa in the well-known legend. Having chased the wheke across the Pacific, Kupe and Ngahue were finally able to corner it near Arapawa Island in Cook Strait, where Kupe managed to kill it. After considerable exploration (*see* Matahourua) the two waka returned to Hawaiki with pounamu and preserved moa meat. The tales of their voyage inspired others to follow in their wake to the newly discovered land.

JPS, Vol. 22, p. 126.
Lore and History of the South Island Maoris, p. 10.
Takitimu, p. 18.
The Coming of the Maori, p. 6.
Treasury of Maori Exploration, p. 23

TEREANINI

Name variations: Rereanini, Rereanani

The waka Tereanini was captained by the brothers Rongomai-tuahu and Pouheni, sons of Paikea, and is said to have landed at Whangara near Gisborne.

JPS, Vol. 12, pp. 129–30.
Maori Art, pp. 35–6.

TIHAUWEA

Chatham Islands

This was a waka of witchcraft. It is debatable whether Tihauwea was an actual waka, or a figure of speech, but either way it was named alongside six others (Tama-kororo, Tupu-ngaherehere, Mata-rangi, Tohoro-i-ongongo, Hape and Karangatai) as having been left behind in Hawaiki when Nga Rauru migrated to the Chatham Islands. The Tihauwea's place in Moriori history has been remembered because the karakia of each of the waka left behind was carried to the Chatham Islands with the immigrants.

JPS, Vol. 5, p. 18.

TIKITERE

The following notes were recorded by the Reverend H.J. Fletcher from 'a very old Maori named Erueti, or Edward, living at Oruanui, Taupo'.

> *The captain of the Tikitere was Kahu-pungapunga whose father was Manaia, brother-in-law to Ngatoroirangi. The chiefs along side him on the voyage from Hawaiki were Nga-roto, Manga-harakeke, Te Muriwai and Ati-a-muri, and the crew was said to number thirty. According to tradition, the waka made land at Hauraki.*

JPS, Vol. 24, pp. 26–8.

TIMUAKI

All that is remembered about the Timuaki is that it was one of the earliest waka to voyage to the South Island.

Traditional Lifeways of the Southern Maori, p. 523.

TINANA

The Tinana (later relaunched as Mamaru) landed at Tauroa near Ahipara at the south end of Ninety Mile Beach. The captain, Tumoana, claimed all the lands between Hokianga and Ahipara on the coast and as far inland as Mangamuka and Maungataniwha. Later, Tumoana returned to Hawaiki in the Tinana, leaving behind his daughter Kahutianui and his son Tamahotu. The waka eventually returned from Hawaiki, landing again at Tauroa. According to tradition it had been adzed out a second time and renamed Mamaru. Tumoana's nephew Te Parata was the captain.

Muriwhenua Fishing Report, p. 259.

TOHORO-I-ONGONGO
Chatham Islands

The memory of this waka was kept alive by way of its karakia. The Nga Rauru people had been forced to abandon the Tohoro-i-ongongo along with five other waka as they fled their enemies and voyaged to the Chatham Islands. (*See* Tihauwea.)

JPS, Vol. 5, p. 18.

TOKAKA

The Tokaka was captained by Huri-tini. The only other information recorded was that Aokehu was a passenger and that he settled at Kura-reia.

JPS, Vol. 16, p. 190.

TOKOMARU
Name variation: Tongamaru

There are two distinct traditions featuring the Tokomaru: the migration tradition, and the legend of Manaia fleeing his enemy Nuku-tama-roro and voyaging to Aotearoa.

The following excerpt from an Atiawa lament, as recorded in *The Coming of the Maori*, suggests that Whata was the captain of the

Tokomaru, and that his navigators were Rakeiora and Tamaariki.

> E iri e te hoa i runga o Tokomaru
> Te waka o Whata,
> Na Rakeiora na Tamaariki
> I hoa mai ki uta.
> Huaina te whare ko Maraerotuhia,
> I tu ki Mohakatino.
>
> Recline O friend on Tokomaru,
> The waka of Whata,
> By Rakeiora and Tamaariki
> It was paddled to land.
> The house was named Maraerotuhia
> It stood by the Mohakatino River.

Comments made by Buck after this extract clearly show his acceptance that this passage accurately portrays the facts, in relation to the 'migration Tokomaru'. His attack on the work of Grey (*Polynesian Mythology and Ancient Traditional History of the New Zealand Race*) is quite scathing. He blames Grey's sources for polluting the Tokomaru tradition:

> *The error of Grey's informant commenced with giving the command of the Tokomaru of the fleet to Manaia. He borrowed the stranded whale and the anchor site in the Mokau River from the Tainui tradition. He landed the waka at the wrong river and his local geography was inaccurate. The few lines of lament I have quoted are worth more than the whole text of his published account and I say this for the guidance of students.*

The Tokomaru is said to have first made land in the Bay of Plenty. From this landfall, the waka was sailed north around North Cape, or in some versions, to Tamaki, where it was hauled across the portage between the Tamaki river and the Manukau harbour, before continuing its voyage to the mouth of the Mohakatino River on the west coast. It was at Mohakatino that the tribal house Maraerotuhia was built. From Mohakatino the descendants of the Tokomaru crew spread north to the Mokau River and south to Onukutaipari, these two localities marking the northern and southern boundaries of their lands.

Those tribes descending from the Tokomaru crew include Ngati Tama, Ngati Mutunga, Ngati Rahiri, Manu-korihi, Puketapu, Te Ati Awa and Ngati Maru.

The tohunga Rakeiora made his home in the vicinity of Mohakatino, where he remained and was later deified as the god of the kumara.

In some versions of the legend, when the Tokomaru made landfall on the Taranaki coast the crew found an aboriginal people dwelling there. In the ensuing battles for the land, the Tokomaru people virtually wiped out the original inhabitants.

Other landing places suggested in various accounts of the Tokomaru are Great Barrier Island, Whangaparaoa, Whangara-mai-tawhiti and Tokomaru (Bay) on the east coast, and after voyaging to the west coast, Waitara, Mokau and Tongaporutu.

The anchor of the Tokomaru also has an interesting history. According to Buck, the anchor was 'kept for centuries on a ridge near the south bank of the Mohakatino. It disappeared in later times but was ploughed up by a cousin of mine in a hollow below the ridge where it had been kept. It had evidently been rolled down and covered over by the old people to save it from curio hunters'.

The second legend, wherein Manaia borrows his brother-in-law's waka, the Tokomaru, and flees Hawaiki with Nuku-tama-roro close behind, is claimed by Buck in *The Coming of the Maori* to be highly inaccurate. He states that Manaia lived well before the voyage of the Tokomaru, and that his waka was Tahatuna. The tradition is nevertheless well known, and has come to be regarded in some circles as a legitimate legend.

(For the Manaia–Tokomaru story, *see also* Tangiapakura, Waimate and Te Houama.)

The Coming of the Maori, pp. 52–4, 337.
Echoes of the Pa, p. 119.
Kahungunu, October 1992.
JPS, Vol. 1, p. 227.
JPS, Vol. 46, p. 83.
Maori and English Dictionary, p. 70.
Maori Lore, p. 296.
The Maori–Polynesian Comparative Dictionary, p. 21.
The Story of Te Waharoa, p. 252.
Treasury of Maori Folklore, pp. 201–2.
Suggestions for a History of the Origin and Migrations of the Maori People, pp. 96–7.
Whakatane and District Historical Society Inc. Memoir #1, p. 77.

TOROA

Only the name remains for the Toroa, and that comes from a scrap of information found in 'The Traditions of the Ngai Tahu'.

The Ancient History of the Maori, Vol. 2, p. 179.

TOROA-I-TAI-PAKIHI

The Toroa-i-tai-pakihi was one of the fleet in which Whakatau-potiki and his fellow tribesmen voyaged to avenge the death of Whakatau's brother, Tuwhakararo, at the hands of the Ati-hapai tribe. (*See* Hakirere.)

Maori Art, p. 37.

TOTARAIKARIA

Name variations: Totaraikeria, Totora-karia, Totara-keria

When Ngatoroirangi needed to return to Hawaiki to avenge a curse that his niece Haunga-roa had overheard from the mouth of Manaia, he had the Totaraikaria built to replace the destroyed waka Te Arawa. The adze used to fashion the Totaraikaria was named Hauhau-te-rangi, and it belonged to Tama-te-kapua. (It is stated that this adze was also used to build Te Arawa.)

The waka was launched with the favouring wind Pungawera and managed to reach Hawaiki without mishap, where the battle named Ihumotomotokia was fought.

After successfully defeating Manaia and his tribe, Ngatoroirangi returned to his pa, Matarehua, on Motiti Island in the Bay of Plenty. Soon after returning to his home, survivors of Manaia's tribe who had followed the Totaraikaria arrived and challenged Ngatoroirangi and his people to another fight. The challenge was accepted, and it was agreed to recommence the fighting the following morning. It was also agreed that the challengers would sleep in their waka.

During the night Ngatoroirangi went to Matarehua to build an altar, where he was able to incite Maui, Tawhirimatea, Kahukura and Tangaroa to combine their powers to destroy his enemy, thus ending the war between Manaia's people and his.

JPS, Vol. 1, p. 213.
JPS, Vol. 2, p. 239.
JPS, Vol. 3, pp. 200–1.
Treasury of Maori Exploration, p. 266.
Tuhoe: Children of the Mist, p. 692.

TUAHIWI-O-ATEA

Name variation: Te Iwi-o-Atea

This was the canoe in which Hui-te-rangiora voyaged across the Pacific during his years exploring the vast ocean. It is unclear whether or not he visited Aotearoa, but in one legend it is claimed that Hui-te-rangiora experienced huge seas and encountered seals, bull-kelp and 'a sea of arrowroot' that later historians have suggested to be an ice-floe.

From Polynesian traditions we can add that Hui-te-rangiora led a migration fleet of seven waka east from his homeland to Tawhiti-roa. Of the seven only five are remembered by name: Tuahiwi-o-Atea, Uru, Te Moana-taupuru, Te Karearea and Kura-nui. An account of the actual waka describes them as being 'all built up and sewn waka, with top sides'.

JPS, Vol. 22, pp. 15, 59.
Treasury of Maori Exploration, p. 17.

TUAROPAKI

The captain of this waka was Te Atua-raunga-nuku, a younger brother of Turi, captain of the Aotea. The descendants from this waka are numbered among Nga Rauru.

JPS, Vol. 16, p. 190.

TUMUWHENUA

This waka was in the fleet known as the Heke-o-Naia, which left Hawaiki with thirteen canoes and voyaged through the Pacific, stopping off at Iva (possibly Nukuhiva), Tahiti and Rarotonga. At Rarotonga the crews of five waka, including the Tumuwhenua, decided to remain and colonise. This left the Tainui, Te Arawa, Mataatua, Kurahaupo, Takitimu, Okotura and Muriwhenua to travel on to Aotearoa. (It is doubtful whether the above-named fleet actually sailed together, and it is generally accepted that the majority of them voyaged to Aotearoa independently.)

JPS, Vol. 11, p. 252.

TU-NUI-A-RANGI

The Tu-nui-a-rangi is credited with bringing the Ngai Tahuhu people to Aotearoa and is said to have landed first at Motu-Kokako in the Bay of Islands, then travelled on along the coast to Ngunguru and to have finally stopped at Whangarei. The tradition of the Ngai Tahuhu migration is as follows.

It was while the ancestors of Ngai Tahuhu and Ngati Awa were living on their island in the Pacific that they noticed that the annual migration and return of the kuaka (curlew) followed a specific route. Knowing it to be a land bird, they deduced that it must be flying to an unknown southern land. It was decided by the chiefs of both tribes to each build a waka to voyage in the direction of the bird's flight to search for the new land. After much argument among Ngai Tahuhu it was decided that the younger brother of the chief Te Kokako would lead the expedition, and Te Kokako himself would stay behind and guard the women, children and the old in the event of trouble. Te Kokako agreed publicly to stay behind to perform the duty given to him, but formed a plan to secretly hide himself in the waka shortly before the voyage was to commence. In all the excitement Te Kokako easily avoided detection as he concealed himself in the bow of the waka, and it wasn't until the trip was well under way that he was detected. It took all of Te Kokako's younger brother's persuasive powers to save Te Kokako from a watery grave — those in the bow argued to throw him overboard for leaving those at home undefended. It was agreed to allow Te Kokako stay on board. Te Kokako however, saw fit to plot his revenge on those who wanted him dead, and quietly sat in the bow section constructing his plan.

The Tu-nui-a-rangi first made land at Motu-Kokako, an island in the Bay of Islands named after Kokako himself, and then voyaged south to Ngunguru, where it was decided to resupply the water stores. Because the seas were running high and it was too dangerous to beach the waka, Te Kokako volunteered to take a handful of men from the bow and swim to shore to fill the empty water containers.

The swimmers managed to reach shore, but were unable to find any water suitable for drinking. Te Kokako, putting his plan into action, thrust his bewitched spear into the sand and instantly a spring appeared. His thirsty companions drank deeply and almost immediately fell to the ground and died. Te Kokako returned to the waka empty handed and told his brother that the waters were poisonous and suggested that they had better sail on. This was agreed to and the Tu-nui-a-rangi sailed south to Whangarei where the crew were able to beach their vessel safely. From here Ngai Tahuhu are said to have spread and inhabited all the land from the Auckland Peninsula to approximately eighty kilometres north of Whangarei.

JPS, Vol. 12, pp. 125–7.

TUPU-NGAHEREHERE
Chatham Islands

This waka is said to have been abandoned by Nga Rauru when they fled to the Chatham Islands. The other waka left behind were Tama-kororo, Mata-rangi, Tohoro-i-ongongo, Hape, Karangatai and Tihauwea (a waka of witchcraft). Only the karakia of each waka was taken to the Chathams by the migrants.

JPS, Vol. 5, p. 18.

TURORE
Chatham Islands

The Turore was a waka of witchcraft (E waka makutu) according to Moriori tradition. No further information was found.

JPS, Vol. 5, pp. 17–18.

TU-TE-PEWA-A-RANGI

Name variations: Hurepureiata, Huripureiata, Nuku-te-pewa-raki, Rangi-pato-roa, Te-o-te-poa-raki, Terehapua, Tu-te-pa-wharangi, Tu-te-paerangi, Tu-te-pewa, Tu-te pewha-raki, Tu-te-pewa-rangi, Tu-te-pewa-wharangi, Tu-te-pe-wawharangi, Tu-te-poa-raki

The above names are given in various accounts as the waka in which

Ruatapu attempted to take his revenge on Uenuku. The story is as follows.

Kahutia-te-rangi (later known as Paikea) and Ruatapu were sons of Uenuku, a high chief in Hawaiki. But while Kahutia was first born and of a chiefly union, Ruatapu had been born of a slave wife. Despite this significant drawback, both sons were accorded the same education from the whare wananga of their people. As the boys grew they developed in different ways, with Kahutia specialising in things tapu, as became his high position in the tribe. Ruatapu, on the other hand, was skilled in many other ways which were thought highly of by the tribesmen, including a great skill with manu-tuku-tuku (kites).

At some point before manhood, Ruatapu brought great shame upon himself and his family. Some say Ruatapu climbed up on the roof of Uenuku's house to retrieve a manu-tukutuku while unbeknown to him Uenuku rested below, thus being seen to trample on the sacred head of Uenuku. In the other well-known version, Ruatapu was caught with Uenuku's sacred comb — also a serious breach of the lore of his tribe and family. Whatever the event, Uenuku could not hold back his rage, and screamed at his son, 'How dare you, child of a slave, do this thing.' Totally humiliated in front of the tribe and with the words still ringing in his ears, Ruatapu formed a plan of revenge. He arranged the use of a large fishing waka from Haeora (Hae-ora), and after carefully cutting a hole in the hull and plugging it, invited all the young chiefs of the tribe to join him in a fishing expedition. As soon as the waka was well out from land, Ruatapu unplugged the hole and let the waka fill with water. In the confusion that followed, Ruatapu was able to kill all the young chiefs except Kahutia, who was able to evade his murderous half-brother by calling out a karakia to two of his ancestors, who sent forth a whale to rescue him. It is this action that led Kahutia-te-rangi to be known as Paikea (the name of the type of whale that saved him) from that time on.

As Kahutia escaped, Ruatapu called after him: 'Tell our people that in the eighth month I will return in some form to fulfil my revenge.' Legend says a great tidal wave swept the land and killed almost all of the people except Paikea and his two sons, Whatuia-te-ramarama and Tahuipotiki, who fled to the highest peak on Hikurangi.

The Tutepawharangi is also named as the waka Tane used to hang the ten heavens above the earth by suspending them one above the other, with the topmost connected to a huge pole. After he had laid the pole across the highest heaven, Tane returned to earth in his waka, Tutepawharangi. His work completed, he gave ownership of the waka to the family of Tama-rereti. It can still be seen as a cluster of stars among the constellations and is known as Te Waka-a-Tama-rarereti. It is said Ruatapu's vessel was named after this waka.

Another piece of related information is recorded as follows:

> *Ruatapu is well known in the South. The name of the waka of which he drew the plug was Tu-te-pewha-raki, and his club was named Kahutia-te-raki. There is an extremely lengthy song about this affair. Extra big waves around the Murihiku coasts are still called 'Ruatapu' in memory of him. [Or rather, in memory of the flood Te tai o Ruatapu.]*

The Ancient History of the Maori, Vol. 3, pp. 14, 23, 48, 50–1.
JPS, Vol. 12, p. 129.
JPS, Vol. 28, p. 50.
Maori Art, pp. 36, 37.
Tikao Talks, pp. 29, 56.
Traditional Lifeways of the Southern Maori, p. 433.

TU-TE-PUEHU

Name variation: Tu-te-pueha

Nothing is known about this waka other than its name, although there is an obvious similarity between this name and that of the Tu-te-pewa-a-rangi.

Maori Art, p. 37.
Treasury of Maori Exploration, p. 266.

TUWHAKARARA

Information about this waka is scarce, although it is remembered that it had voyaged to Aotearoa 'flying on the wings of the wind' in the very earliest of times, and that the crew placed two huge sharks, Mako-tipua and Mako-horopekapeka, in their wake to try and prevent anyone from following them. It is also claimed that the crew of the Tuwhakarara fought with Maui's men in Hawaiki, either before or after the voyage.

Our Southernmost Maoris, p. 157.
Treasury of Maori Exploration, p. 12.

TUWHENUA

There are two waka with this name: one brought leprosy to Aotearoa and landed in Northland (*see* Moe-Karaka), while the second landed in the Bay of Plenty. Tamatea-mai-tawhiti is said to have been its captain, and he found a tribe at Motu living under the protection of the chiefs Tu-whara-nui and Manawa-ki-aitu.

Tuhoe: Children of the Mist, p. 685.

UANGA-KI-O-KUPE, TE

Only the name of this waka has been recorded.

A Leaf from the Natural History of New Zealand, p. 49.

URIWERA

No information was found other than that it was a waka belonging to Ngati Awa.

Maori Art, p. 37.

URUAO

Name variation: Uruao-kapua-rangi

The full name of this waka, Uruao-kapua-rangi, is given in a karakia that was supposedly recited during its construction. The two adzes used to shape the waka are also named: Te Hae-mata and Whiro-nui. It is stated that these adzes belonged to Uru-te-ngangana. The name Urunui features in the same karakia, and it has been suggested that the Uruao may have been double-hulled; if so, then Urunui was probably the name of the second hull.

The Uruao was originally owned by Tai-te-whenua of Te Kahui-tipua. Tai-te-whenua later gave the waka to Matiti, who in time gifted it to a man of the Waitaha tribe named Rakaihautu (Rakaihaitu), who had married his daughter Waiariki-o-Aio.

Legend states that some time after the voyage of the waka Huruhurumanu to Aotearoa, it was decided by Rakaihautu to migrate to the great southern land. This is backed up by the following statement recorded in *Traditional Lifeways of the Southern Maori*: 'the Huruhurumanu is said to have smoothed out the seas for the Uruao and all other waka to follow'.

Those of note on board the Uruao were Rakaihautu and his wife Waiariki-o-Aio; their son Raki-houia and his wife Tapu-iti; and Matiti. Also accompanying them were several crewmen, of whom Noti and Nota have been remembered by name. Tribes descending from the Uruao are Waitaha, Te Kahui-tipua and Te Kahui-roko, and it is claimed that they were 'the same kind of people as Toi and Rauru' (from the same island?). Te Kahui-tipua carried with them the kauru (cabbage-tree root) and Te Kahui-roko had kumara.

Before leaving Hawaiki, Matiti is said to have travelled to Tautari-nui-o-Matariki to learn from Takopa the lore of the stars. He was told that the stars Wero-i-te-ninihi, Wero-i-te-kokoto and Wero-i-te-aumaria portend a season of fair weather and signalled an ideal time for voyaging. (There is no indication of the time of year that these three stars were present, but it was probably in the southern hemisphere's early summer months). During the long voyage south it is recorded that the people on board recited karakia at night, and each morning rainbows appeared to point the way to their destination.

The following quote was found in an article commenting on the genealogy of Rakaihautu and refers to the voyage of the Uruao.

This waka was brought hither from the Tapahanga-a-Taiehu, over the waves of the sea. As they approached they found the sea connected with the sky. The axes which were used in severing them were named Kapa-ki-tua and Tua-uru-rangi: by their means the waka got through, and this land was settled.

According to tradition the Uruao first made landfall in the north, but found the island to be fully inhabited by Te Ope-ruarangi. After sailing down the east coast of the North Island the waka finally made landfall in the South Island. Kai-koura was the first named South Island stopping place for the Uruao, and it was possibly there that three shrines were established: Te Puna-hau-aitu, Te Puna-maria and Te Puna-karikari. It has been suggested that one of these shrines may have been erected for Matua-a-rua, the god entrusted with protecting the waka and crew during the voyage.

Also at Kai-koura, Rakaihautu and several of the crew left the waka and travelled inland. During the journey, Rakaihautu is credited with creating several of the South Island lakes with his ko (digging stick), Tu-whakaroria. The most prominant were Rotoiti and Rotoroa in the Nelson District; Pukaki, Ohau and Tekapo in South Canterbury; Wanaka and Hawea in Otago, and Wakatipu and Te Anau in Southland. From Te Anau, Rakaihautu and his group ventured down the Waiau River until they reached the ocean at Te Ara-a-Kiwa (Foveaux Strait). In the vicinity of Te Waewae Bay on the southern coast, Rahaihautu left Noti and Nota to look after the newly explored lands. Those remaining in the group now turned north and proceeded along the coastal plains where they found the going much easier.

In the meantime, the Uruao had been left with the reduced crew to sail further south under Raki-houia. At least two places were named during this southern leg of the waka's voyage. Te Whata-kai-o-Raki-houia (the food storehouse of Raki-houia) was the name given to the cliffs at Kai-koura, after the crew had gathered bird eggs from the cliffs to supplement their provisions. Still further south a species of eel called hao was caught by the crew at the mouth of a river, which was subsequently named Waihao. This part of the Canterbury coastline was later called Nga Poupou-o-te-Raki-houia after the posts used to build the eel weirs. It was while Raki-houia and his companions were busy catching eels in the South Canterbury rivers, that they were reunited with Rakaihautu and the rest of the crew as they made their way along the flat plains of the eastern seaboard.

The following description of the crew accompanies a rare claim that the Uruao made landfall at Wharekahika, Hicks Bay: 'this waka was manned by a crew of very dark-skinned people, speaking a foreign language, who settled at Matakaoa but were quickly absorbed by the local inhabitants, viz, the Wahine-iti'. (The statement that the crew were quickly absorbed by the Wahine-iti is almost certainly incorrect, however, as in every other tradition the crew settle in the South Island.)

Echoes of the Pa, p. 121.
JPS, Vol. 3, p. 14.
JPS, Vol. 22, pp. 19–20.
JPS, Vol. 27, p. 138–40, 142, 145.
Maori Place Names, p. 122.
Traditional Lifeways of the Southern Maori, p. 202.
Treasury of Maori Exploration, p. 52.
Treasury of Maori Folklore, p. 418.

URUNUI

This waka is remembered in a karakia by name only, but notes after the text suggest it may have been the second hull of the Uruao.

JPS, Vol. 22, p. 20.

WAI-KERERE

The only mention of the Wai-kerere states that it was lost at sea during the voyage from Hawaiki to Aotearoa.

Maori Art, p. 37.

WAI-MATE

The Waimate was one of three waka used by Nuku-tama-roro to chase Manaia, in his waka Tokomaru, to Aotearoa. It is described as having been a double waka and capable of transporting a large number of warriors. (*See* Houama for an account of the voyage to Aotearoa and the outcome of the hostilities between Manaia's force and that of Nuku-tama-roro.)

JPS, Vol. 23, p. 13.

WAIPAPA

The Waipapa was commanded jointly by Kai-whetu and Wai-rere, and it made land on the northern shores. The exact point of landing is contested. Traditions place the final resting place as alternatively Rangiaowhio, Taipa or Oruru, all places within the sheltered waters of Doubtless Bay.

Treasury of Maori Exploration, p. 266.

WAKA-A-AORANGI

Name variation: Waka-a-Aoraki

It is said that after the separation of Rangi-nui-e-tu-nei and Papa-tu-a-nuku (sky father and earth mother), some of their offspring voyaged down to earth in a waka named Te Waka-a-Aorangi. Those that are remembered from the crew are Aorangi, Rangiroa, Rangirua and Rarangiroa, each of whom had a South Island mountain named after them (Mount Cook, Mount Dampier, Mount Teichelmann and Mount Silberhorn respectively).

In some versions of the tradition it is claimed that the waka became the South Island, and the crew are still sitting in their positions to form each of the mountains named.

Treasury of Maori Folklore, p. 53.
Two Worlds, p. 239.

WAKA-A-RANGI

Name variation: Waka-a-raki

The Waka-a-rangi features strongly in South Island legends. It was a very early visitor to Aotearoa and like so many of the earlier waka, its history has been largely forgotten. Tradition does not name where the Waka-a-rangi made landfall when it reached Aotearoa, but claims that it was transported to the sky by Tane, where it is apparently still visible as a constellation in the southern night sky. The group of stars was known variously to the Maori as Te Waka-ahua-a-raki, Te Whakaahua-o-te-waka-a-raki and, by some, Te Waka-a-tama-rereti. S. Percy Smith and Hare Hongi suggested that the constellation was Scorpio.

In one South Island account, it has been stated that this waka came from a place remembered as Patu-nui-o-aio, and was renamed Wakahuruhuru after its launching due to its buoyancy and speed.

Maori Place Names, p. 120.
Traditional Lifeways of the Southern Maori, p. 426.

WAKAATUA

Wakaatua is the name given by southern Maori to one of the very first waka to visit Aotearoa. Kopuwai, Pouakai, Pukutuaro, Komakohua and Te Karara-haurau were among the crew, and each of them has been remembered in folklore.

Our Southernmost Maoris, p. 156.

WAKANUI

Nothing is known of the Wakanui other than that it landed in the Bay of Plenty.

Treasury of Maori Exploration, p. 266.

WAKAORUREA

Name variation: Wakaororua

The Wakaorurea, captained by Te Huruhuru-manu and Te Potiki-tautahi, is said to have landed at Te Awamutu, near Lake Forsyth on Banks Peninsula. The crew settled in North Canterbury. The district to the west of present-day Christchurch was known as Te Whenua-o-Huruhuru-manu, while the eastern seaboard and surrounding land was known as Te Whenua-o-Te-Potiki-tautahi (these areas are now known as Ohurumanu and Otautahi respectively).

While Te Potiki-tautahi remained in the general vicinity of Te Awamutu, Te Huruhuru-manu explored further afield in the Wakaorurea, sailing to the west coast. It was while Te Huruhuru-manu was sailing along the coast that his waka was wrecked at Big Reef (approximately halfway between Awarua and Cascade Point, just to the south of Jackson Bay). Apparently no one was lost during the wrecking, and the survivors were able to live in peace on the lands adjacent to the reef.

It was quite some time after this mishap that Te Huruhuru-manu moved north to Central Westland to live out his days. Legend says that the petrified waka is still visible as part of the reef.

Our Southernmost Maoris, pp. 156–7.
Treasury of Maori Exploration, pp. 7–8.

WAKARINGARINGA

The captain of the Wakaringaringa was Mawakeroa, and the waka landed near the mouth of the Kaupokonui River on the South Taranaki coast. The descendants of the crew are Ngati Ruanui.

JPS, Vol. 16, p. 190.
Maori Lore, p. 296.

WAKATANE

The only information recorded about this waka is that it landed at a spot called Whakapoukorero, to the west of Matata.

Treasury of Maori Exploration, p. 266.

WAKIRERE

Name variation: Whakirere

It is unclear why this waka should be remembered in Maori tradition, as it is claimed that it voyaged only as far as Mata-te-ra in order to obtain taro root for cultivation, and then returned to Hawaiki without landing in Aotearoa. One possible reason is that it is claimed that the Waki-rere was the last waka to leave Hawaiki, and therefore must have reached Aotearoa for its story to be known.

Maori Lore, p. 296.
Treasury of Maori Exploration, p. 266.

WAO, TE

Te Wao was the waka in which Whatonga and Tu-rahui were lost at sea during a race at Hawaiki. The race had started promisingly enough for Whatonga, Tu-rahui and their crew, with their skill at sailing and the speed of Te Wao seeing them well out in front. As the race continued and the day wore on, the winds began to strengthen alarmingly, and before they could return to land they were caught in a fierce gale. The crew had more than enough to do trying to keep Te Wao afloat in the strong winds and raging seas, and when night came with a thick fog, they found themselves hopelessly lost. The waka was buffeted before the storm for some time before the crew was finally able to make landfall on an island often named in tradition as Rangiatea. Here they stayed and intermarried with the local people.

In the meantime the grandfather of Whatonga and Turahui, Toi-te-tuatahi, had commenced a search in his waka Paepae-ki-Rarotonga for Te Wao, voyaging first to Rarotonga, then on to Samoa, south to the Chatham Islands and finally on to Aotearoa, where he touched land at Hauraki. The waka was then sailed to Whakatane, where Toi-te-tuatahi and his crew built the pa named Kapu-te-rangi and settled down.

Whatonga and Tu-rahui eventually decided to return to Hawaiki.

With sufficient provisions for the return voyage they set off with those others in the crew who also wished to return. After an uneventful journey, the returning crew had an emotional homecoming, at which time the voyage of Toi-te-tuatahi was conveyed to Whatonga and Tu-rahui. It was decided that the two grandsons would search for Toi and his crew, and soon another of Whatonga's waka, Te Hawai was readied to follow Toi's journey.

(*See also* Te Hawai and Kurahaupo.)

The Maoris of the South Island, pp. 15–16.
Treasury of Maori Exploration, p. 62.

WHAKAREWAREWA

The Whakarewarewa is one of several waka mentioned by Hetaraka Tautahi during an interview with S. Percy Smith conducted in 1900. The following list of waka are all claimed by Tautahi to have been ancestral waka of the Nga Rauru tribe: Takere-o-Toitahi, Rangi-tako, Hakirere, Karamu-raunui, Tatataiore, Whakarewarewa, Rangi-totohu, Rangi-kekero and Pahi-tonoa.

JPS, Vol. 9, p. 213.

WHAKA-TERETERE-TE-URU-RANGI

It was from the Whaka-teretere-te-uru-rangi that Tama-nui-a-raki killed his unfaithful wife, Rukutia, as she swam out to him. Rukutia had run off with a man named Tu-te-koro-panga, but was soon disillusioned as he continually beat her. She managed to contact Tama-nui-a-rangi and asked him to take her back. It was arranged that he would call on a pre-arranged night and Rukutia would swim out to the waiting waka. On the chosen night the waka arrived and Rukutia swam out to it, but as she approached it Tama-nui-a-rangi grabbed her hair and with one blow of his adze severed her head from her body. The waka was given the name Whaka-teretere-te-uru-rangi after the beauty of the red garments that Tama-nui-a-rangi wore on this occasion.

The Ancient History of the Maori, Vol. 2, p. 45.

WHATU-RANGA-NUKU

Name variations: Whatu-a-ranga-ngutu, Whatu-a-ranga-nuku, Whatu-a-rangi-nuku

The crew of this waka are believed to have comprised those who could not be transported on Te Arawa due to numbers. The Whatu-ranga-nuku landed on the Wairarapa coast where it was met by hostile inhabitants who badly burned the chief Tauwera (Tahuwera). It is not known what happened to the waka, but the crew are said to have carried Tauwera overland on a litter to Otamarakau in the Bay of Plenty where they settled. The tribe was later renamed Waitaha-Turauta.

JPS, Vol. 12, p. 59.
Maori Art, p. 37.
Te Arawa, p. 491.

WHATU-TE-IHI

In the Nga Puhi tradition of Whiro, Whatu-te-ihi was the waka that was being built when Whiro murdered the boy Ngana-te-irihia and hid his corpse among the discarded wood chips. Before long the boy's body was discovered and a fierce battle commenced between Whiro's people and those of the boy's father. In the battle Whiro and his warriors virtually annihilated their enemy. (*See also* Hotu-taihi-rangi.)

JPS, Vol. 7, pp. 36–7.

WHIRITOA

The Whiritoa was one of five waka used when Whakatau-potiki and his warriors sailed to Hawaiki to avenge the death of Whakatau-potiki's brother Tuwhakararo. (*See also* Hakirere.)

Maori Art, p. 37.

NGA WAKA A MAUI

Auraro-tuia
Hauraro-tuia
Mahatu-ki-te-raki
Mahunui
Mahutu-ki-te-raki
Mahutu-ki-te-rangi
Nukutaimehameha
Nuku-tai-memeha
Nuku-tai-mimiha
Pirita-o-te-rangi, te
Riu-o-mahu
Riu-o-mahue
Rua-o-mahu
Rui-o-mahui
Tahu-a-rangi
Tama-rereti
Tane-a-rangi
Tau-rangi

The above waka are all linked to the great Maui, voyager of the Pacific, and with each comes a different angle on the story of Maui and his voyage to Aotearoa. In the case of the Auraro-tuia, it is said that Tutaranaki was the builder of both this waka and the Tane-a-rangi (Tahu-a-rangi or Tau-rangi) and that they were hewn from the trunk of one tree: 'It was in this waka, Auraro-tuia, that Maui was fishing with his hook Piki-rawea, with its barb Awenga (Awhenga) or Maire-hua-kai, when he fished up land. He is said to have used alternatively his own blood, or the body of a man named Aki or Heke for bait, and his line Tiri-tiri-ki-matangi to haul up his catch.' A second version, collected and recorded in the same volume of *Ancient History of the Maori*, says that 'Tahu-a-rangi was the name of the waka in which Maui sat when he pulled the land up out of the ocean, and Tonganui was the name of his fish hook'.

In the centennial publication *Tahi Rau Tau o te Marae o Mohaka*, Maui's waka is named as Nukutaimehameha, and its resting place is atop Hikurangi.

According to our ancestors 'Hui te Rangiora' sailed the oceans of Tangaroa in his waka 'Tuahiwi o Atia' . . . He returned to Hawaiki & told the people of the lands he had seen. This inspired his mokopuna Maui to sail the ocean for his king 'Ama tai Atea'. His route was south to Tupuai, Rurutu, Rimatara, Rarotonga, Rimitera & Aotearoa. Ngati Porou say his waka Nukutaimehameha is on 'Hikurangi te Maunga'. The people of this waka were Mamoe, Tuehu, Tahurangi, Pokepoke, Hamoamoa, Patupaiarehe & Tuepe. These people were the custodians of Maui's fish. They were collectively known as Ngati Ui (Kui, Pui, Hui) depending on dialect.

In *Nga Moteatea* there is a waiata from Ngati Kahungunu which starts:

Alas, that you should die upon this new waka,
Here is your waka, 'tis Nuku-tai-memeha,
The waka befitting your journey to the hereafter.
That waka was of your ancestor Maui,
From which he fished up this widespread land.

In Ngata's explanations following the waiata he states: 'Nuku-tai-memeha.— The waka of Maui-potiki from which he fished up the Fish-of-Maui (North Island of New Zealand)'.

Another waka associated with Maui is Mahunui. Hukateke is remembered as the tohuka (tohunga) on the Mahunui, and it is said he uttered a karakia known as Ranga Whenua during the long weary search west and south. After Maui returned to Hawaiki he sent back the Mahunui to Aotearoa under the command of Tara-o-tu with instructions to place the waka in the exact centre of the South Island, where it is sometimes said to remain in a petrified state in the Harper Range. Other crew remembered as having voyaged with Maui are Ui and Wi, who were left to guard the land. Their names are remembered through landmarks at the mouths of the Oreti River and Mataura River respectively. Kui is another name listed which is very possibly a variation of Ui.

In Beattie's book *The Maoris and Fiordland* the following passage is given:

> *It is interesting to know that Maui's two sailing masters, Te Hehe and Te Whena, came from a maritime tribe with the intriguing name of Kati-hau-itiiti (people of the slight breeze). This brings up the involved story of Maui's waka for this voyage, and I record it subject to correction. As far as I can piece it together the story runs that in a land beyond the sky a waka with a name like Mahu-tu-ki-te-raki belonged to Te Hehe (also called Hehe-ue), who was the seventh in descent from the great god of war, Tu-mata-ueka, and he brought it to Maui, who renamed it Mahunui, and set off on an exploring voyage.*

James Cowan adds the following short note in an article on names for the South Island:

> *Mahutu-ki-te-rangi, said by the Moeraki Maoris to be an ancient name of the Middle Island, and was originally that of a waka. It is mentioned in the following fragment of an old haka:* —
>   'Kowai tou waka e —
>   E Heu E! i manu atu ai —
>   Ko Te Raka-a-matua a-i —
>   Ko Mahutu-ki-te-rangi e.'
> *By some Maoris this waka is said to be identical with that called Mahunui.*

It should also be noted that there was a waka by the name of Mahuhu-ki-te-rangi which landed in the Tai Tokerau district, and it is possible that that waka and the one mentioned in the quote above are the same, with the facts and spelling of the name having altered slightly over time in the two South Island traditions.

Ancient History of the Maori, Vol. 2, pp. 114, 116–17.
JPS, Vol. 14, p. 46.
Maori Art, p. 31.
The Maoris and Fiordland, p. 15.
Nga Moteatea, Vol. 3, p. 283.
Our Southernmost Maoris, pp. 145, 156.
Tahi Rau Tau o te Marae o Mohaka, p. 4.
Tikao Talks, p. 64.
Treasury of Maori Folklore, p. 135.
Tuhoe: Children of the Mist, p. 940.

NGA WAKA A RATA

Aniu-waru
Aniwa-niwa
Niwa-reka
Niwa-ru
Niwharu
Pakawai
Puniu
Punui
Punui-o-Rata
Riwaru
Riwharu
Tuirangi

These waka are all named as belonging to the well-known Rata. According to one version, Rata built his waka because his grand father Tawhaki had been killed by Matuku-tangotango and Pou-a-hao-kai, and he was desperate to voyage to their land and avenge Tawhaki's death. Rata, determined to build a voyaging waka, entered the sacred domain of Tane-Mahuta to cut down a massive tree. He was so impatient that he neglected the appropriate incantations and sacred rites before felling one of Tane's trees. That night, as Rata slept, Tane was so furious at this unimaginable insult that he ordered the creatures of the forest to stand the tree once again in its former magnificence among the other trees.

In the morning, when Rata returned to the site of the tree he had laboured over for so long the previous day, he found to his astonishment that it was standing as if no adze had ever touched it. Enraged that all his work had been undone, he immediately began to cut at the tree with his adze. After a second long day of toil, the great tree again lay on the forest floor and once again Rata returned to his whare to rest and sleep. The next morning he returned to his work site yet again only to see the massive tree standing proud as if it had not been touched in a thousand years.

Once again he laboured throughout the day to prepare the tree he was so desperate to have, and as he laboured at his work, he devised a plan to discover who had been interfering with the tree each night. As night fell he left the site as usual, but instead of returning to his whare to sleep, he hid himself in the nearby bush, waiting eagerly. Soon after his departure the insects and birds returned to piece together the many woodchips that littered the surrounding forest floor. Rata confronted the workers of Tane and demanded an explanation as to why they were repeatedly disrupting his efforts to build a waka. The birds and insects advised him of his gross insult to Tane-Mahuta and of the order to re-erect the tree each day. Rata, totally shamed by his actions, returned to his village to learn the appropriate incantations and rituals. In due course he returned to the great tree and after completing the correct ceremony cut down the giant tree easily. That night, as Rata lay sleeping, Tane's creatures constructed a great voyaging waka for him, which he named Aniu-waru.

A further note in *Maori Art* says that Rata's waka had three names, marking three stages in the waka's contruction: Riwharu, Tuirangi and Pakawai, respectively.

The Ancient History of the Maori, Vol. 1, p. 77.
The Ancient History of the Maori, Vol. 3, p. 3.
JPS, Vol. 7, p. 39.
Maori Art, p. 29.
Nga Moteatea, Vol. 3, p. 441.
Treasury of Maori Folklore, p. 180.

THE MAPS

The maps on the following pages provide a rough guide to the locations of the main places referred to in the text.

Map 1: Northern North Island
Map 2: Western North Island
Map 3: Eastern North Island
Map 4: Southern North Island/Northern South Island
Map 5: Southern South Island
Map 6: Chatham Island

Not all places have been located.

THE MAPS

Map 1

Map 2

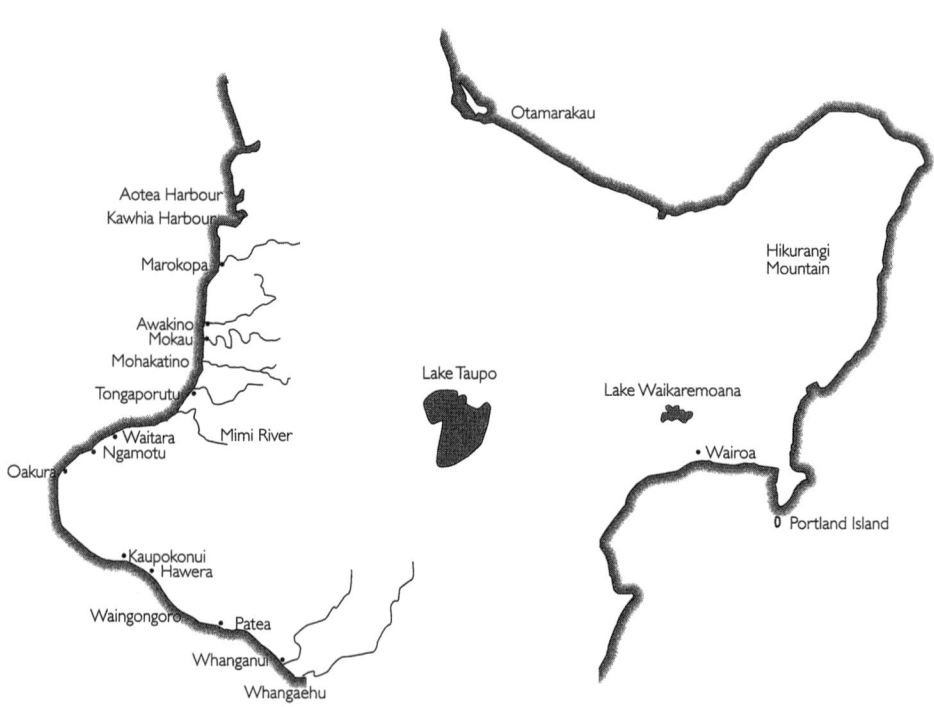

Map 3

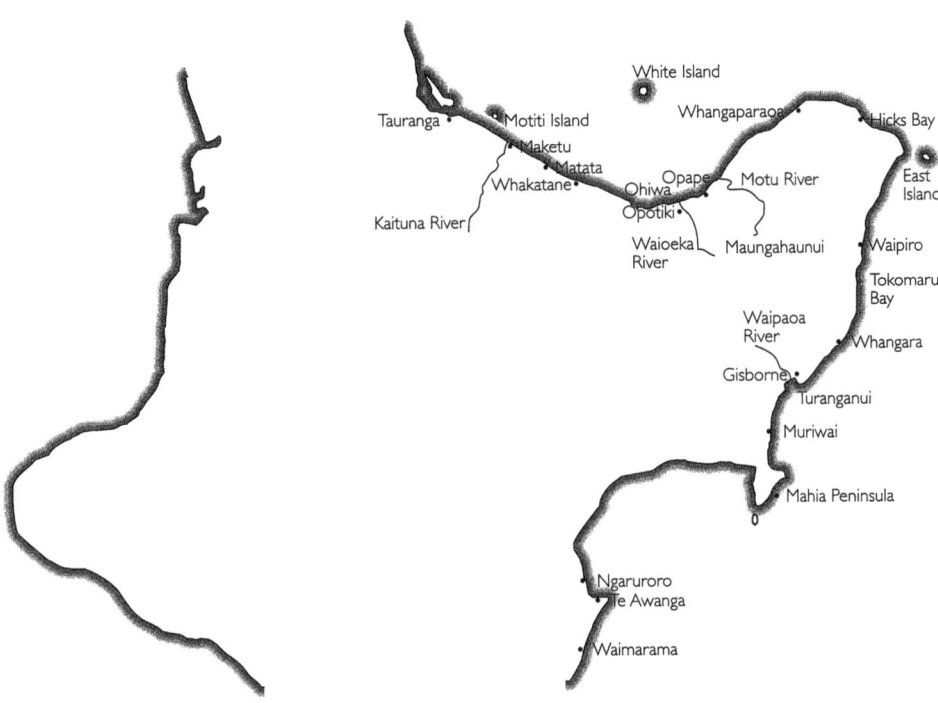

NGA WAKA O NEHERA — The first voyaging canoes

Map 4

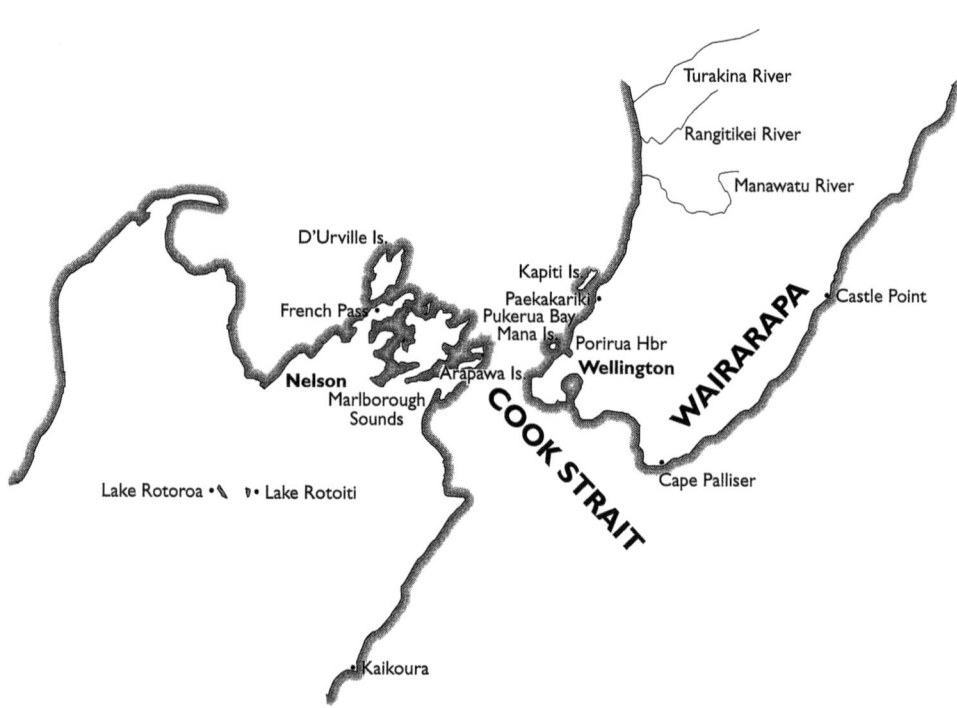

Map 5

Map 6

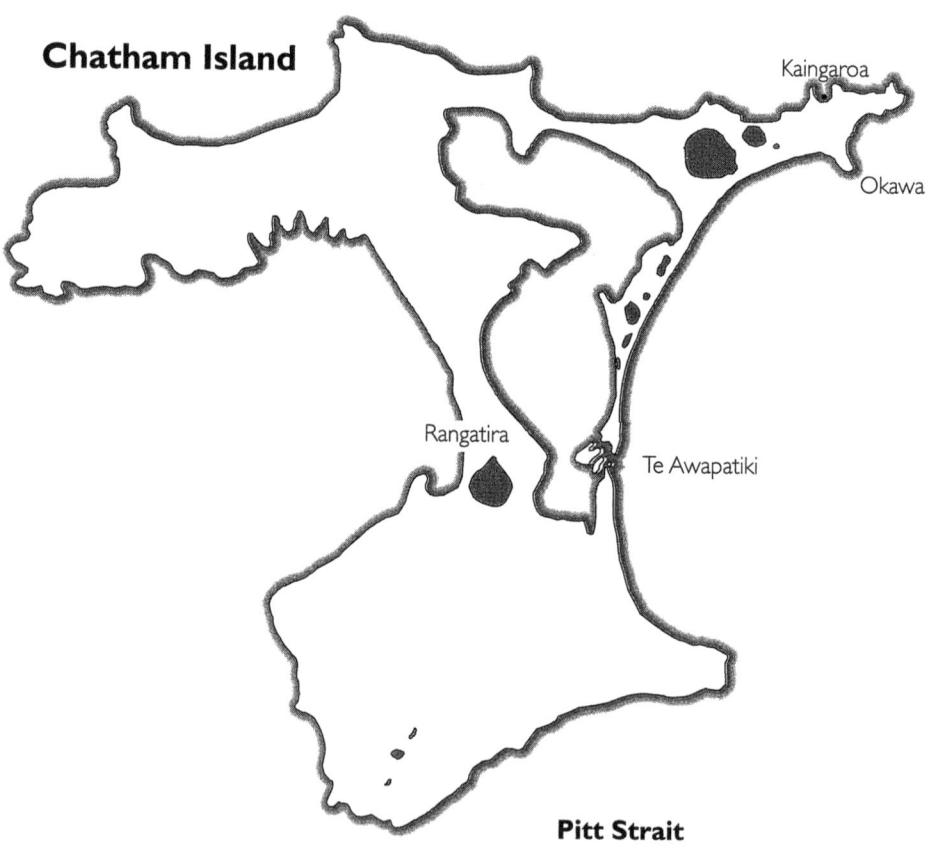

BIBLIOGRAPHY

Note: This bibliography is arranged alphabetically by title rather than author, to reflect the references in the main text. Books are listed first, followed by volumes of the Journal of the Polynesian Society, Whakatane and District Historical Society Memoirs and other publications.

Books

The Ancient History of the Maori, Volumes 1-5, Best, E., 1886, Wellington, Government Printer.

The Astronomical Knowledge of the Maori, Best, E., 1886, Wellington, Government Printer.

The Coming of the Maori, Buck, P., 1987, Wellington, Whitcoulls Limited.

Echoes of the Pa, Proceedings of the Tairawhiti Maori Association, 1932, Gisborne, Gisborne Publishing Company.

Fishing Methods and Devices of the Maori, Best, E., 1977, Wellington, Government Printer.

Folklore and Fairytales of the Canterbury Maori, Beattie, J.H., 1957, Otago, Otago Daily Times.

Forest Lore of the Maori, Best, E., 1977, Wellington, Government Printer.

Fragments of Ancient Maori History, Aoterangi, W., 1923, Auckland, Champtaloup and Edmiston.

The Great New Zealand Myth, Simmons, D.R., 1976, Wellington, A.H. & A.W. Reed.

Hawaiki: A New Approach to Maori Traditions, Orbel, M., 1985, Christchurch, Canterbury University Press

Hawaiki: The Original Home of the Maoris, Smith, S., 1921, Auckland, Whitcombe and Tombs

Historic Maketu, Tapsell, E., 1940, Rotorua, Rotorua Morning Post Printing House.

History and Traditions of the Taranaki Coast, Smith, S.P., 1910, New Plymouth, Thomas Avery.

How the Maoris Came to Aotearoa, Dansey, H.D.B., 1947, Wellington, A.H. & A.W. Reed.

In Ancient Maori Land, Best, E., 1896, Rotorua, F.F. Watt, Hot Lakes Chronicle Office.

A Leaf From the Natural History of New Zealand, Taylor, R., 1848, Auckland, J. Williamson.

Legends of the Maori, Vol. 2, Pomare, M., 1987, Papakura, Southern Reprints.

Lore and History of the South Island Maoris, Taylor, W.A., 1952, Christchurch, Bascands Limited.

The Lore of the Whare Wananga, Vol. 2, Smith, S. Percy, 1915, New Plymouth, Thomas Avery.

The Maori, Best, E., 1924, Wellington, Harry H. Tombs Limited.

Maori Agriculture, Best, E., 1976, Wellington, Government Printer.

Maori and English Dictionary, Taylor, Rev. R., 1848, Auckland, George T. Chapman, Publisher.

Maori Art, Hamilton, A., 1896, Wellington, The New Zealand Institute.

The Maori as He Was, Best, E., 1924, Wellington, Dominion Museum.

Maori Life in Old Taranaki, Houston, J., 1965, Wellington, A.H. & A.W. Reed.

Maori Lore: The traditions of the Maori people, with the more important of their legends, Izett, J., 1904, Wellington, Government Printer.

Maori Place Names, Andersen, J., 1942, Wellington, The Polynesian Society of New Zealand.

Maori Religion and Mythology, Vol. 1, Best, E., 1976, Wellington, Government Printer,

Maori Religion and Mythology, Vol. 2, Best, E., 1982, Wellington, Government Printer.

The Maori Waka, Best, E., 1976, Wellington, Government Printer.

The Maori–Polynesian Comparative Dictionary, Tregear, E., 1891, Wellington, Lyon and Blair.

The Maoris and Fiordland, Beattie, J.H., 1949, Dunedin, Otago

BIBLIOGRAPHY

Daily Times and Witness Newspapers Co. Limited.
The Maoris of the South Island, Pybus, T.A., 1954, Wellington, A.H. & A.W. Reed.
Moriori: A People Rediscovered, King, M., 1989, Auckland, Viking.
The Morioris of the South Island, Beattie, J.H., 1941, Dunedin, Otago Daily Times and Witness Newspapers Co. Limited.
Nga Iwi o Tainui, Biggs, B., 1995, Auckland, Auckland University Press.
Nga Moteatea, Vol. 2, Ngata, A., 1974, Wellington, A.H. & A.W. Reed.
Nga Moteatea, Vol. 3, Ngata, A., 1970, New Plymouth, Masterprint Press Limited.
Nga Waka Maori, Nelson, A., 1991, Wellington, IPL Publishing Group.
Our Southernmost Maoris, Beattie, J.H., 1954, Dunedin, Otago Daily Times and Witness Newspapers Co. Limited.
The Peopling of the North, Smith, S.P., 1898, Wellington, Whitcombe and Tombs Limited.
Polynesian Mythology and Ancient Traditional History of the New Zealand Race, Grey, G., 1885, Auckland, H. Brett, Evening Star Office.
Rangitane, McEwen, J.M., 1990, Auckland, Heinemann Reed.
Sir Apirana Ngata Memorial Tribute, The Polynesian Society, 1951, Wellington, The Polynesian Society.
Sketches of Ancient Maori Life and History, Wilson, J.A., 1894, Auckland, Champtaloup and Cooper.
Songs and Tales of the Sea Kings, Stimson, J.F., 1957, Portland, Maine, The Anthoensen Press.
The Story of Aotea, Hammond, Rev. T.G., 1924, Christchurch, Lyttelton Times Co. Limited.
The Story of Te Waharoa, Wilson, J.A., 1907, Christchurch, Whitcombe and Tombs Limited.
Suggestions for a History of the Origin and Migrations of the Maori People, Fenton, F.D., 1885, Auckland, H. Brett, Evening Star Office.
Tahi Rau Tau o te Marae o Mohaka, Mohaka Marae and Centennial Committee, 1986, Mohaka, Mohaka Marae and Centennial Committee.
The Tail of the Fish, Kereama, M., 1968, Auckland, Maxwell Printing Co. (N.Z.) Limited.
Tainui, Kelly, L.G., 1949, Wellington, The Polynesian Society.

Tainui Sexcentennial Waka Celebration, Winiata, M., 1950, Hamilton, Turangawaewae Maori Adult Education Committee and Tainui Sexcentennial Waka Celebrations Committee.
Tai Tokerau, Keene, F., 1988, Whangarei, F. Keene.
Takao Talks, Beattie, J.H., 1990, Auckland, Penguin Books.
Takitimu, Mitchell, J., 1944, Wellington, A.H. & A.W. Reed.
Te Arawa, Stafford, D., 1991, Auckland, Reed Books.
Te Ika a Maui, Taylor, Rev. R., 1974, Wellington, A.H. & A.W. Reed.
Te Roroa, Waitangi Tribunal Reports, 1992, Wellington, Brooker and Friend Limited.
Thames and the Coromandel Peninsula 2000 Years, Williams, Z. and J., 1994, Thames, Williams Publishers
Traditional Lifeways of the Southern Maori, Beattie, J.H., 1994, Otago, University of Otago Press.
Treasury of Maori Exploration, Reed, A.W., 1977, Wellington, A.W. & A.H. Reed.
Treasury of Maori Folklore, Reed, A.W., 1963, Wellington, A.W. & A.H. Reed.
Tuhoe: Children of the Mist, Best, E., 1925, New Plymouth, Thomas Avery and Sons Limited.
Tuwharetoa, Grace, J.T., 1992, Auckland, Reed Publishing.
Two Worlds, Salmond, A., 1991, Auckland, Viking.
We the Navigators, Lewis, D., 1972, Wellington, A.H.& A.W. Reed.

Journal of the Polynesian Society

Volume 1.212, *Maori Migrations to New Zealand*, Gudgeon, W.E., 1892.
Volume 2.25, *The Genealogy of the Pomare Family of Tahiti*, from the papers of the Rev. J. M. Orsmond, 1893.
Volume 2.109, *Notes on the Paper by Timi Wata Rimini, on the fall of Pukehina and other pas*, Gudgeon, W.E., 1893.
Volume 2.119, *He Waiata Whanai Ariki, a chant at the offering of first-fruits*, Hare Hongi, 1893.
Volume 2.149, *The Coming of Kupe From Hawaiki to New Zealand*, Te Whetu, 1893.
Volume 2.186, *The Kurahaupo Waka*, Te Kahui Karaehe, 1893.

Volume 2.231, *The Coming of Te Arawa and Tainui Waka From Hawaiki to New Zealand*, Takaanui Tarakawa (translated by S. Percy Smith), 1893.
Volume 3.9, *Genealogy of Te Mamaru Family of Moeraki*, Northern Otago, New Zealand, Smith, S. Percy, 1894.
Volume 3.46, *Maori Migrations*, no. 2, Gudgeon, W.E., 1894.
Volume 3.65, *The Coming of Mata-atua, Kurahaupo, and Other Waka From Hawaiki to New Zealand*, Takaanui Tarakawa (translated by S.Percy Smith), 1894.
Volume 3.105, *The Taro*, Hammond, Rev. T.G., 1894.
Volume 3.199, *Explanation of Some Matters Referred to in the Paper, 'The Coming of the Arawa and Tainui Waka From Hawaiki to New Zealand'*, Takaanui Tarakawa, (translated by S. Percy Smith), 1894.
Volume 4.33, *The Moriori People of the Chatham Islands: Their Traditions and History*, Shand, A., 1895.
Volume 5.16, *The Moriori People of the Chatham Islands: Their Traditions and History*, Shand, A., 1896.
Volume 5.113, *The Lament of Te Rangi-Mauri for Tonga-Awhikau*, Karepa-te-Whetu, (translated by Hare Hongi), 1896.
Volume 7.32, *Notes on T. Tarakawa's 'The Coming of the Mata-atua Waka From Hawaiki'*, Tutaka-Ngahau, 1898.
Volume 7.36, *Concerning Whare-kura: Its Philosophies and Teachings*, Hare Hongi, 1898.
Volume 7.59, *Te Tatau-o-te-po*, W. Te Kahui Kararehe (translated by S. Percy Smith), 1898.
Volume 7.111, *Kiwa, the Navigator*, Tregear, E., 1898.
Volume 9.211, *The Aotea Waka*, Hetaraka Tautahi and Werahiko Taipuhi, (translated by S. Percy Smith), 1900.
Volume 10.107, *Te Whanga-nui-a-Tara*, Best. E., 1901.
Volume 11.179, *The Whence of the Maori*, part 1, Gudgeon, W.E., 1902.
Volume 11.252, *The Whence of the Maori*, part 2, Gudgeon, W.E., 1902.
Volume 12.51, *The Whence of the Maori*, part 3, Gudgeon, W.E., 1903.
Volume 12.120, *The Whence of the Maori*, part 4, Gudgeon, W.E., 1903.
Volume 12.166, *The Whence of the Maori*, part 5, Gudgeon, W.E., 1903.

Volume 14.46, *Some Middle Island, N.Z, Place Names*, Cowan, J., 1905.
Volume 14.96, *The Coming of Tainui*, Cowan, J., 1905.
Volume 14.167, *Maori Superstition*, Gudgeon, W.E., 1905.
Volume 16.134, *History and Traditions of the Taranaki Coast*, Chapter two, Smith, S. Percy, 1907.
Volume 16.189, *History and Traditions of the Taranaki Coast*, Chapter five, Smith, S. Percy, 1907.
Volume 16.221, *The Story of the Takitimu*, Cowan, J., 1907.
Volume 17.1, *History and Traditions of the Taranaki Coast*, Chapter seven, Smith, S. Percy, 1908.
Volume 17.99, *The Story of the Takitimu Waka*, Hare Hongi, 1908.
Volume 19.142, *The Rarotongan Version of the Story of Rata*, Savage, S., 1910.
Volume 19.206, *The Moriori People of the Chatham Islands: Their Traditions and History*, Shand, A., 1910.
Volume 21.26, *The Return of Takitimu Waka to Rarotonga*, Smith, S. Percy, 1912.
Volume 21.39, *Extracts From Dr. Wyatt Gill's Papers*, Gill, Rev. W.W., 1912.
Volume 21.152, *The History of Horouta Waka and the Introduction of the Kumara into New Zealand*, Mohi Turei, 1912.
Volume 22.8, *The Lore of the Whare Wananga*, Chapter one, H.T. Whatahoro (translated by S. Percy Smith), 1913.
Volume 22.118, *The Lore of the Whare Wananga*, Chapter three, H.T. Whatahoro (translated by S. Percy Smith), 1913.
Volume 22.196, *The Lore of the Whare Wananga*, Chapter five, H.T. Whatahoro (translated by S. Percy Smith), 1913.
Volume 23.9, *The Lore of the Whare Wananga*, Chapter six, H.T. Whatahoro (translated by S. Percy Smith), 1914.
Volume 23.70, *The Lore of the Whare Wananga*, Chapter seven, H.T. Whatahoro (translated by S. Percy Smith), 1914.
Volume 23.198, *The Lore of the Whare Wananga*, Chapter nine, H.T. Whatahoro (translated by S. Percy Smith), 1914.
Volume 24.12, *The Lore of the Whare Wananga*, Chapter ten, H.T. Whatahoro (translated by S. Percy Smith), 1915.
Volume 24.26, The Story of Kahu-Pungapunga, Fletcher, Rev. H.J., 1915.
Volume 24.42, *The Lore of the Whare Wananga*, Chapter eleven, H.T. Whatahoro (translated by S. Percy Smith), 1915.
Volume 24.98, *Traditions and Legends Collected From the Natives*

Volume 24.98, *Traditions and Legends Collected From the Natives of Murihiku*, Beattie, J.H., 1915.
Volume 26.144, *The Land of Tara and They Who Settled It*, Best, E., 1917.
Volume 27.10, *The Land of Tara and They Who Settled It*, Best, E., 1918.
Volume 27.137, *Traditions and Legends Collected From the Natives of Murihiku*, Beattie, J.H., 1918.
Volume 28.48, *Traditions and Legends Collected From the Natives of Murihiku*, Beattie, J.H., 1919.
Volume 28.111, *The Account of Kupe and Tainui*, Graham, G., 1919.
Volume 29.162, *Two Hawaiki Place Names at Kaikoura*, South Island, N.Z., Cowan, J., 1920.
Volume 29.215, *Uvea and Futuna Islands*, Smith, S.P., 1929.
Volume 31.56, *Te Ngutu-au*, Graham, G., 1922.
Volume 34.177, *Te Toka-tu-whenua*, Graham, G., 1925.
Volume 34.292, *The Burning of Te Arawa*, Best, E.,1925.
Volume 34.386, *Toi and Rakaihaitu*, (notes and queries, no author named), 1925.
Volume 44.36, *Aotea*, Houston, J., 1935.
Volume 46.37, *The Stone Anchors of the Matahorua, Tokomaru and Tainui Waka.*, Godber, A.P., 1937.
Volume 46.83, *'Correspondence'*, Skinner, W.H., 1937.
Volume 48.186, *Mahuhu*, Graham, G., 1939.
Volume 59.335, *The Io Cult — Early Migration-Puzzle of the Waka*, Ngata, A.T, 1950.
Volume 60.80, *Tainui*, Graham, G., 1950.
Volume 64.189, *Cook Island Origin of the Maori*, Kelly, L.G., 1955.
Volume 66.232, *The Story of Kupe*, Himiona Kaamira (translated by Bruce Biggs), 1957.
Volume 75.189, *The Early Tradition of the Whakatane District*, Roberton, J.B.W., 1966.

Transactions of the New Zealand Institute

Volume 1.446, *Proceedings*, Tareha, 1868.
Volume 4.94, *Third Paper on Moas and Moa Hunters*, Haast, J., 1872.

Volume 7.91, *On a Moa-hunter Encampment*, Haast, J., 1874.
Volume 9.15, *Notes on the Traditions and Manners and Customs of the Mori-oris*, Travers, W.T.L., 1876.
Volume 22.75, *The Moriori*, Tregear. E., 1889.
Volume 32.352, *The Ceremony of Rahui: Part Two*, White, T., 1899.
Volume 37.121, *Notes on Ancient Polynesian Migrants*, Best, E., 1904.
Volume 37.159, *The Early History of the Morioris*, Mair, G., 1904.
Volume 48.447, *Maori Voyagers and Their Vessels*, Best, E., 1915.

Whakatane and District Historical Society

Te Tini o Toi, Halbert, R.W., 1961, Whakatane, Whakatane and District Historical Society Inc. Memoir #1.
Traditions and History, Roberton, J.B.W., 1964, Whakatane, Whakatane and District Historical Society Inc. Memoir #3.
A Consecutive Account of the Traditional History of the Whakatane District, Roberton, J.B.W., 1975, Whakatane, Whakatane and District Historical Society Inc. Memoir #4.
The Mataatua Question, Lyall, A.C., 1975, Whakatane, Whakatane and District Historical Society Inc. Memoir #7.
Te Whakatohea: A Part History, Lyall, A.C., 1974, Whakatane, Whakatane and District Historical Society Inc. Memoir #8.
Some Notes on Bay of Plenty Traditions Relating to Archaic People, Stafford, D.M., 1960, Whakatane, Whakatane and District Historical Society Inc. Vol. 8.

Magazines and other publications

Kahungunu Magazine, October, 1992, Havelock North, Kahungunu Publications Limited.
Kahungunu Magazine, November/December, 1992, Havelock North, Kahungunu Publications Limited.
Muriwhenua Fishing Report, Waitangi Tribunal Reports, 1989, Wellington, Government Printer,

INDEX

Note: This index is in three parts. The first part contains place names referred to in the text; the second contains name variants for the waka in the main alphabetical listing; and the third part is an index to the Chatham Islands waka.

Places

Admiralty Bay 97
Ahipara 81, 176
Ahuahu 54, 55, 93, 94, 99, 138
Ahuahu (Mangaia) 111
Ahuriri 156
Aitutaki 64, 104, 150
Aotea 19, 22, 23, 117, 128, 147
Aotea (Great Barrier Island) 93, 111, 178
Arahura 99, 110, 115, 157
Arahura River 65, 152
Arapawa Island 61, 171, 174
Araura (Aitutaki) 64, 104, 150
Aropaki 89
Atiu 152
Aurere 169
Avaiki 47
Awaawakino 108
Awakino 114, 149
Awanui 156
Awanui-a-rangi River 94
Awarua 15, 190

Banks Peninsula 190
Barretts Reef 97, 98
Bay of Islands 94, 181
Bay of Plenty 44, 71, 185, 190, 193
Big Reef 190

Cape Colville 38
Cape Palliser (Te Kawakawa) 97, 98
Cape Rodney 102
Cape Runaway 38, 138
Cascade Point 190
Castlepoint (Rangi-whakaoma) 97

Chatham Islands 24, 50, 67, 69, 70, 83, 85, 101, 109, 110, 111, 115, 119, 120, 121, 122, 125, 129, 130, 131, 170, 171, 175, 176, 182, 191,
Cook Islands 26, 82, 149, 152, 165, 173
Cook Strait (Raukawa) 61, 93, 94, 99, 171, 174
Cuvier Island (Repanga) 38, 77, 93

D'Urville Island 61
Devonport 139
Doubtless Bay 82, 188

East Cape 67, 78, 82
East Coast 71, 93, 112
East Island (Whanga-o-kena) 82

Fiji 84
Flat Island (Tuhua) 114
Forsyth, Lake 190
Foveaux Strait (Te Ara-a-Kiwa) 168, 187
French Pass (Te Au-miti) 129

Gisborne 156, 175
Great Barrier Island (Aotea) 93, 111, 178
Great Mercury Island (Ahauhu) 54, 55, 93, 94, 99, 138
Greytown 97

Ha-wai 139
Hampden 25
Harper Range 196

215

Hataitai Beach 98
Haupapa-nui-a-tau 65, 109
Haupapanuiatau 132
Hauraki 175, 191
Hauraki Gulf (Tekapamoana) 44, 45, 139, 145, 147
Hawaiki 16, 19, 24, 25, 26, 27, 28, 31, 32, 38, 40, 45, 46, 48, 50, 51, 52, 54, 56, 59, 61, 62, 67, 68, 71, 74, 75, 79, 80, 84, 86, 89, 99, 100, 101, 103, 104, 106, 107, 108, 109, 110, 110, 112, 113, 114, 115, 116, 117, 118, 120, 123, 125, 128, 128, 130, 131, 137, 141, 143, 153, 154, 158, 160, 161, 163, 165, 170, 171, 172, 173, 174, 175, 176, 178, 179, 180, 183, 184, 186, 188, 195-6, 193, 195
Hawaiki Rangi-atea 49
Hawaiki-rangi 95
Hawea 187
Hawera 47
Hawke's Bay 164
Henderson Valley 111
Herekino 93
Heretaunga 55
Hicks Bay 187
Hikurangi 114, 130, 183, 195
Hiwi-ki-Matatera 161
Hohonu 152
Hokanui hills 161
Hokianga 68, 80, 99, 104, 105, 147, 160, 172, 176
Hokianga Harbour 105
Horanui-a-tau 65, 109, 132
Horowhenua 72
Huiakama 54
Huka Falls 68
Hukarangi 121

Island Bay 94
Iva 47, 100, 103, 180
Iva-nui 63

Jackson Bay 190
Jacksons Head 97

Kaihau-o-Kupe 99
Kai-hinaki 25
Kaikohe 169
Kaikoura 55, 114, 164, 186, 187
Kaikoura Coast (Te Ahi-kaikoura-a-Tama-ki-te-rangi) 152
Kaingaroa 171
Kaipara 23
Kaipara Heads 77, 79
Kaitaia 156
Kaituna River 39
Kapiti Island 67, 114
Karikari Peninsula 81
Katikati 39
Kaupokonui River 190
Kawa 148
Kawhia 19, 22, 45, 114, 137, 140, 146, 147, 148, 149
Kerikeri 98
Kermadec Islands 22, 75, 88, 129
Kirikino 28
Koharau 165
Kohi Point 89
Kotiwhatiwha 22
Kuporu (Upolu of Samoa) 84
Kura-reia 176

Lyall Bay 98
Lyttelton 160

Mahia 71, 113
Mahia Peninsula 68, 73, 156
Mahia-mai-Tawhiti (Mahia Peninsula) 68
Makaro (Ward Island) 98
Makeakea 156
Maketu 38, 39, 45, 46, 71, 116
Mana Island 62, 98, 99, 171
Mana-aotea 122
Manawatu 73, 114
Mangaia 111
Mangamuka 176
Mangati 20
Mangonui 131
Mangonui Harbour 131
Manuae 64, 150, 114, 146, 147

INDEX

Manukau Harbour 23, 139, 145, 147, 148, 177
Maraekura 23
Maraetai 145
Marlborough 75
Marokopa 114
Marquesas 47
Mata-te-ra 78
Matakaea (Shag Point) 25, 168
Matakaoa 187
Matakitaki 97
Matarehua 179
Matata 47, 59, 112, 130, 191
Matata Lagoon 88
Mataura River 196
Matauri Bay 91
Matiu (Somes Island) 98
Maungahaumi 55
Maunga-roa 133
Maungataniwha 176
Mercury Bay 24, 56
Milford Sound 114
Mimi 149
Mimi River 140
Moehau 38, 45, 114
Mohakatino 178
Mohakatino River 177
Moharuru (Maketu) 71
Moioio Island 97
Mokau 20, 114, 140, 149, 178
Mokau River 140, 177
Moreroa 122
Motiti Island 179
Motiwhatiwha 22, 75
Motu 32, 55, 139, 185
Motu-Kokaka 181
Motutapu 44, 139
Motutaputeranga 94
Mount Cook 189
Mount Dampier 189
Mount Silberhorn 189
Mount Smart (Rarotonga) 139, 145
Mount Takitimu 169
Mount Teichelmann 189
Murihiku 164, 184

Muriwai 55
Muriwai lagoon 56
Muriwhenua 71, 88, 93, 160

Nelson 22, 117, 129
New Plymouth 149
Ngamotu 64, 109, 114, 132
Nga Poitu-o-te-kupenga-a-Taramainuku 45
Nga Poupou-o-te-Raki-houia 187
Nga Rango-e-rua-o-Tainui 148
Nga-ra-o-Takitimu 161
Ngaruroro River 156
Ngaruru-kai-whatiwhati 31
Niao 46
Ninety Mile Beach 156
North Cape 54, 63, 71, 78, 79, 145, 147, 156, 160, 177
Northland 71, 185
Nui-o-Wara 95
Nui-o-Whiti 95
Nuku-te-Varovaro (Rarotonga) 111
Nukuhiva 47, 180
Nuku-roa 84
Nukutaotao 122
Nukutaurua 55, 73, 113, 122, 156, 160

Oakura 20, 23, 72, 101, 174
Oeunuku 148
Ohau 187
Ohiwa 74, 78, 111, 123
Ohiwa Harbour 31, 112
Ohuri 172
Ohurumanu (Te Whenua-o-Huruhuru-manu) 190
Okahu 120
Okawa 122
Okoutuku 48
Omamari 81
Omeheu 59
Onukutaipari 177
Opape 108, 173
Opotiki 31, 108, 112, 139, 147, 173
O-potiki-mai-tawhiti 32

Opotiki River 112
Oraka 156
Oreti River 196
Oruanui 175
Oruru 188
Otago Heads 127
Otahuhu 139, 139, 147
Otamarakau 193
Otamatea Stream 161
Otamete 161
Otautahi (Te Whenua-o-Te-Potiki-tau-tahi) 190
Otengi 81, 131

Paekakariki 62
Pakarae 154
Pae-kawa 157, 158
Pakirikiri 56
Palliser Bay 97
Papa-a-waka-o-Tamatea-ariki 67
Pararae River 156
Paremata 98
Parengarenga 78
Paringatai 149
Pari-nui-te-ra 31
Patea 20, 22, 23, 47, 70, 99, 100, 114, 128
Patea River 22, 128
Patu-nui-o-aio 63
Pikopiko-i-whiti 56, 95, 106, 118, 137, 142, 155, 158
Piopiotahi 115
Pitt's Strait 110
Pokerekere 108
Pokotakina 93
Poretu 122
Porirua Harbour 98
Portland Island (Waikawa) 156
Pouakai Ranges 101
Poverty Bay 52, 164
Pukaki 187
Puke-hapopo 57, 118
Purakau 89
Putiki 67

Queen Charlotte Sound 97

Raglan Harbour 147
Rangatapu 125, 126
Rangaunu 79, 169
Rangaunu Harbour 82
Rangiaowhio 188
Rangiatea 191
Rangiawhia 81
Rangi-kapua 129
Rangiora Point 98
Rangitahua 19, 22, 72, 73, 74, 75, 88, 129
Rangi-tahuahua 22
Rangitaiki River 59, 88
Rangi-tawhi (Sunday Island) 129
Rangitikei 114
Rangitikei River 170
Rangitira 122
Rangitoto 44, 145
Rangi-whaka-oma 66, 126
Rangi-whakaoma (Castlepoint) 97
Rarotonga 24, 43, 47, 47, 67, 71, 72, 85, 88, 100, 103, 114, 119, 137, 144, 145, 160, 163, 167, 171, 180, 191, 195
Rarotonga (Mount Smart) 139
Rarotonga (Nuku-te-Varovaro) 111
Raukawa (Cook Strait) 61, 93, 94, 99, 171, 174
Rehuroa 154
Rekohu 121
Reponga (Cuvier Island) 38, 77, 93
Rimatara 195
Rimitera 195
Riripo Beach 81
Rongo-rupe 22
Rotoiti 187
Rotoroa 187
Rurima 117
Rurutu 195

Samoa 111, 191
Shag Point (Matakaea) 25
Sinclairs Head 98
Somes Island (Matiu) 98
South Bay 152
South Canterbury 67

INDEX

Sunday Island (Rangi-tawhi) 22, 88, 129

Tahiti 47, 61, 100, 103, 180
Tahuarangi 89
Tahurimanuka 109, 123, 125, 131
Tai-harakeke 67
Taipa 81, 131, 188
Taiti 64, 150
Taiti-iva-iti 63, 149
Tai-Tokerau district 81
Takapaukura 75
Takitimu Ranges 164
Takou 78, 88, 94
Takou Stream 91
Tama-i-ea (Te Rangaatamatea) 129
Tamaki 116, 139, 139, 145, 147, 177
Tamaki Isthmus 111
Tamaki River 139
Tamaki West Head 145
Tamaki-Manakau 147
Tama-totea 160
Taporapora 79
Tapuae-o-Rongo-kako 160
Tapuwae o Rongokako 169
Tarahaukapiti 169
Taranaki 14, 64, 66, 70, 71, 93, 93, 99, 109, 110, 113, 115, 125, 148
Taranaki Coast 64, 178
Tara-o-Muturangi 112
Tararu 139
Taumata-apanui Point 138, 147
Taupo 68, 175
Tauranga 156, 164
Taurere 139
Tauroa 176
Tawhiti-roa 180
Tawhiuwhiu 128
Te Ahi-kaikoura-a-Tama-ki-te-rangi (Kaikoura Coast) 152
Te Anau 187
Te Ara-a-Kiwa (Foveaux Strait) 168, 187
Te Atea 89
Te Au-miti (French Pass) 129
Te Au-o-kura 75

Te Awa-a-te-atau 46
Te Awamutu 190
Te Awanga River 156
Te Awa-nui-a-Taikehu 22
Te-awa-o-te-atua 88
Te Awapatiki 122
Te Haukapua (Torpedo Bay) 145
Te Inuwai o Tainui 146
Tekapamoana (Hauraki Gulf) 145
Tekapo 187
Te Kapurangi 108
Te Karaka 139
Te Kawakawa (Cape Palliser) 97, 98
Te Ko Tukutuku 108
Te Kurae-a-Tura 139
Te Mahia 146
Te Mawahi 160
Te Mawhai 169
Te Pakaroa 157
Te Papa 156
Te Papa-o-karewa 149
Te Poito-o-te-kupenga-a-Taramainuku 38
Te Puna-i-te-ao-marama 99
Te Ra-o-Tainui 139
Te Rae-o-Tawhiti 152
Te Rangaatamatea (Tama-i-ea) 129
Te Rangi 108
Te Rangitoto-o-Tama-te-kapua 145
Te Rimurapa 98
Te Tapotu-o-Tainui 148
Te Teko 59
Te-upoko-ta-marimari 114
Te Waewae Bay 160, 168, 187
Te Wai-iti 149, 156
Te-waka-tu-whenua 102
Te Whaka-whitinga 55
Te Whata-kai-o-Raki-houia 187
Te Whenua-o-Huruhuru-manu (Ohurumanu) 190
Te Whenua-o-Te-Potiki-tautahi (Otautahi) 190
Te-whetu-matarau 155
Three Kings 139
Tikapa 139
Titirangi 154, 156

219

Toka-ahuru 169
Tokomaru Bay 178
Tonga 64, 150
Tonga-porutu 71, 178
Tongariro 45, 67
Torpedo Bay (Te Haukapua) 145
Tory Channel 97
Tuamotu islands 150, 170
Tuanaki 22
Tuara-hiwi-otienga 68
Tuhua (Flat Island) 111, 114
Tupuai 195
Tura's Point 139
Turakina 114
Turanga 51, 55, 63
Turanganui 51, 55, 71, 92, 130

Upolu, Samoa 84
Ure-nui 20
Ureia 149

Vairoa 64
Vairoa River 64, 150

Waerota 78
Waerota Island 75
Waeroti 78
Waiapu 55, 78
Waiarohe 145
Waiau 161
Waiau River 160, 164, 187
Waiaua 107
Waiaua River 108
Waihaha 148
Waihao River 187
Waihihi 145, 148
Waihou River 70
Waikare River 157
Waikaremoana 132
Waikaretu 79
Waikato 114
Waikato River 26
Waikawa (Portland Island) 156
Waimarama 156
Waimate 168
Waimate Plain 47

Waimatuhirangi 15
Waimeha Plains 161
Waimeha Stream 161
Waimimi 146
Waingongoro 20
Waingongoro River 125
Waioeka 55
Waiotahi Beach 31
Wai-o-Taiki 139, 145
Wai-o-weka 108
Waipaoa 55
Wai-pare-ira Stream 111
Waipiro 67
Waipiropiro-a-Whiro 174
Wairakei Stream 38
Wairarapa 117
Wairarapa Coast 157, 193
Wairau River 97
Wairere waterfall 87
Wairoa River 156
Wairuangangana 49
Waitakere Ranges 102
Waitaki River 25
Waitamata Harbour 23
Waitangi Stream 75
Wai-tara 20
Waitara 47, 178
Waitekura Stream 43
Wai-whakapukuhanga 139
Wakatipu 187
Wanaka 187
Wanganui 67
Ward Island (Makaro) 98
Wellington Harbour 97
Westfield 148
Westland 152
Whaingaroa 114
Whakaari (White Island) 128
Whakapoukorero 191
Whakatane 26, 45, 52, 71, 89, 92, 94, 111, 118
Whakatane River 27, 87, 88, 89, 164
Whanga lagoon 122
Whanga-o-kena (East Island) 82
Whangaehu 72, 114
Whangaimakau 139

Whanganui 99, 114
Whanganui River 67
Whanganui-a-Tara 114, 160, 164
Whanganui-o-Hei (Mercury Bay) 24
Whangaparaoa 38, 45, 55, 77, 88, 114, 138, 146, 160
Whangape 93
Whangara 44, 45, 55, 88, 92, 145, 154, 156, 157, 175
Whangara-mai-tawhiti 178
Whangarei 181, 182
Whangaroa 78, 96, 98, 102
Whangaroa Harbour 96
Whare-kawa 139
Wharekahika 187
Wharenga 139
Wharepapa 89, 109, 123, 125, 131
Whenuakura 35, 75
Whirinaki River 98
White Bluff 97
White Island (Whakaari) 128
Whitianga 56, 139
Whitianga-te-ra 25

Waka name variants

Aniu-waru 198
Aniwa-niwa 198
Ara Umauma 31
Arai-te-tonga 24
Arai-uru 24
Auraro-tuia 195
Awatea 79

Hauraro-tuia 195
Hotu-te-ihi 60
Hotu-te-ihi-rangi 60
Hotu-te-ihu-rangi 60
Hurepureiata 182
Huripureiata 182

Kahui-mounga 64
Kawhao-mata-rua 94
Kopua-horahora 66
Kura-pau-popo 71
Kura-te-po 71
Kura-wau-po 71
Kuraaupo 71
Kurawhapo 71
Kuruatepo 71
Kuruhaupo 71

Mahanga-a-Tuamatua 32
Mahatu-ki-te-raki 195
Mahuhu 77

Mahunu 79
Mahunui 195
Mahutu-ki-te-raki 195
Mahutu-ki-te-rangi 195
Mamamaru 81
Manu-ka-rere 84
Manuka-tai 83
Mataharua 94
Matahoru 94
Matahorua 94
Matahoura 94
Mataorua 94
Matatua 86
Matawhaoru 94
Matawhaorua 94
Moana-waewae 101
Moetekakara 102
Motumotu 102
Muri-enua 103

Naenaemoko 103
Nga-tai-a-Kupe 51
Ngaio 103
Niwa-reka 198
Niwa-ru 198
Niwharu 198
Nuku-tai-memeha 195
Nuku-tai-mimiha 195
Nuku-te-pewa-raki 182
Nukutaimehameha 195

Okoturu 109
Orouta 52
Otu-rere 110

Pakawai 198
Papakatoro 113
Papakatoru 113
Pauiraira 114
Pauiraraira 114
Pauiriraiira 114
Piniu 198
Pirita-o-te-rangi, Te 195
Pongatoru 113
Poutini 65
Pukanui 116
Pukateawainui 116
Pukatewainui 116
Pukeatuawainui 116
Puketeawainui 116
Punui 198
Punui-o-Rata 198

Rangi-aoao-nunui 13
Rangi-mata-wai 121
Rangi-mutu 125
Rangi-na-mutu 125
Rangi-pato-roa 182
Rangi-ua-mate 125
Rangihoana 120
Rangimatoro 123
Rereanani 174
Rereanini 174
Rimu-rapa 128
Ringamatoro 123
Ringamatoru 123
Ringauamotu 125
Ringauamutu 125
Riu-o-mahu 195
Riu-o-mahue 195
Riuhakara 102
Riukakara 102
Riukaramea 130
Riwaru 198
Riwharu 198
Ronawaiwai 101
Roua-waewae 101

Ru-nakia 102
Ru-ngakia 102
Rua-o-mahu 195
Rui-o-mahui 195
Runga-ki-a 102

Tahatura 131
Tahirirangi 174
Tahu-a-rangi 195
Taikorea 132
Tairea 125
Taiwirirangi 174
Takare-aotea 153
Takareira 67
Takaria 67
Taki-te-uru 24
Takitumu 153
Tama-rereti 195
Tane 170
Tane-a-rangi 195
Tane-kaha 170
Tanetewa 170
Tapatapa-nukarere 172
Tatataeore 173
Tau-rangi 195
Tawaowao 174
Tawhiri-kura 174
Tawhiri-rangi 174
Tawhitirangi 174
Te Iwi-o-Atea 180
Te-o-te-poa-raki 182
Terehapua 182
Tongamaru 176
Totara-keria 179
Totaraikeria 179
Totora-karia 179
Tu-te-pa-wharangi 182
Tu-te-paerangi 182
Tu-te-pe-wawharangi 182
Tu-te-pewa 182
Tu-te-pewa-rangi 182
Tu-te-pewa-wharangi 182
Tu-te-pewha-raki 182
Tu-te-poa-raki 182
Tu-te-pueha 184

Tuhua 65
Tuirangi 198
Turereao 110
Tutara-kauika 51
Tuwhenua 102

Uruao-kapua-rangi 185
Utupawa 127

Waka-a-Aoraki 188
Waka-a-raki 189

Wakahuruhuru 62
Wakahuruhurumanu 62
Wakahurumanu 62
Wakaororua 190
Whakahuruhurumanu 62
Whakirere 191
Whatu-a-ranga-ngutu 192
Whatu-a-ranga-nuku 192
Whatu-a-rangi-nuku 192
Whatu-purangi 117

Chatham Islands

Hape 50

Karangatai 69
Katoko 69
Kimi 70

Mano 83
Manu-kau-moana 85
Mapouriki 85
Mata-rangi 101

Okahu 109
Oropuke 109

Poreitua 115
Pou-ariki 115

Rangiahua 119
Rangihoua 120
Rangimata 121
Rangi-tane 125
Rangi-tu-makohakoha, Te 125
Ruapuke 131

Tama-kororo 170
Tanewai 170
Tihauwea 175
Tohoro-i-ongongo 176
Tupu-ngaherehere 182
Turore 182

www.ingramcontent.com/pod-product-compliance
Ingram Content Group UK Ltd.
Pitfield, Milton Keynes, MK11 3LW, UK
UKHW051652180426
11947UKWH00021B/1918